Slavery in Yorkshire

Richard Oastler and the campaign against child labour in the Industrial Revolution

EDITED BY
JOHN A. HARGREAVES
& E. A. HILARY HAIGH

Published by University of Huddersfield Press

University of Huddersfield Press
The University of Huddersfield
Queensgate
Huddersfield HD1 3DH
Email enquiries university.press@hud.ac.uk

First published 2012
Text © The Authors 2012
Images © as attributed

A CIP catalogue record for this book is available
from the British Library.
ISBN 978-1-86218-107-6

Designed and printed by
Jeremy Mills Publishing Limited
113 Lidget Street
Lindley
Huddersfield HD3 3JR
www.jeremymillspublishing.co.uk

COVER IMAGE:
Factory Children depicted in an original watercolour
by George Walker for the first edition of his *The
Costume of Yorkshire*, published in 1814 (Yorkshire
Archaeological Society).

Contents

Foreword

INDERJIT BHOGAL

I WELCOME THIS book with its broad perspective as an important contribution to making us all more informed on the whole theme of slavery today. Slavery, past and present, exists where people with power seize or secure others, often women and children, and make or force them to carry out work or other actions. The scandal is that while there were around ten million people in slavery worldwide two hundred years ago, there are around twenty million in slavery worldwide today.

As a social and economic reality slavery has existed from ancient times around the world and is known in texts like the Bible. Biblical witness begins with the affirmation that God is Creator, and that human beings are created – male and female – in the image of God. This Creation story also acknowledges that as soon as there is human community, issues of dominance and power come into play in human relationships. Perverted and exploitative selfishness promotes self-preservation at the expense of others. Man exploits woman and brother overpowers brother (*Genesis* 1-4). Although the Jewish Law was to forbid the enslavement of the poor (*Leviticus* 25:39), slavery is nevertheless part of the Biblical story. For example, Hagar is referred to as Abraham's 'bondwoman' (*Genesis* 16 and 21:13), Joseph was sold into slavery by his brothers for twenty pieces of silver (*Genesis* 37:28) and the children of Israel were enslaved by Rameses II as building workers in Egypt (*Exodus* 1). Jesus did not specifically address the issue of slavery but his lifestyle and life experiences offer important insights.

He chose to serve others and to commend a life of service to his disciples while speaking out against authoritarian relationships (*Luke* 22: 25-27). Paul accepted slavery as a fact in the Graeco-Roman world but also proclaimed the equality of bond and free before God (*Galatians* 3:28).

Though the Bible, which is the basis of Christian faith and records stories of both human failings and of God's faithfulness, has been used by some Christians to sanction, support or justify injustices, not least the transatlantic slave trade, there has also been a strong tradition of Christian opposition to injustices such as the slave trade. Members of the Society of Friends (Quakers) and people like John Wesley wrote and preached against the 'horrid' slave trade, and William Wilberforce and his fellow Evangelicals, including Richard Oastler, campaigned for legislation against forms of slavery and exploitation at home and abroad. Africans themselves challenged and shared in the struggle. Having gained his freedom from slavery, Olaudah Equiano went on to play a powerfully eloquent role in the abolition of the slave trade. Later, in the United States, escaped slaves like Harriet Tubman helped run the subversive, secret 'underground railroad' to rescue slaves while Frederick Douglass campaigned internationally for racial equality and equal rights for all men and women. Equiano wrote an autobiography outlining his experiences which concludes with these words:

> After all, what makes any event important, unless by its observation we become better and wiser, and learn 'to do justly, to love mercy, and to walk humbly before God?'

Despite such a plea there is today more slavery and economic exploitation than ever, including debt bondage, child labour, sex trafficking, people trafficking for labour, cheap migrant labour, cheap house cleaners and unjust trade rules. In September 2011 more than twenty men were rescued by the police from slavery in Bedfordshire, England. Some of the men had been kept there so long that that they were described as 'institutionalised' slaves. And the lasting legacy of the transatlantic slave trade still lingers in the scandal of racism that continues to degrade black people. The contemporary world can scarcely be understood without taking this legacy into account. Slavery – in all its forms – remains a disgrace to civilisation, and still needs the campaigning vigour shown by a Wilberforce, an Equiano or an Oastler to make a difference. Jubilee 2000, and movements like the Trade Justice Campaign, and Make Poverty History have demonstrated how power can be exerted to challenge the public conscience and government policy; and prophetic organisations such as Anti-Slavery International and Dalit Solidarity continue working hard to bring today's slavery to an end. The issues discussed in this book are not confined to the past. We can no more turn aside from the suffering of others than Oastler and others could nearly two centuries ago. Humanitarian moral decency and Christian discipleship still calls us, as it called them, to share the burden of the cross and to work for freedom and fullness of life for all.

INDERJIT BHOGAL IS a Methodist Minister currently working as Leader of Corrymeela Community, Northern Ireland. He is a former President of the British Methodist Conference, and is Founder and National Chair of City of Sanctuary. He was Chair of the Churches Together initiative Set All Free to mark the Bi-Centenary of the Act to Abolish the Transatlantic Slave Trade (2007). Inderjit was also Chief Executive of the Yorkshire and Humber Faiths Forum, and was awarded the OBE for his work in Interfaith Relations.

Preface

TIM THORNTON, UNIVERSITY OF HUDDERSFIELD

IN RESPONDING TO the bicentenary of the abolition of the transatlantic slave trade in 1807, this collection of essays and the conference in 2007 from which it springs have helped to remind us of important resonances of that momentous legislation. Centrally, the book provides a rounded evaluation of the contribution of Richard Oastler to the broader movement for emancipation. This is conceived without geographical or cultural barriers, as a way in which some in the nineteenth century responded both to slavery as then conventionally defined and to the situation, especially for children and women, amongst those working in the newly emerged industries of Britain in that period.

It was a particular privilege to be able to host the conference and to support publication at the University of Huddersfield, an institution where those resonances were and are particularly strong: in a town which Oastler knew so well and where he was so enthusiastically hailed as 'Factory King', and in a university which incorporates a training college formerly known as Oastler College in his honour. It was striking that the conference brought together a large and enthusiastic audience and one which approached Oastler from many different perspectives, reflective of his meanings in the contemporary world. I am confident that this book will have a similarly broad appeal. It is also appropriate that the university is an international community of scholars and students, reflecting the global implications for Oastler's message, whether in the nineteenth century or now in the twenty-first. Oastler's memory and that of the cause for which he stood have been strong in this area, and the conference and book stand as an excellent testimony to the role of rigorous scholarship in reviving and renewing our understanding of that memory and its relevance to contemporary issues in Huddersfield, Yorkshire, and around the world.

The interconnectedness of the economies and cultures of slavery on both sides of the Atlantic; the importance of religious faith, and especially of Wesleyan Methodism and of New Connexion Methodism, in shaping responses to human exploitation; the dynamics of the factory movement, especially in Huddersfield itself; the mechanisms of the campaign Oastler waged, whether in the press or in his personal appearances; and the character of the man himself – our understanding of all these aspects is enhanced in this excellent book.

TIM THORNTON STUDIED at New College, Oxford. In 1997 he was awarded the Royal Historical Society's David Berry Prize for his work on the Isle of Man; in 1999 he was proxime accessit for the Society's Alexander Prize for an essay on the palatinate of Durham. He was the first scholar based in a new University to win one of the Society's prizes. Tim works on the late medieval and early modern political and social history of the British Isles, spanning the period c. 1400–1650, and his many books and papers include *Cheshire and the Tudor State, 1480–1560* (2000), *The Charters of Guernsey* (2004), and *Prophecy, Politics and the People in Early Modern England* (2006); his monograph on *The Channel Islands, 1370–1640: Between England and Normandy* is due for publication in 2012.

Appointed Head of the Department of History, English, Languages and Media at the University of Huddersfield in 2003, Tim was on secondment as Head of University Centre Barnsley during 2005–6 and became Dean of the School of Music, Humanities and Media in October 2006. He was appointed Pro Vice-Chancellor (Teaching and Learning) at the University in October 2008.

Acknowledgements

JOHN A. HARGREAVES AND E.A. HILARY HAIGH

THE PUBLICATION OF this book has been facilitated by the encouragement and support of many people and the generous support of the Heritage Lottery Fund. The content of the book is largely derived from contributions to a conference, which formed part of the University of Huddersfield Archives Department's Heritage Lottery funded project '*Yorkshire Slavery; the campaign for the release of the oppressed*', supplemented by articles developing the theme of the conference by Dr John Halstead, Dr Janette Martin and Professor James Walvin and a Foreword from the Revd Dr Inderjit Bhogal OBE, Chair of the Set All Free initiative in 2007.

Thanks are due to everyone involved in that Conference, notably Dr Fiona Spiers, the Yorkshire and the Humber Regional Director of the Heritage Lottery Fund, who gave the opening address, and Professor Timothy Thornton, Pro Vice Chancellor of the University of Huddersfield, who chaired the proceedings and has provided the Preface for this volume.

Huddersfield Local History Society, Kirklees Museums and Galleries, Kirklees Libraries, West Yorkshire Archive Service, St John's Church, Kirkheaton, Christ Church Woodhouse and the Hudawi Centre, Huddersfield, were all active supporters of the Yorkshire Slavery project. Grateful thanks are also due to the following individuals for their generous and enthusiastic participation: Richard Butterfield, Joanne Catlow, the Revd Sue Clarke, Robert Frost, Katy

Goodrum, George Matheson, Nicola Pullan, Neil Pye, Pam Riding, Howard Robinson, George Smith, the Revd Richard Steel and Sylvia Thomas.

Richard Oastler lived at Fixby Hall during his employment as steward to Thomas Thornhill. Until recent times the agent for the Thornhill Estate was Mr Richard Crowther, and the generous time and assistance given by both Mr and Mrs Crowther, especially in the early stages of this project, is gratefully acknowledged. Fixby Hall is now home to Huddersfield Golf Club, and the assistance of the Club Secretary and the Club Archivist, George Smith, is gratefully acknowledged.

Illustrations have been provided by the following: Professor Malcolm Chase, Dr P. Forsaith, Mrs A. Hansen, Mr C.D. Helme, Mr Peter Pearson, Bradford Libraries, Hampshire Record Office, Huddersfield Local Studies Library, Hull Museums, Kirklees Image Archive, Kirklees Museums and Galleries, the Mary Evans Picture Library, West Yorkshire Archive Service and the Yorkshire Archaeological Society.

At the University of Huddersfield, the Director of Computing and Library Services, Professor John Lancaster, his successor Sue White, Graham Stone and the University of Huddersfield Press Editorial Board have all encouraged and enabled the publication of this volume. We are also indebted to the staff of Jeremy Mills Publishing, and especially the Publishing Manager, Hazel Goodes for steering it through the publishing process and to all the contributors to this volume for their forbearance and enthusiasm. As ever, grateful thanks are due to the families of all the authors and editors, without whose encouragement and support this volume would not have appeared. Finally the editors and contributors accept responsibility for any errors within the text which may have escaped their scrutiny.

List of Illustrations

Introduction: 'Victims of slavery even on the threshold of our homes': Richard Oastler and Yorkshire Slavery

JOHN A. HARGREAVES

IN HIS CELEBRATED open letter to the *Leeds Mercury* of 29 September 1830 on 'Yorkshire Slavery', Richard Oastler alerted the readers of Yorkshire's highest circulation provincial newspaper to the desperate plight of those 'victims of slavery even on the threshold of our own homes', the child workers in the worsted spinning mills around Bradford.[1] His letter was penned, perhaps surprisingly, not from the industrial heartland of Bradford, but, somewhat incongruously, from the arcadian fastnesses of Fixby Hall, an elegant Georgian, country house on the rural periphery of Huddersfield, where its author had served for a decade as land agent for the estate's owners, an absentee gentry family since 1809. Indeed, Oastler had come to be regarded by many of his contemporaries as the surrogate squire of Fixby on account of the prolonged absences of his employer, Thomas W. Thornhill (1780–1844). However his more mundane and onerous responsibilities included the management of his employer's vast estates extending across a large swathe of West Yorkshire, with a rent roll of £20,000 in

---

1. D. Read, *Press and People 1790–1850*, (London: Edward Arnold, 1961), appendix, pp. 209–18 reveals that the *Leeds Mercury* had a weekly circulation of 5,200 in *c*.1830 significantly higher than its nearest rivals the *Leeds Intelligencer* (1,500) and the *Leeds Patriot* (*c*. 1,200), and over ten times greater than the *Sheffield Independent* (*c*. 500). I am grateful to Professor Edward Royle and Professor Keith Laybourn for their comments on a preliminary draft of this chapter.

1830, encompassing some thousand tenancies, including cottages, farms, four collieries, some two dozen quarries and numerous turnpike investments. Moreover, many of them were poised to produce higher revenues for the estate as the urban and industrial centres of Halifax, Huddersfield, Leeds and Bradford and their hinterlands began to expand with the acceleration of industrialisation.[2]

1:1 Fixby Hall, home of Richard Oastler from 1821 until 1838 (Photograph: E.A.H. Haigh).

Hand-delivered by Oastler on horseback, his sensational letter was eventually published on 16 October 1830, after an agonising delay whilst the editor, Edward Baines, had pondered its potential impact on the paper's predominantly dissenting, middle-class readership and added an accompanying editorial explicitly critical of Oastler's belligerent prose. The letter appeared on the back page of the pioneering,

2. P. Roebuck, *Yorkshire Baronets 1640–1760*, (Hull: University of Hull, 1980), p. 308; C. Driver, *Tory Radical. The Life of Richard Oastler*, (New York: Oxford University Press, 1946, reprinted New York: Octagon Books, 1970), p. 25. Driver's biography of Oastler draws extensively on Yorkshire sources, acknowledging the invaluable contribution of the historical and topographical knowledge of the Huddersfield local historian Philip Ahier, ibid., p. 521.

SLAVERY IN YORKSHIRE.

TO THE EDITORS OF THE LEEDS MERCURY.

"It is the pride of Britain that a Slave cannot exist on her soil; and if I read the genius of her constitution aright, I find that Slavery is most abhorrent to it—that the air which Britons breath is free—the ground on which they tread is sacred to liberty."—*Rev. R. W. Hamilton's Speech at the Meeting held in the Cloth-hall Yard, Sept. 22d, 1830.*

GENTLEMEN,—No heart responded with truer accents to the sounds of liberty which were heard in the Leeds Cloth-hall yard, on the 22d inst. than did mine, and from none could more sincere and earnest prayers arise to the throne of Heaven, that hereafter Slavery might only be known to Britain in the pages of her history. One shade alone obscured my pleasure, arising not from any difference in principle, but from the want of application of the general principle *to the whole Empire*. The pious and able champions of *Negro* liberty and *Colonial* rights should, if I mistake not, have gone farther than they did; or perhaps, to speak more correctly, before they had travelled so far as the West Indies, should, at least for a few moments, have sojourned in our own immediate neighbourhood, and have directed the attention of the meeting to scenes of misery, acts of oppression and victims of Slavery, even on the threshold of our homes!

Let truth speak out, appalling as the statements may appear. The fact is true. Thousands of our fellow-creatures and fellow-subjects, both male and female, the miserable inhabitants of a *Yorkshire town*, (Yorkshire now represented in Parliament by the giant of anti-slavery principles,) are this very moment existing in a state of Slavery *more horrid* than are the victims of that hellish system—"*Colonial Slavery.*" These innocent creatures drawl out unpitied their short but miserable existence, in a place famed for its profession of religious zeal, whose inhabitants are ever foremost in *professing* "Temperance" and "Reformation," and are striving to outrun their neighbours in Missionary exertions, and would fain send the Bible to the farthest corner of the globe—nay, in the very place where the anti-slavery fever rages most furiously, her *apparent charity*, is not more admired on earth, than her *real cruelty* is abhorred in heaven. The very streets which receive the droppings of an "Anti Slavery Society" are every morning wet by the tears of innocent victims at the accursed shrine of avarice, who are *compelled* (not *by* the art-whip of the negro slave-driver) but by the dread of the equally appalling thong or strap of the overlooker, to hasten, half-dressed, *but not half-fed*, to those magazines of British Infantile Slavery—*the Worsted Mills in the town and neighbourhood of Bradford!!!*

Would that I had Brougham's eloquence, that I might rouse the hearts of the nation, and make every Briton swear "These innocents shall be free!"

Thousands of little children, both male and female, *but principally female*, from SEVEN to fourteen years of age, are daily compelled to labour from six o'clock in the morning to seven in the evening, with only—Britons blush whilst you read it!—*with only thirty minutes allowed for eating and recreation!*—Poor infants! ye are indeed sacrificed at the shrine of avarice, *without even the solace of the negro slave*—ye are no more than he is, *free agents*; ye are compelled to work as long as the *necessity* of your needy parents may require, or the cold-blooded avarice of your worse than barbarian masters *may demand!* Ye live in the boasted land of Freedom, and *feel* and mourn that *ye are Slaves*, and slaves without the only comfort which the Negro has. He knows it is his sordid mercenary master's INTEREST that he should *live*, be *strong* and *healthy. Not so with you.* Ye are doomed to labour from morn till night for one who cares not how soon your weak and tender frames are stretched to breaking! You are not mercifully valued at so much per head; this would assure you at least (even with the worst and most cruel masters) of the mercy shown to their own labouring beasts. No, no! your soft and delicate limbs are tired, and fagged, and jaded at only so much *per week*; and when your joints can act no longer, your emaciated frames are cast aside, the boards on which you lately toiled and wasted life away, are instantly supplied with other victims, who in this boasted land of liberty are HIRED—not sold—as Slaves, and daily forced to *hear* that they are free. Oh! Duncombe! Thou hatest Slavery—I know thou dost resolve that "Yorkshire children shall no more be slaves." And Morpeth! who justly gloriest in the Christian faith—Oh Morpeth listen to the cries and count the tears of these poor babes, and let St. Stephen's hear thee swear—"they shall no longer groan in Slavery!" And Bethell, too! who swears eternal hatred to the name of Slave, whene'er thy manly voice is heard in Britain's senate, assert the rights and liberty of Yorkshire Youths. And Brougham! Thou who art the chosen champion of liberty in every clime! Oh bend thy giant's mind, and listen to the sorrowing accents of these poor Yorkshire little ones, and note their tears; then let thy voice rehearse their woes, and touch that chord thou only holdest—the chord that sounds above the silvery notes in praise of heavenly liberty, and down descending at thy will, groans in the horrid caverns of the deep in muttering sounds of misery accursed to hellish bondage; and as thou soundst these notes, let Yorkshire hear thee swear "Her children shall be free!" Yes, all ye four protectors of our rights, chosen by freemen to destroy oppression's rod,

"Vow one by one, vow altogether, vow
"With heart and voice, eternal enmity
"Against oppression by your brethren's hands;
"Till man nor woman under Britain's laws,
"Nor son nor daughter born within her empire,
"Shall buy, or sell, or HIRE, or BE a Slave!"

The nation is now most resolutely determined that Negroes shall be free. Let them, however, not forget that Briton's have common rights with Afric's sons. The blacks may be fairly compared to beasts of burden, *kept for their master's use.* The whites to those *which others keep and let for hire!* If I have succeeded in calling the attention of your readers to the horrid and abominable system on which the worsted mills in and near Bradford are conducted, I have done some good. Why should not children working in them be protected by legislative enactments, as well as those who work in cotton mills? Christians should feel and act for those whom Christ so eminently loved and declared that "of such is the kingdom of heaven."

Your insertion of the above in the *Leeds Mercury*, at your earliest convenience, will oblige, Gentlemen,

Your most obedient servant,
RICHARD OASTLER.

Fixby-Hall, near Huddersfield, Sept. 29th, 1830.

1:2 Facsimile of Richard Oastler's letter on 'Slavery in Yorkshire' published in the *Leeds Mercury* 16 October 1830.

progressive, Whig-Liberal, Leeds newspaper, whose commercial readership was already well acquainted with the long running campaign to end colonial slavery. It was the first of four persistent letters to the *Leeds*

1:3 Portrait of Richard Oastler by Benjamin Garside, engraved by James Posselwhite and published at Leeds, 1838. At Oastler's side are two volumes entitled *White Slavery* and *Marcus*. Commissioned by Feargus O'Connor, this engraving was distributed with copies of the *Northern Star*, 12 December 1840 (Private collection).[3]

3. I am indebted to Professor Malcolm Chase of the University of Leeds for this information.

Mercury written by Oastler highlighting the problem of child labour in West Yorkshire's mills and it came to be regarded as one of the most momentous letters ever published in a Yorkshire newspaper on account of its far-reaching impact.[4]

Indeed, with the deft stroke of his quill pen, possibly that later depicted emblematically resting on Oastler's desk in the engraving of the factory reformer by James Posselwhite, based on Benjamin Garside's oil portrait, it associated the faltering movement to regulate the employment of young children in factories with the extraordinarily successful campaign to end transatlantic slavery, championed by Yorkshire's Tory Member of Parliament, William Wilberforce.[5] Moreover, as Cecil Driver observed in his monumental biography of Oastler published in 1946, it not only launched Oastler's career as a factory reformer, which ultimately was to earn him the soubriquet of 'Factory King', but it also proved to be a major turning point in British social and economic history. By reinvigorating the languishing factory movement it helped to secure a series of legislative enactments between 1833 and 1853 which, together with the establishment of a factory inspectorate, resulted in a more effective and wide-ranging regulatory system of factory employment than had existed before 1830.[6]

Oastler's widely publicised letter followed his Damascene conversion to the cause of factory reform during an illuminating, overnight visit to the now demolished Horton Hall, Bradford, formerly the home of John Wood, Bradford's largest worsted spinner, an evangelical Tory and enlightened, paternalistic employer. Wood's sprawling industrial premises employing 527 workers, covering seven acres in Goodman's End between Bridge Street and Bowling Beck, became one of the leading worsted spinning enterprises in Britain during the first quarter

---

4. Read, *Press and People*, pp. 59–60, 118–36.
5. Before the emergence of Oastler's ten-hour movement in the 1830s, Short Time Committees had been widely established in both Lancashire and Yorkshire in the late 1820s to support the radical M.P. Sir John Cam Hobhouse's efforts to limit the working day for children and young persons, which succeeded only in obtaining minor improvements to existing legislation in 1825 and 1829 in the cotton industry, see G.B.A.M. Finlayson, *England in the 1830s*, (London: Edward Arnold, 1969), pp. 38–39 and D.G. Wright, *Popular Radicalism. The Working-Class Experience 1780–1880*, (London: Longman, 1988), p. 100.
6. Driver, *Tory Radical*, p. 42; E. Crooks, *The Factory Inspectors. A Legacy of the Industrial Revolution*, (Stroud: Tempus Publishing Limited, 2005), pp. 16–23.

1:4 Horton Hall, home of the Bradford worsted spinner John Wood, where Oastler first became acquainted with the problem of child labour (Blunt Family Album).

of the nineteenth century. Deeply frustrated by the lack of enthusiasm of his fellow Bradford mill owners for any form of self-imposed regulation of child labour, Wood had urged Oastler to launch a campaign for a statutory ten-hour day on the grounds that since adult workers were dependent on the assistance of child workers, the restriction of adult working hours would necessitate the reduction of the working hours of children. Indeed, Wood shared his concerns with Oastler long into the night of 28 September 1830 and again in the early hours of the following morning before Oastler departed at dawn, henceforward resolutely determined to champion the plight of the child workers.[7]

Cryptically headed 'Slavery in Yorkshire' it appeared in print three weeks later. Oastler's controversial letter deliberately appropriated the evocative analogy of transatlantic slavery to revive the hitherto faltering factory movement. Moreover, some of its most memorable and evocative

---

7. A. Hansen, *Sharp to Blunt. The Story of Horton Hall, Bradford and Some of its Occupants*, (Bradford: Bradford Libraries, 2000), pp. 46–49, estimates the size of the workforce as 3,000, but I am grateful to Professor Keith Laybourn for drawing my attention to the figure of 527 operatives recorded by factory inspectors in 1833. J.T. Ward, *The Factory Movement* 1830–1855, (London: Macmillan, 1962), p. 34 described Wood as 'the greatest worsted spinner in Britain'.

phrases such as 'doomed to labour from morning to night' have passed into everyday discourse and are still heard today nearly 200 years after they first appeared in print. Other highly charged phrases, notably references to child workers as 'victims at the accursed shrine of avarice' in 'those magazines of British infantile slavery' in that 'horrid and abominable system on which the worsted mills in and near Bradford is conducted' became the war cries of Oastler's platform oratory and the campaign slogans of the revived ten-hour movement. They reverberated throughout its intense campaign which continued intermittently even beyond the enactment of the Ten Hours Act of 1847 until adequate safeguards were introduced in 1853 to ensure the effective statutory regulation of conditions of work for children in textile factories.

Oastler's professed justification for his emotive letter had been to challenge the complacency of the Revd R.W. Hamilton, the formidable

1:5 Portrait of John Wood, Bradford worsted spinner and factory reformer (Hampshire Record Office: 17M48/506).

dissenting ministerial incumbent of the pulpits at the Albion and
Belgrave Independent Chapels in Leeds between 1814 and 1848. He
had claimed in a speech at a recent public meeting at the Leeds Cloth
Hall Yard on 22 September 1830 that 'it is the pride of Britain that a
slave cannot exist' on British soil. Oastler declared that, on the
contrary, 'thousands of our fellow-creatures and fellow-subjects, both
male and female, the miserable inhabitants of a Yorkshire town … are
this very moment existing in a state of slavery, more horrid than are
the victims of that hellish system "colonial slavery"'.[8] Moreover, Oastler
contended that this situation was even more intolerable given that
'Yorkshire was currently represented in Parliament by none other than
William Wilberforce, that 'giant of anti-slavery principles'. It was also
unacceptable, he insisted, since Bradford, the town in question, was 'a
place famed for its profession of religious zeal, whose inhabitants are
ever foremost in professing "temperance" and "reformation" and are
striving to outrun their neighbours in missionary exertions' where
'anti-slavery fever rages most furiously.' Exposing the hypocrisy of
Bradford's millocracy and that of Yorkshire's current anti-slavery
Members of Parliament, Duncombe, Morpeth, Bethell and Brougham,
Oastler declared that the pious and able champions of *negro* liberty
and *colonial* rights' should 'before they had travelled so far as the West
Indies' have 'sojourned in our own immediate neighbourhood, and
have directed the attention of the meeting to scenes of misery, acts of
oppression, and victims of slavery, even on the threshold of our
homes'.[9]

---

8. For the Revd R.W. Hamilton see N. Yates, 'The religious life of Victorian Leeds'
    in *A History of Modern Leeds*, ed. by D. Fraser, (Manchester: Manchester
    University Press, 1980), p. 251.
9. Richard Oastler, 'Yorkshire Slavery' letter to the editors of the *Leeds Mercury*,
    Fixby Hall, near Huddersfield, 29 September 1830, cited in Driver, *Tory
    Radical*. There are discrepancies between the signature of the version of Oastler's
    letter cited in Driver, *Tory Radical*, pp. 42–44 and that published in the *Leeds
    Mercury* of 16 October 1830 in that the latter does not appear anonymously
    with the generically patriotic pseudonym of 'A Briton' as its signature as it does
    in Driver's account, but appends the name of Richard Oastler as the signatory of
    the letter. However, transcripts of the published letter in secondary sources have
    invariably followed Driver's version, for example, G.D.H. Cole and A.W. Filson,
    British Working Class Movements Selected Documents 1789–1875, (London:
    Macmillan, 1951, reprinted 1965), pp. 315–17. pp. 42–44.

SLAVERY IN YORKSHIRE

———

TO THE EDITORS OF THE LEEDS MERCURY

"It is the pride of Britain that a slave cannot exist on her soil; and if I read the genius of her constitution aright, I find that slavery is most abhorrent to it – that the air which Britons breath is free – the ground on which they tread is sacred to liberty" – Rev. R.W. HAMILTON's *Speech at the Meeting held in the Cloth-hall Yard*, Sept. 22d, 1830.

———

GENTLEMEN, – No heart responded with truer accents to the sounds of liberty which were heard in the Leeds Cloth-hall yard, on the 22d inst. than did mine, and from none could more sincere and earnest prayers arise to the throne of Heaven, that hereafter Slavery might only be known to Britain in the pages of her history. One shade alone obscured my pleasure, arising not from any difference in principle, but from the want of application of the general principle to the whole Empire. The pious and able champions of Negro liberty and Colonial rights should, if I mistake not, have gone farther than they did; or perhaps, to speak more correctly, before they had travelled so far as the West Indies, should, at least for a few moments, have sojourned in our own immediate neighbourhood, and have directed the attention of the meeting to scenes of misery, acts of oppression, and victims of slavery, even on the threshold of our homes!

Let truth speak out, appalling as the statement may appear. The fact is true. Thousands of our fellow-creatures and fellow-subjects, both male and female, the miserable inhabitants of a Yorkshire town; (Yorkshire now represented in Parliament by the giant of anti-slavery principles,) are this very moment existing in a state of Slavery more horrid than are victims of that hellish system – "Colonial Slavery." These innocent creatures drawl out unpitied, their short but miserable existence, in a place famed for its profession of religious zeal, whose inhabitants are ever foremost in professing "Temperance" and "Reformation," and are striving to outrun their neighbours in Missionary exertions, and would fain send the Bible to the farthest corner of the globe – aye in the very place where the anti-slavery fever rages most furiously, her apparent charity, is not more admired on earth, than her real cruelty is abhorred in heaven. The very streets which receive the droppings of an "Anti-Slavery Society" are every morning wet by the tears of innocent victims at the accursed shrine of avarice, who are compelled (not by the cart-whip of the negro slave-driver) but by the dread of the equally appalling thong or strap of the overlooker, to hasten, half-dressed, but not half-fed, to those magazines

1:6 'Slavery in Yorkshire': transcript of Richard Oastler's letter to the *Leeds Mercury* published 16 October 1830 (British Library).

of British Infantile Slavery – the Worsted Mills in the town and
neighbourhood of Bradford!!!

Would that I had Brougham's eloquence, that I might rouse the hearts
of the nation, and make every Briton swear "These innocents shall be
free!"

Thousands of little children, both male and female, but principally
female, from SEVEN to fourteen years of age, are daily compelled to
labour from six o'clock in the morning to seven in the evening, with
only – Britons, blush while you read it! – with only thirty minutes
allowed for eating and recreation! – Poor infants! ye are indeed
sacrificed at the shrine of avarice, without even the solace of the negro
slave: ye are no more than he is, free agents – ye are compelled to work
as long as the necessity of your needy parents may require, or the cold-
blooded avarice of your worse than barbarian masters may demand! Ye
live in the boasted land of freedom, and feel and mourn that ye are
Slaves, and slaves without the only comfort which the Negro has. He
knows it is his sordid mercenary master's INTEREST that he should
live, be strong and healthy. Not so with you. Ye are doomed to labour
from morn till night for one who cares not how soon your weak and
tender frames are stretched to breaking! You are not mercifully valued
at so much per head; this would assure you at least (even with the worst
and most cruel masters), of the mercy shown to their own labouring
beasts. No, no! your soft and delicate limbs are tired, and fagged, and
jaded at only so much per week; and when your joints can act no longer,
your emaciated frames are cast aside, the boards on which you lately
toiled and wasted life away, are instantly supplied with other victims,
who in this boasted land of liberty are HIRED – not sold – as Slaves,
and daily forced to hear that they are free. Oh! Duncombe! Thou hatest
Slavery – I know thou dost resolve that "Yorkshire children shall no
more be slaves." And Morpeth! Who justly gloriest in Christian faith
– Oh Morpeth listen to the cries and count the tears of these poor babes
and let St. Stephen's hear thee swear – "they shall no longer groan in
Slavery!" And Bethell too! who swears eternal hatred to the name of
Slave, whene'er thy manly voice is heard in Britain's senate, assert the
rights and liberty of Yorkshire Youths. And Brougham! Thou who art
the chosen champion of liberty in every clime! Oh bend thy giant's
mind, and listen to the sorrowing accents of these poor Yorkshire little
ones, and note their tears; then let thy voice rehearse their woes, and
touch the chord thou only holdest – the chord that sounds above the
silvery notes in praise of heavenly liberty, and down descending at thy
will, groans in the horrid caverns of the deep in muttering sounds of
misery accursed to hellish bondage; and as thou soundst these notes,
let Yorkshire hear, thee swear "Her children shall be free!" Yes, all ye
four protectors of our rights, chosen by freemen to destroy oppression's
rod,

"Vow one by one, vow altogether, vow
"With heart and voice, eternal enmity
"Against oppression by your brethren's hands;
"Till man nor woman under Britain's laws,
"Nor son nor daughter born within her empire,
"Shall buy or see, or HIRE, or BE A SLAVE!"

The nation is now most resolutely determined that Negroes shall be free. Let them, however, not forget that Briton's have common rights with Afric[a]'s sons.

The blacks may be fairly compared to beasts of burden, kept for their master's use. The whites to those which others keep and let for hire! If I have succeeded in calling the attention of your readers to the horrid and abominable system on which the worsted mills in and near Bradford are conducted, I have done some good. Why should not children working in them be protected by legislative enactments, as well as those who work in cotton mills? Christians should feel and act for those whom Christ so eminently loved, and declared that "of such is the kingdom of heaven."

Your insertion of the above in the Leeds Mercury, at your earliest convenience, will oblige, Gentlemen,

Your most obedient servant,
RICHARD OASTLER.

Fixby-Hall, near Huddersfield, Sept. 29th, 1830.

This volume of essays is based on a conference held at the University of Huddersfield on Saturday 17 November 2007 to commemorate the bicentenary of the abolition of the slave trade in 1807 and to celebrate Huddersfield's heritage as the historic springboard for the launch of the ten-hour movement in Yorkshire under Oastler's leadership in 1830.[10] It explores the links between the anti-slavery movement in

---

10. The conference on the theme of 'Yorkshire Slavery; the campaign for the release of the oppressed', supported by a 'Your Heritage' grant from the Heritage Lottery Fund, was hosted by the University of Huddersfield and supported by the West Yorkshire Branch of the Historical Association. Chaired by Professor Tim Thornton, the speakers included Dr Fiona Spiers, Mr D. Colin Dews, Professor Edward Royle, Dr John A. Hargreaves and Mr Jonathan Blagbrough of Anti-Slavery International.

Yorkshire and the re-invigorated campaign for factory regulation, which emerged in the county following the publication of Richard Oastler's sensational letter exposing the evils of child slavery in Bradford's worsted mills in the *Leeds Mercury* in October 1830. It provides an opportunity to revisit a theme first explored in depth in twentieth-century historiography in the United States of America by Cecil Driver at Yale University in 1946 in a monumental biographical study of Richard Oastler and in the United Kingdom by the Leeds-born historian, Professor J.T. Ward, in his seminal study of the factory movement published in 1962, based on his Cambridge doctoral thesis, and supplemented by a series of related articles in regional publications in Bradford and Leeds.[11]

These trailblazing studies have stimulated a wide-ranging debate around the issue of child labour in the late twentieth and early twenty-first centuries mainly in academic journals and monographs and increasingly within the context of an emerging international concern for the global welfare of children. This has been evidenced in comparative studies of childhood exemplified by the work of the American historian Professor Peter N. Stearns, reflecting that 'for many children' in the world today 'still in the labour force, rather than primarily focused on schooling, key experiences resemble what children in Western Europe, the United States and Japan encountered a century or a century and a half ago.[12] However, media reports continue to provide shocking reminders that there can be no room for complacency even in western societies about the problem of child labour and the abuse of children more generally. For example, one British newspaper in October 2010, reporting under the headline 'Child "slaves" found working on a farm', revealed that a group of Romanian children, some as young as nine, had been taken into police protection after having been found working as 'slave labourers' picking spring onions in a field

---

11. Driver, *Tory Radical*; J.T. Ward, 'The Factory Movement', PhD thesis, University of Cambridge, 1956, published as *The Factory Movement* in 1962; J.T. Ward, ed., *Popular Movements c. 1830–1850*, (London: Macmillan, 1970), pp. 1–30, 54–77; J.T. Ward, 'Bradford and Factory Reform', *Bradford Textile Society Journal*, 1961; 'Leeds and the Factory Reform Movement', *Thoresby Society Miscellany*, 1961, 46, pp. 87–118.
12. Peter N. Stearns, *Childhood in World History*, (London: Routledge, 2006, second edition 2011).

in Worcestershire following an international trafficking operation. Moreover, the most notable recent historian of childhood and child labour in the British industrial revolution, Jane Humphries, Professor of Economic History at Oxford University, reminds her readers in her groundbreaking study lamenting the invisibility in modern economic history of 'the children who toiled in the early mills [and] mines' that 'as the dismal catalogue of recent cases of appalling abuse makes clear', even 'rich economies with well-developed welfare states' have not yet gained immunity from the global problem of child neglect and abuse. This remains a challenging and disturbing indictment almost two centuries after Oastler penned his controversial letter.[13]

Other issues, which have emerged in the historical debate about child labour during this period, have been gender related. Although Oastler's letter expressed a particular concern about the employment of young girls in Bradford factories, the late Katrina Honeyman, Professor of Social and Economic History at Leeds University, maintained that 'women played a low-key role in the factory campaigns of the early 1830s' where their participation in demonstrations for shorter hours was motivated 'primarily by a desire to protect their children'. Indeed, she has contended that the factory movement in the West Riding continued to be male dominated at least until the passage of the 1844 Factory Act restricted the labour of women to twelve hours. Thereafter, she recognised that female support became more evident especially in the 'relatively gender-unified weaving districts' where women's 'perception of their rights as workers evolved through their employment as power-loom operatives'. Morcover, Honeyman has insisted that, notwithstanding Oastler's primary concern to eradicate the exploitation of children within the factory system, his aim 'to enhance the welfare of the working-class family was founded on a commitment to re-establish "traditional" gender roles, especially female domesticity' since Oastler had declared:

> We want to see woman in her right place … on her own hearth-stone making it ready to be comfortable for her industrious husband when he returns to his house to meals, and to his bed at night.[14]

---

13. *Daily Telegraph*, 25 October 2010; Jane Humphries, *Childhood and Child Labour in the British Industrial Revolution*, (Cambridge: Cambridge University Press, 2010), pp. xi, 1.

However, Honeyman acknowledged that by 1844 a different emphasis was emerging, characterised by the description of the ten-hour movement as 'this arduous and important struggle for the liberty of our sex, and the protection of our children'.

Indeed, there is even earlier evidence of attempts by the ten-hour movement to engage directly with women across the social spectrum in 1833 when George Crabtree, the Huddersfield mill operative entrusted by Oastler to collect evidence of conditions in the mills of the Calder Valley, addressed both the 'Ladies of Halifax', who though 'alive to the emancipation of the Negro ... 'forget, or else turn a deaf ear to the wretched condition of the Factory Children' and then concluded:

> Mothers of Halifax and its neighbourhood, rouse yourselves in your children's cause; if the RICH ladies won't use their influence to emancipate your infants, you as mothers ought to be alive to the amelioration of their condition.[15]

Moreover, women were strongly in evidence in contemporary prints in the vast crowds welcoming Oastler home to Huddersfield on 12 July 1832 after giving evidence to Sadler's Committee in July 1832. Women in shawls also appear to be listening attentively to Oastler when he addressed a crowded open-air meeting in Huddersfield after his release from prison on 20 February 1844, when *The Times* also reported 'ladies in private carriages' accompanying his procession into the town. Many women were impressed by Oastler for his role in the anti-Poor Law movement and showed their disapproval of his dismissal from his stewardship at Fixby Hall in August 1838, 'waving a flag condemning the bastardy clause of the Poor Law' and they organised Oastler festivals in 1841 to support him during his imprisonment, suggesting that Oastler's views on female domesticity may have

---

14. K. Honeyman, *Women, Gender and Industrialisation in England, 1700–1870*, (Basingstoke: Macmillan, 2000), p. 128; see also Colin Creighton, 'Richard Oastler, Factory Legislation and the Working-Class Family', *Journal of Historical Sociology*, vol. 5, no. 3, September 1992, pp. 292–320.

15. G. Crabtree, *Brief Description of a Tour through Calder Dale*, 1833, (Huddersfield: 1833), pp. 25–26.

1:7 Factory Children depicted in an original watercolour by George Walker for the first edition of his *The Costume of Yorkshire*, published in 1814 (Yorkshire Archaeological Society).

appeared distinctly less controversial to contemporaries than some later feminist historians and historical sociologists have recognised.[16]

Contemporary observers of Yorkshire society were well aware of the phenomenon of child labour under both the domestic and factory systems of production. Daniel Defoe's classic account of the proto-industrial landscape of the Calder Valley and its tributaries in the early eighteenth century as he approached Halifax from Blackstone Edge commented positively on the 'spectacle of the most exemplary industry' with 'no hand being unemployed … even from the youngest to the ancient'. Indeed, Defoe invariably wrote approvingly of child labour even commenting enthusiastically on children usefully employed scarcely 'above four years old'.[17] A century later, George Walker (1781-

16. *Times*, 22 February 1844, *Leeds Mercury*, 1 September 1838, *Leeds Intelligencer*, 30 January 1838, 17 April 1838; M.I. Thomis and Jennifer Grimmett, *Women in Protest 1800–1850*, (London: Croom Helm, 1982), p. 61.
17. Daniel Defoe, *A Tour Through the Whole Island of Great Britain*, ed. by P.N. Furbank, W.R. Owens and A.J. Coulson, (London: Yale University Press, 1991), pp. x-xi.

1856) the artist of Killingbeck Hall, Leeds, included in his collection of coloured drawings of Yorkshire costume a sketch of two rather forlorn looking children with pallid complexions. Wearing brats and carrying lunch baskets, they were depicted against a backcloth of a recently constructed factory filling the atmosphere with clouds of thick black smoke. Published in 1814, when, the artist commented, 'a great part of the West Riding of Yorkshire abounds with cotton mills, cloth manufactories and other large buildings appropriated to trade'

THE FACTORY GIRL.

DEDICATED TO JOHN WOOD, ESQ.,

BY ROBERT DIBB, DEWSBURY.

Who is she with pallid face?
That slowly moves with languid pace,
Her limbs bespeak her wearied frame
She seems in suff"ring, grief, and pain!
" A little child"—with list'ning ear,
Approach'd me with a falling tear
     And said—'tis Jane the Factory Girl!

I took her by her little hand—
Though from fatigue, she scarce could stand,
I tried to soothe her tender grief
By friendship's pow'r to give relief;
And ask'd in accents most sincere
What caus'd the anguish so severe?
     Of Jane—the Village Factory Girl!

She answer'd!—near that little wood,
Once liv'd my mother—kind—and good:
My father died upon that morn,
When I unhappily was born:
And now one only sister dear
Is left—the broken heart to cheer
     Of Jane—the Orphan Factory Girl!

Oh! Sir! we work from morning's light
Till darkness settles at the night:
No rest we know—no parents come
To welcome our return to home,
We call on Heaven to bless our cot
For earthly friends have all forgot
     The poor neglected Factory Girl!

The overlooker—many a time,
Without a fault—without a crime,
Has beat me with such savage might
That scarce could I reach home at night:
Oh! then I've wept in anguish deep,
And blest those parents now asleep
     Who lov'd poor Jane, the FactoryGirl!

Oh! yes! upon their lowly bier
Oft have I shed a mournful tear!
And wish'd that I alas could sleep
No more to suffer, nor to weep:
But soon I feel that welcome death
Will claim the last—the parting breath
     Of Jane, the wretched Factory Girl!

She cast her eyes with wildness round,
Then sunk exhausted on the ground:
I clasp'd the sufferer to my breast,
But she—poor girl—was now at rest!!
No cruel tyrant now could place
A tear upon the snowy face
     Of Jane, the lifeless Factory Girl!

Ye! who alone on Gold are bent,
Blush! at the Murder'd Innocent,
Let not Old England's glorious pride
Be stain'd by black Infanticide !!
But let Humanity's bright Ray
Protect from greedy Tyrant's sway
     The poor defenceless Factory Girl!

PRICE 1d.—*The profits arising therefrom to go towards forwarding the*
TEN HOURS BILL!!!

E. WILLAN, PRINTER, DEWSBURY,

1:8 'The Factory Girl': ballad by Robert Dibb of Dewsbury, dedicated to factory reformer John Wood, c. 1836 (West Yorkshire Archive Service, Bradford: DB27/C1/47/1).

furnishing 'employment, food and raiment to thousands of poor industrious individuals', Walker maintained that the 'little blue dirty group' depicted alongside a stunted tree stump was an authentic representation. Moreover, he enquired pessimistically 'where in their complexions would the painter discover the blooming carnations of youth?'. However, he declined to condemn the manufacturers as a class, commending the 'many proprietors of factories' who had remedied 'these evils by a strict attention to the morals, behaviour and cleanliness of the children'.[18]

By contrast, George Crabtree, albeit a committed ten-hour movement propagandist, concluded his report of his tour of the Calder Valley with the observation:

> during our perambulation in the parish of Halifax, we found that the master manufacturers were dead to every feeling but of *interest* – the 'cursed lust of gold' has so engrossed their minds, and absorbed their whole hearts, that they view their work people as part of those inanimate machines by which they amass that wealth which is their pride and boast, even the infant portion of their slaves shares not their protection and regard![19]

Moreover, the evidence provided by Joseph Habergam, a crippled seventeen-year old operative, of his employment since the age of seven in a succession of factories in Huddersfield to the Select Committee on Factories chaired by Oastler's friend, Michael Sadler, which was published in 1833, revealed a catalogue of harrowing abuse. It referred to some fifty children of his age who had often been 'sick and poorly as a result of excessive labour' at Bradley Mill and 'about a dozen of the children who had died shortly after leaving work'. Habergam was later regarded as an 'unimpeachable' witness when the effects of his employment were made evident by the treatment he received at the Huddersfield Infirmary from Dr Walker and at the Leeds Infirmary which he attended following the personal intervention of Richard

18. George Walker, *The Costume of Yorkshire*, (Firle: Caliban Books, 1978), pp. 96–97.
19. Crabtree, *Tour*, p. 23.

Oastler. Habergam remarked that when he had heard the condition of West Indies slaves described, he had reflected 'that there could not be worse slaves than those who worked in factories' in Huddersfield.[20]

It is revealing that even the Benthamite, Edwin Chadwick, author of the Royal Commission Report on Factories which followed the publication of Sadler's Report, whilst critical of Sadler's evidence and clearly favouring the economic arguments of the manufacturers, accepted, nonetheless, that children needed protection from employers who overworked them. He also confirmed that the problem of factory children was 'rapidly increasing' and comprehended 'a very considerable proportion of the infant population'. In 1833 Lord Althorp's Factory Act, secured by parliamentary pressure under the leadership of Lord Ashley (1801–85), later the seventh Earl of Shaftesbury, extended an earlier ban in 1819 on the employment of children under nine in cotton mills to all textile factories and limited the hours of work of children aged between nine and thirteen to nine hours a day and between twelve and eighteen to twelve a day. It also imposed a daily requirement of two hours schooling on factory children and created an inspectorate to enforce the regulations.[21]

The practice of child labour which had long been a characteristic of the domestic system of cloth manufacture in the West Riding appears to have become well-established in the emerging factory system in the half-century before it became the focus of Oastler's campaign in the 1830s. Katrina Honeyman has shown how the employment of pauper apprentices helped to meet a growing demand for juveniles to augment the workforces of many early textile mills.[22] John, Thomas

---

20. PP, 1831–32, XV: 'Report from the Committee on the Bill to regulate the Labour of Children in the Mills and Factories of the United Kingdom'; A. Gardiner, *The Industrial Revolution and Child Slavery*, (Slaithwaite: A.T. Green and Company, 1948), pp. 19–21. Joseph Habergam's evidence is included in Alan Whitworth, *Huddersfield As They Saw It*, (Huddersfield: Culva House Enterprises, 2008), pp. 22–28. For the context see J.T. Ward, *Factory Movement, 1830–1855*, pp. 60–63 and Finlayson, *England in the 1830s*, pp. 39–41.

21. E.J. Evans, *The Forging of the Modern State*, (London: Longman, 3rd edition, 2001), p. 288, Ward, *Factory Movement*, pp. 101–104.

22. K. Honeyman, *Child Workers in England, 1780–1820: Parish Apprentices and the Making of the Early Industrial Labour Force*, (Aldershot: Ashgate, 2007); J. Humphries, *Childhood and Child Labour in the British Industrial Revolution*, (Cambridge: Cambridge University Press, 2010), pp. 2, 301, 367.

and Samuel Haigh of Marsden near Huddersfield, for example, employed pauper apprentices from the parishes of St Margaret and St John, Westminster and St Mary, Lambeth in their Marsden cotton mills between 1792 and 1803. They were generally between the ages of nine and fourteen, but also included at least two six-year-old boys. Indeed, 'having lost so many of his London apprentices' after they had evidently absconded from the factories, John Haigh approached the overseers of Halstead in Essex for replacements to maintain his labour supply. A surviving indenture for Sarah Stock, 'a poor child of the parish of Halstead' aged about fourteen, reveals that she was required to serve John Haigh as an apprentice until she attained the age of twenty-one and that, for his part, Haigh was required to ensure that she was 'taught and instructed in the best way and manner that he can' and to 'provide sufficient meat, drink, apparel, lodging and washing and other things necessary and fit for an apprentice'.[23] In remote mills the maturation of the apprentice labour force contributed to a gradual decline in the demand for pauper apprentices over the early decades of the nineteenth century, reinforced by amending legislation in 1816 restricting the distance over which apprentices could be indentured.[24]

Recent analysis of the structure of the textile labour force from government inquiries and other contemporary surveys has led economic historians such as Carolyn Tuttle to suggest extremely high relative employment levels of children and young people, comprising between one third and two-thirds of all workers in many textile mills by 1833, when the reinvigorated ten-hour movement under Oastler's leadership was seeking to raise awareness of the problem. Moreover, Jane Humphries' pioneering prosopographical analysis of no fewer than 617 working-class autobiographies has also identified astonishingly high levels of child labour throughout this early period of industrialisation, underlining, as one reviewer of her study was quick to point out, that Britain's industrial revolution – the first in the world – might 'never have happened without child labour'.[25] Professor

---

23. J. Thorpe, *Marsden Children their work in the mills and the history of their schools*, (Marsden: Marsden History Group, 2010).
24. P. Kirby, *Child Labour in Britain, 1750–1870*, (Basingstoke: Macmillan, 2003), p. 40.
25. David Keys, *BBC History Magazine*, vol. 11, 8, August 2010, p. 15.

Humphries, whilst emphasizing the continuing significance of mechanisation and division of labour as other key factors driving change, has nevertheless demonstrated that, whereas for most of the eighteenth century only around thirty-five per cent of ten year-old working-class boys were in the labour force, the figure rose dramatically to fifty-five per cent between 1791 and 1820 and almost sixty per cent between 1821 and 1850, challenging the claims of Peter Kirby that very young child working was 'never widespread' in Britain, though Kirby recognised the problems associated with the sparsity of reliable quantitative data.[26]

However, it has also become increasingly clear that factory reform did not command universal support among factory workers, as the American neo-classical economic historian Clark Nardinelli recognised, arguing controversially but influentially that since child workers and their families apparently opted for employment by choice, child labour must have been a preferred option for significant numbers of families, though his views have been criticised as presenting 'an over optimistic view of work in the mills' by the British social historian Pamela Horn.[27] Nardinelli has also criticised Oastler rather churlishly for allegedly subordinating other welfare issues such as educational, sanitary and health provisions to his preoccupation with the single-issue campaign to secure a reduction of working hours, which Oastler clearly regarded as intrinsically linked with child welfare, whilst Peter Kirby has concluded somewhat tendentiously that 'humanitarian campaigns against child labour … should be viewed realistically as the product of a convergence of political interests rather than an attempt to improve the long-term welfare of most working children'.[28] Nardinelli's emphasis on the importance of technical change as a significant driving factor in the decline of child employment has, however, attracted more widespread support even from those historians like Humphries who

---

26. Ibid.; J. Humphries, *Childhood and Child Labour in the British Industrial Revolution*, pp. 2–3, 12, 42–48, 367; Kirby, *Child Labour*, p. 131.
27. C. Nardinelli, *Child Labor and the Industrial Revolution*, (Bloomington: Indiana University Press, 1990); Pamela Horn, *Children's Work and Welfare, 1780–1880s*, (Basingstoke: Macmillan, Economic History Society, 1994), p. 98.
28. Kirby, *Child Labour*, pp. 132–33.

seek to re-emphasize the role of children in bearing 'many of the social and economic costs of the industrial revolution'.[29]

The essays in this volume aim to inform both those with an interest in regional, local and family history and research students interested in exploring broader themes of British social and economic history within a global context. They utilise a wide range of sources and illustrations, many drawn from local and regional archive collections and offer fresh interpretations of the role of Richard Oastler, who remains a relatively neglected figure in British social and economic history, described by his twentieth-century biographer as England's forgotten 'Factory King'.[30] This collection of essays seeks to re-assess the significance of this extraordinary provincial figure, whose identification of the campaign for factory regulation with the astonishingly successful anti-slavery movement had such a far-reaching impact on the social history of nineteenth century Britain. These essays also endeavour to explore the relationship of the factory movement to the trailblazing anti-slavery campaign; its associations with Evangelicalism both in its paternalistic expressions within Anglicanism and its more radical expressions within Nonconformity, and its connections with embryonic trade unionism and Owenite socialism, particularly in Huddersfield and its vicinity. They also assess the significance of the regional media campaign and of well-publicised, carefully-planned demonstrations and processions in contributing to the success of the movement.

Chronologically, the book spans the period from the emergence of the anti-slavery movement in Yorkshire in 1787 until the death of the last veteran of Oastler's campaign in 1876. However the volume focuses predominantly on the four decades between 1807 and 1847, from the abolition of the slave trade in 1807 to the introduction of the Ten Hours Act for factory workers in 1847. Geographically, Huddersfield, which became the springboard for the re-launch of the ten-hour movement under Oastler's leadership in the 1830s, assumes centre stage for a significant proportion of the book, but the social and economic context in which the factory movement re-emerged during this decade in many other localities across the West Yorkshire textile

---

29. Humphries, *Childhood and Child Labour*, pp. 1, 7, 42, 245–46, 373.
30. Driver, *Tory Radical*, p. 520.

belt is also explored. Its links are recognised with a radical tradition dating from the American and French Revolutions, which embraced Yorkshire Luddism and the years of radical protest following the wars with Revolutionary and Napoleonic France and the later struggle for parliamentary reform between 1829 to 1832.[31] The impact of this extraordinarily passionate campaign on the post-reform politics of the 1830s and its significance in the development of legislative factory regulation restricting the working hours of children, requiring educational provision and the establishment of a factory inspectorate to ensure compliance with the law, is analysed and glimpses of its contribution to other contemporary extra-parliamentary protests, notably the anti-Poor Law movement and Chartism, are revealed, though not fully explored in this volume.

The history of this movement has a distinctively Yorkshire ambience. Richard Oastler, has frequently been characterised as an archetypal Yorkshireman: blunt, forthright and rarely reluctant to invoke his Yorkshire identity in the furtherance of his campaigning objectives. Moreover, he developed strong personal connections with an unusually broad spectrum of Yorkshire society in a variety of sharply contrasting communities within the county of his birth. The yeomen-farming, Anglican, paternal ancestry of his father, Robert Oastler (1748–1820), connected him with the secluded Swaledale village of Kirby Wiske, until his father's adolescent conversion to Wesleyanism obliged him to leave the family home and seek refuge in the bustling market town of Thirsk in North Yorkshire with his two uncles, John and Samson Oastler, prosperous Wesleyan Methodists. They had built the new chapel in Thirsk opened by John Wesley in April 1766, thereby introducing Robert and ultimately his son Richard to a vibrant North Riding Wesleyanism and a close relationship with its founder, who reputedly later took the young Richard in his arms and blessed him during a visit to the family home.[32]

Richard's maternal ancestry connected him with the West Riding town of Leeds, an emerging industrial centre, where his father had commenced cloth trading in the late 1780s and where a blue plaque

---

31. See also John A. Hargreaves, '"A Metropolis of Discontent" Popular Protest in Huddersfield c.1780–c.1850 in *Huddersfield. A Most Handsome Town*, ed. by E. A. Hilary Haigh (Huddersfield: Kirklees Cultural Services, 1992), pp. 189–220.
32. Driver, *Tory Radical*, pp. 4–5.

located close to the nucleus of the BBC's regional television and radio network in St Peter's Square, commemorates his birth to Sarah Oastler, daughter of Joseph Scurr of Leeds.[33] Richard's education connected him with the nearby Moravian settlement of Fulneck at Pudsey, which he attended between 1798 and 1806 and to which he made frequent return visits in later life, for example, his unexpected arrival at a centenary jubilee celebration in 1855 'grey-haired and stooping with age'. On this occasion he recounted how the religious teaching of the school especially that provided by his 'learned tutor, kind monitor and faithful friend', Henry Steinhauer, had 'often supplied him with support amid the conflicts of life'.[34] After a failed attempt to enter the legal profession and an abortive apprenticeship to a distinguished architect, Charles Watson, in Wakefield, curtailed because of problems with eyestrain, Oastler briefly entered the business world as a commission agent, liaising between Leeds wholesalers and retailers in towns and villages across the West Riding, and engaging in a variety of business activities as a 'drysalter, oilman, general dealer and chapman' until he was declared bankrupt in 1820. During these tumultuous years in Leeds, Oastler developed a close personal friendship with Michael Sadler, a Leeds linen merchant and energetic Church Methodist, who helped shape the young Oastler's emerging evangelical humanitarianism, Tory radicalism and commitment to the anti-slavery movement. Oastler's lifelong association with Leeds, where he was buried at St Stephen's Kirkstall in 1861, was recognised at the opening of the new Leeds Infirmary on 19 May 1868 in a commemorative booklet which listed Oastler among the most eminent figures in the history of Leeds and contained a rare extant photograph of Oastler in his later years.[35] A rectangular brass mural tablet, financed

33. Driver, *Tory Radical*, pp. 5–6.
34. J.P. Libby, *Celebration of the Centenary Jubilee of the Congregation of the United Brethren in Wyke, Mirfield, Gomersal and Fulneck*, April 1855, pp. 89–90, Fulneck School Archives, PC 533. Earlier references to his schooldays appear in entries of the Fulneck Elders' Conference, for 3 April 1802, where reference is made to a letter from his father testifying to the 'progress he finds his sons have made while they have attended the Fulneck Schools'. I am grateful to Ruth Strong for arranging for me to consult material in the archives relating to Richard Oastler.
35. C.S. Spence, *Memoirs of Eminent Men of Leeds*, (Leeds: D. Green and Sons, 1868).

1:9 Matthew
Balme (1813–1884),
Bradford factory
reformer (Yorkshire
Archaeological
Society).

by public subscriptions in remembrance of Richard Oastler, 'The
Factory King', was unveiled in Leeds Parish Church many years later
in 1925.[36] Today the Oastler Centre in New Market Street, Leeds,
recognised by the West Yorkshire Ecumenical Council in 2006 'as an
ecumenical instrument to foster and forward the mission of the

36. M. Pullan, *The Monuments of the Parish Church of St Peter-at-Leeds*, Thoresby
    Society/Leeds Philosophical and Literary Society, 2007, p. 183.

Church as it relates to the workplace and to the economic life of Leeds,' commemorates Oastler's historic links with the city.[37]

After his father's death and the failure of his own business in Leeds in 1820, employment opportunities drew Richard Oastler to Fixby near Huddersfield. After paying his creditors in full, he succeeded his father as land steward to the absentee Thornhill family at Fixby Hall. However, his management of the more distant Thornhill West Riding estates at Calverley bordering both Leeds and Bradford, enabled him to maintain his Leeds contacts and also develop close relationships with other key figures in the factory movement as it emerged under his leadership, not least the Revd George Stringer Bull, a former West African missionary, now Vicar of Bierley, and his protégé, the Bradford schoolmaster, Matthew Balme.[38]

In his new employment at Fixby he soon cut his teeth as a radical agitator by leading a highly effective, if deeply acrimonious, tithe war on behalf of his new employer, Thomas Thornhill, against the new Vicar of Halifax, the Revd Charles Musgrave, in whose parish Fixby was located, succeeding in resisting his attempt to double his tithe income.[39] In the process he established his first campaigning organisation, published his first substantial polemical tract and consequently received many invitations to speak on the factory question in the ancient parish of Halifax. Here he encountered some of his fiercest opposition from the millowners in Halifax led by the Akroyds and in the Calder Valley led by Messrs Edmondson, Walker and Hinchliffe of Cragg Vale, whom Oastler described as 'more Tyrannical and more Hypocritical than the Slave Drivers in the West Indies'. In retaliation, a vituperative poster dubbed Oastler 'that great Mountebank' and the Revd G.S. Bull of Bierley 'the noted

---

37. Philip Bee, *The Oastler Centre for Faith in Economic Life*, (Leeds: n.d.).
38. Driver, *Tory Radical*, pp. 19–23, 25–35; for Bull *see* J.C. Gill, *Parson Bull of Byerley*, (London: S.P.C.K., 1963) and for Balme, see John A. Hargreaves, 'Matthew Balme (1813–1884), factory reformer, *Oxford Dictionary of National Biography*, (Oxford: Oxford University Press, 2004).
39. R. Oastler, *Vicarial Tithes*, (Halifax: Holden, 1827); E.J. Evans, *The Contentious Tithe. The tithe problem and English agriculture, 1750–1850*, (London: Routledge, Kegan Paul, 1976), pp. 48–49.

Mountebank Parson' in advance of a meeting they were scheduled to
address at Hebden Bridge in August 1833 for 'seeking to shorten the
hours of labour'.[40]

Fixby, despite its historic links with the parish of Halifax,
overlooked the emerging industrial townscape of Huddersfield and its
hinterland, and is today the home of the Huddersfield Golf Club. It
was with the working men of Huddersfield on Sunday 19 June 1831
that Oastler established with six leading local radicals the famous Fixby
Hall compact, which committed both parties to setting aside their
sectarian and political differences to work together for the common
cause of factory reform.[41] Oastler was often personally identified with
the Huddersfield radical protesters, arriving at both the Easter
pilgrimage to York in April 1833 and at a demonstration at Wibsey
Moor on 1 July 1833 with 'Oastler's Own' Huddersfield contingent,
incorporating supporters from Holmfirth, Honley, Deighton and
Brighouse.[42] He twice stood for election to the post-reform Parliament
at Huddersfield and came within an ace of securing victory as a Tory
Radical in what has been described as a Whig pocket borough
under the control of the Ramsden family.[43] When he was obliged to
leave Fixby Hall after Thornhill dismissed him for his financial
mismanagement in 1838, Richard and Sarah Oastler were accompanied
by a procession of sympathetic tenantry, and ten-hour and anti-Poor
Law movement protesters organised by the Huddersfield Short Time
Committee. Scarcely a month after his subsequent imprisonment in

---

40. Driver, *Tory Radical*, pp. 547–50; *Letter to the Factory Masters in Cragg Dale,
    who have challenged Richard Oastler without publishing their names*, broadsheet
    published by Joshua Hobson, Huddersfield, 15 July 1833; George Crabtree,
    Tour, passim; for the Cragg Vale controversy see the extensive collection of
    posters in the Richard Oastler 'White Slavery' Collection at Goldsmith's
    College, University of London, including: 'An Appeal to the Public by the
    Factory Masters in Cragg Valley', Todmorden, 9 July 1833; 'To the Nameless
    Factory Masters in the Cragg Valley', Bradford Short Time Committee, 2
    August 1833 and 'Unrivalled Performances! That great Mountebank, R. Oastler
    will exhibit to the public at Hebden Bridge', 22 August, 1833.
41. Driver, *Tory Radical*, pp. 86–89, 395, 420.
42. Ward, *Factory Movement*, pp. 104–05, 157.
43. Felix Driver, 'Tory Radicalism? Ideology, Strategy and Locality in Popular
    Politics during the Eighteen-Thirties', *Northern History*, vol. xxvii, 1991, pp.
    120–38.

1:10 Statue of
Richard Oastler by
John Birnie Phillips,
Bradford, n.d. (West
Yorkshire Archive
Service, Bradford:
38D96 folio 39).

the metropolitan Fleet debtor's prison, his 'Huddersfield Boys' held an
Oastler festival in the Philosophical Hall at Huddersfield attended by
over 600 supporters, followed by music and dancing which resulted
in a cheque for £23 being forwarded to Oastler for sustenance.[44]

44. Driver, *Tory Radical*, pp. 420–21.

STATUE OF RICHARD OASTLER AT BRADFORD.

1:11 Depiction of the statue of Richard Oastler with two factory children, *Illustrated London News* 15 May 1869 (University of Huddersfield Special Collections).

Indeed, he regularly received hampers of food sent from Huddersfield during his incarceration, commenting in his weekly *Fleet Papers* which he edited from his prison cell that 'a Huddersfield friend sent me a box of preserves. The fruit was grown in his Fixby gardens!'[45] Just

45. R. Oastler, *Fleet Papers*, vol. II, 41, 8 October 1842, cited in J. Horsfall Turner, (Bradford: *Halifax Books and Authors*, 1906), p. 195.

prior to his release from prison in 1844 Oastler informed his close friend and supporter, Lawrence Pitkethly that he had declined an invitation to attend a public dinner and subsequently recuperate in 'the North Riding', insisting that he must return to 'Huddersfield first'.[46] Unsurprisingly, he received a rapturous welcome on his return to Huddersfield following his release.[47] Whilst residing at Fixby Hall from 1820 to 1838, he worshipped at nearby Christ Church, Woodhouse, where his association was later commemorated by a monument, financed by contributions from Huddersfield factory operatives, which bore an inscription proclaiming that Richard Oastler, 'the Factory King ... lives in the hearts of thousands'.[48]

Oastler's dramatic conversion at the age of forty to the cause of factory reform at Horton Hall, the home of the worsted manufacturer John Wood, connected him to Bradford, which for most of the factory movement's history became the Yorkshire headquarters of the campaign since his famous letter on Yorkshire Slavery had explicitly

1:12 Opening of the Oastler Memorial Playground, Greenhead Park, Huddersfield, which was handed over to the County Borough Council in December 1926. The inscription on the plaque describes Oastler as 'the Factory King' who 'laboured and suffered for poor children' (Kirklees Image Archive k013103).

46. Letter from Richard Oastler to Lawrence Pitkethly, 1 February 1844, WYAS Kirklees, KC 1040, 5/4-5/5.
47. See below, chapter 6.
48. A. Porritt, 'Richard Oastler', *Transactions of the Halifax Antiquarian Society*, 1965, p. 44.

criticised conditions in Bradford's worsted mills.[49] Indeed subsequent criticism of Oastler in 1834 by the liberal *Bradford Observer* provoked one of the most stinging rebukes Oastler ever delivered in a vitriolic pamphlet accusing the dissenting manufacturing shareholders of the *Bradford Observer*, 'Messrs. Get-all, Keep-all, Grasp-all', of the most outrageous hypocrisy, professing piety in their chapels while maintaining appalling conditions in their mills.[50] However, later an Oastler festival was also organised entirely by operatives in Bradford to support the leader of the movement during his imprisonment.[51] Moreover, after his death an imposing bronze statue by John Birnie Phillips, depicting Oastler with two factory children on a plinth of polished granite, was unveiled in his memory by the Earl of Shaftesbury on 15 May 1869 in Forster Square opposite the railway station, after an overwhelming majority of 1,472 subscribers to the memorial fund had favoured a Bradford location for the statue.[52]

The initiative for the memorial, one of the earliest provincial statues depicting children in the public realm, had come from the trade unions and Short Time Committees of Yorkshire and Lancashire and an estimated hundred thousand people gathered for the ceremony, prompting Shaftesbury to record in his diary that 'the throng was immense ... their enthusiasm knew no bounds'.[53]

Oastler was also associated with the county city of York, the location for the Easter pilgrimage in support of factory reform at the culmination of his most famous, county-wide campaign in April 1833; and Wakefield, where he led one of the largest protests by anti-Poor Law protesters from all parts of the West Riding ever held in the town.

---

49. Ward, *Bradford Textile Society Journal*, 1961, p. 41.
50. Driver, *Tory Radical*, pp. 298-99.
51. Driver, *Tory Radical*, p. 421.
52. The Memorial Committee had originally proposed that the monument be erected in Leeds but a ballot of subscribers resulted in a decisive vote in favour of Bradford (1,472) considerably ahead of Leeds (119), Huddersfield (88) and Halifax (5), see A. Porritt, 'Richard Oastler', *Transactions of the Halifax Antiquarian Society*, 1965, pp. 42–43. The statue was subsequently moved to Rawson Square in 1920 to facilitate the development of the tramway terminus and to its present location off Northgate in 1968.
53. Driver, *Tory Radical*, p. 520; E. Hodder, *Life and Work of the Seventh Earl of Shaftesbury*, (London: Cassell, 1892), p. 636.

1:13 The Rastrick
Ten-hour Movement
Banner, inscribed
on the obverse:
OASTLER is our
Champion. The
TEN HOURS
BILL, And We are
Determined to
have it (Tolson
Memorial Museum,
Huddersfield).

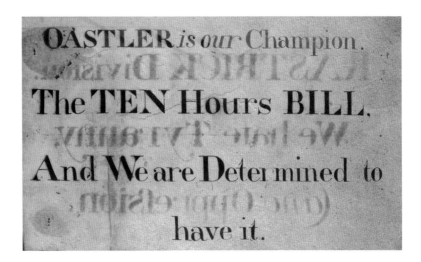

The occasion for the latter demonstration was the hustings for the West Riding constituency, the largest in England, for the county election on Monday 31 July in 1837, called following the dissolution of Parliament on the accession of Queen Victoria. Although narrowly defeated in the recently held Huddersfield borough election of that year, Oastler's appeal for opposition to 'this horrible Bastille law' resulted in some 30,000 supporters and their opponents descending on Wakefield to hear Oastler and others address the crowds. In the ensuing riot there were two fatalities and Oastler himself suffered personal injury.[54]

Oastler's marriage to Mary Tatham, a woman of delicate health hailing from a wealthy Nottingham Wesleyan family of lace makers, had produced two children, Sarah and Robert, both of whom had died shortly after birth in 1819.[55] After his wife's death in 1845, Richard Oastler spent his declining years in rural Surrey living in a small cottage outside Guildford, cared for by his niece, collating records of the factory movement for posterity. However, he died in the county of his birth at a hotel in Harrogate after collapsing with a heart attack as his train approached Harrogate station on 22 August 1861. His old adversary, the young Edward Baines, drew on a host of superlatives to extol Oastler's passing, proclaiming that 'he has died without an enemy

54. Driver, *Tory Radical*, pp. 362–63.
55. Driver, *Tory Radical*, p. 23.

and that the news of his death will be received with tears in many a poor man's dwelling.' He concluded that 'there can be no doubt that the factory operatives' condition is now vastly superior to what it was in 1830'.[56] Indeed, Oastler himself had lived to witness from the gallery of the House of Commons the debates that had led to legislation in 1853 which ensured the demise of the relay system by which employers had been able to circumvent the implementation of the Ten Hours Act of 1847. The surviving Huddersfield working men who had made the Fixby Hall compact with Richard Oastler three decades earlier carried the most persistent champion of their cause to his grave at St Stephen's Church, Kirkstall, eight years later and a memorial sermon was subsequently preached at Huddersfield Parish Church in the presence of a vast congregation, by the Revd G.S. Bull of Bierley who had also conducted Oastler's funeral, when the churchyard of St Stephen's at Kirkstall and the roads leading to it had been thronged with thousands of mourners.[57]

Although he had spent much of his retirement in Surrey, Richard Oastler's commitment to the twin campaigns to abolish colonial slavery and end the abuses to children in factories linked him irrevocably with West Yorkshire, and especially with Huddersfield's hinterland from where he had penned his celebrated 'Slavery in Yorkshire' letter to the *Leeds Mercury* three decades previously. Appropriately a suburban street

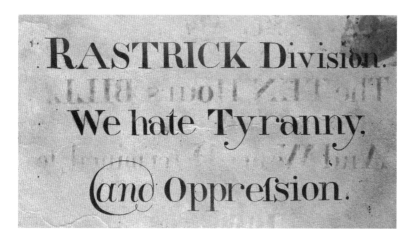

1:14 The Rastrick Ten-hour Movement Banner, inscribed on the reverse: RASTRICK Division. We hate Tyranny and Oppression (Tolson Memorial Museum, Huddersfield).

---

56. Driver, *Tory Radical*, pp. 519–20.
57. Driver, *Tory Radical*, p. 520.

(Oastler Avenue), a former teacher training college (Oastler College) and a children's playground in the town's Greenhead Park were named in his honour in Huddersfield, where he was remembered affectionately by Huddersfield politicians from across the political spectrum. Indeed, Arthur Gardiner (1889–1971), the Huddersfield wool and cotton dyer, a founder member of the Huddersfield Socialist Party in 1910, a conscientious objector during the First World War and member of the Labour Party from 1918, who served subsequently as Huddersfield councillor (1927–30, 1933–67), alderman (1935) and mayor (1941–42), receiving the Freedom of the Borough in 1960, commented in his study of *The Industrial Revolution and Child Labour* in 1948:

> There is one monument in Huddersfield that I never pass without a warm glow of affection and respect. It is the small memorial, erected outside the Children's Playground in Greenhead Park (what a delightfully appropriate place) to the memory of Richard Oastler, 'The Factory King'. Oastler sacrificed his health and his fortune in fighting the battle of the child-slaves. May his memory remain green in the hearts and minds of those who love their fellow-man.[58]

The Rastrick flag which was carried by 'Oastler's Own' Huddersfield contingent on the Easter pilgrimage to York in 1833 hangs proudly in a gallery of the Tolson Museum at Ravensknowle Park, Huddersfield, which also exhibits commemorative medals struck by Oastler's friends to help pay off his debts, a commemorative ceramic blue and white jug dedicated to Oastler the 'Friend of the Poor' and other memorabilia associated with 'the Factory King', including a receipt bearing his distinctive florid signature.

This book focusing on Richard Oastler, Yorkshire Slavery and the campaign against child labour in Britain continues the commemorative

---

58. A. Gardiner, *The Industrial Revolution and Child Slavery*, (Slaithwaite: A.T. Green and Company, 1948), p. 43; For details of Gardiner see C. Pearce, *Comrades in Conscience. The story of an English community's opposition to the Great War*, (London: Francis Boutle Publishers, 2001), p. 296 and passim and *Huddersfield Directory*, 21937, xxxvii; D. Griffiths, *Secured for the Town. The story of Huddersfield's Greenhead Park*, (Huddersfield: Friends of Greenhead Park, 2011), pp. 41, 44, 49. The playground was moved to a new location within the park in 2010 during the park's restoration.

tradition, exploring the cross-fertilisation between the trans-Atlantic anti-slavery movement whose parliamentary campaign was led by William Wilberforce and the campaign against child labour whose extra-parliamentary campaign was led by Richard Oastler, both natives of Yorkshire. James Walvin, a leading contributor to the commemoration of the bi-centenary of the ending of the trans-Atlantic slave trade, provides an overview of the anti-slavery movement. He discusses the dependence of Yorkshire's economy and its landed estates, not least the Lascelles estate at Harewood, on the notorious triangular slave trade. He then traces the emergence of the anti-slavery movement in Yorkshire in 1787 and its impact within the county, before considering the continuing campaign to end the institution of slavery in the British Empire and the controversial system of colonial apprenticeship which continued until 1840, seven years after Wilberforce's death. He emphasizes the significance of humanitarian and evangelical support for the anti-slavery cause, which Wilberforce received from Tory Evangelicals like Richard Oastler, who on one occasion heroically defended Wilberforce from brickbats hurled at him at the hustings at Wakefield in the West Riding election of 1807.[59] He identifies some

1:15
Commemorative medal inscribed on the obverse 'THE OASTLER NATIONAL TESTIMONIAL 1838' and on the reverse 'DWELL LONG IN THE LAND AND VERILY THOU SHALT BE FED: LIVE AND LET LIVE' (Tolson Memorial Museum, Huddersfield).

---

59. Driver, *Tory Radical*, p. 19

1:16 Oastler
commemorative jug,
describing Richard
Oastler as the 'Friend
of the Poor' (Tolson
Memorial Museum,
Huddersfield).

of the key sources available for the study of the movement, its historiography and central interpretative issues and indicates areas which need further research particularly at regional and local level.

Colin Dews of the Wesley Historical Society (Yorkshire) explains the Methodist influences in Yorkshire which helped shape Oastler's evangelical toryism. He focuses upon the significance of the relatively neglected radical Methodist New Connexion influences as well as the more familiar formative Wesleyan Methodist influences deriving from his family background and strengthened by his friendship with Michael Sadler, a Leeds linen merchant and devout Methodist, which helped to shape Oastler's emergence as a radical campaigner and social philanthropist. Utilising sources unavailable to Oastler's biographer Cecil Driver in 1946, Dews explains Oastler's father Robert's instrumental role in the establishment of the Methodist New Connexion in Leeds. He notes how during this period he developed a friendship with the dissenting editor of the *Leeds Mercury*, Edward Baines, and how he emerged as a supporter of the radical secessionist

New Connexion Methodists following the traumatic experience of the loss of a sibling in a horrifying factory fire at Marshall's flax spinning mill in Holbeck, Leeds, on 13 February 1796. The 'dreadful conflagration', which caused the collapse of a wall injuring some twenty workers and killing seven others including Richard's twelve-year-old brother, Robert, opened a rift between the Oastler family and the Wesleyan superintendent minister the Revd Joseph Benson (1748–1821), who advised burial in the parochial churchyard, which was becoming an increasingly acceptable practice for Nonconformists by the late eighteenth century.[60] In the event the chapel trustees overruled their minister and the young Robert Oastler's funeral was conducted by a Baptist minister in the Old Boggard chapel burial ground, the first interment at the chapel which defected to the Methodist New Connexion in 1797 thereby undoubtedly strengthening support for the Kilhamite secession in Leeds.

Fires continued to occur with disturbing frequency in textile factories into the nineteenth century, adding to the toll of juvenile casualties. The fire at Thomas Atkinson's cotton factory at Colne Bridge Mills, Huddersfield, before dawn on the morning of 14 February 1818 was described in the *Leeds Mercury* as 'a most destructive and calamitous fire ... in which the lives of seventeen female children were lost'. Cotton and carded laps appear to have been ignited from the naked flame of a candle by a young boy sent down to the card room for rovings. Desperate attempts to reach the stranded girls by a ladder to a small upstairs window proved unsuccessful when the roof and floors collapsed and within half an hour 'the entire building, all the machinery and every article of stock was destroyed'. Of the twenty-six employees at the mill, only nine escaped and the ages of those who perished in the inferno ranged from nine to eighteen.[61] Curiously, Richard Oastler does not appear to have alluded publicly to this terrifying inferno, which must have remained strong in the popular memory of the town when he took up the cause of factory reform. Was this because of the painful memory of his own

---

60. W. Gibson, *Religion and Society in England and Wales, 1689–1800*, (London: Leicester University Press, 1998), p. 129.
61. *Leeds Mercury*, 21 February 1818, cited in J. Addy, *The Textile Revolution*, (London: Longman, 1976), pp. 98–99.

Find ant

personal loss of his brother in the disastrous fire at Holbeck or was it that this fire in a cotton factory fell outside the remit of his current campaign, namely the ending of child labour in the still unregulated worsted mills? The Colne Bridge fire was instrumental in securing the 1819 Factory Act, but this legislation applied only to cotton factories and not the worsted factories of the West Riding. Oastler's campaign was designed to rectify that omission.

John Halstead of the University of Sheffield provides an in-depth analysis of the factory movement from the grass roots focusing upon the membership, influence and significance of the Huddersfield Short Time Committee until the death of its last surviving member in 1876. Utilising a wide range of sources and employing painstaking detective work he identifies many of the less well-known figures in the movement. Focus on high politics and the drama of the parliamentary campaign has often consigned the Short Time Committees a peripheral role in the movement, but in Halstead's analysis the Huddersfield Short Time Committee occupies centre stage. Analysis of its composition by age and occupation reveals that a remarkably high proportion of members of the committee were in-comers, illustrating the rapid migration of population into Huddersfield and its hinterland in the first three decades of the nineteenth century. However, relatively fewer of its members than those of the Leeds Short Time Committee were employed in factories since Huddersfield was still more a marketing than a manufacturing centre.

Edward Royle of the University of York in a chapter entitled 'Press and People: Oastler's Yorkshire Slavery Campaign, 1830–32' offers an evaluation of the significance of the campaign which Oastler waged through the Leeds press, in the movement to secure improved factory regulation. He demonstrates how Oastler was able to exploit the rivalries of the Leeds newspaper editors to become one of the most successful newspaper propagandists of his day in both the factory and anti-Poor Law movements. He also reveals how Joshua Hobson, one of the Huddersfield working men who had met Oastler at Fixby Hall in June 1831 to seek his support for the factory movement, became a leading figure in the campaign for the unstamped press through *The Voice of the West Riding* between the reform struggle of 1830–32 and the rise of Chartism when he published the *Northern Star and Leeds General Advertiser*, which became the mouthpiece of Feargus O'Connor and the emerging campaign for the People's Charter after

1837. He records the vivid childhood recollections of the Honley
postmistress and local historian, Mary Jagger, of stories of Oastler's
memorable campaign, linking concerns which continued beyond her
own day into the twenty-first century 'with its own experience of child
exploitation on a global scale and the continued subjection of the weak
to the power of the strong'.[62]

Janette Martin of the University of Huddersfield focuses upon
Richard Oastler's triumphal entry into Huddersfield in 1844 following
his release from prison, which she argues was an event skilfully
orchestrated to re-invigorate support for the languishing factory
movement not only in its Huddersfield heartland but also much
further afield, since reports of the event were widely disseminated. She
examines the detailed planning of the carefully staged event and
examines its significance within the context of radical demonstrations
after Peterloo. She explores Oastler's reception in his adopted town of
Huddersfield, evaluates his use of oratory in gaining public support
and examines the significance of the reporting of this later episode both
within and beyond Huddersfield. She argues that the demonstration
of support for Richard Oastler vindicated his public career as an
outspoken critic of factory exploitation and the New Poor Law, given
the politically motivated nature of his imprisonment as a result of
deteriorating relations with his former employer, Thomas Thornhill.

A concluding chapter by John A. Hargreaves of the University of
Huddersfield re-assesses the historical significance of Richard Oastler
and challenges the portrayal of Oastler as a quasi-revolutionary
demagogue by his twenty-first century biographer, Stewart Angas
Weaver.[63] It argues that although Oastler's oratory was often intemperate
in highlighting the injustices of child labour in factories and the
inhumane operation of the New Poor Law, occasionally inviting
misrepresentation of his motives by his opponents when he appeared
to advocate or condone criminality and violence, in reality his rhetoric
hardly amounted to a sustained challenge to the state in which 'he trod

---

62. Mary A. Jagger, *The Early Reminiscences of Mrs Jagger* (Honley: Dightam, 1934),
    (reprinted from articles in the *Huddersfield Weekly Examiner*, January
    and February 1931), p. 12.
63. S.A. Weaver, 'Richard Oastler', *Oxford Dictionary of National Biography*,
    (Oxford: Oxford University Press, 2004).

the edges of revolution' for 'ten turbulent years'. Indeed, it concludes that he is more aptly characterised as a Tory Radical than as a Revolutionary Tory or even as a Tory humanitarian in his devotion to the preservation of 'altar, throne and cottage' and in his opposition to aspects of the new industrial society which he deemed oppressive and of the new political economy of laissez-faire and utilitarianism which he viewed as inhumane.[64] This placed him well to the right on the ideological spectrum re-defined by the Jacobinism of the era of the French Revolution, which began to resonate across Europe, and indeed beyond, in the year of Richard Oastler's birth, stimulating a slave insurrection in the French colony of St Domingue by 1791. It was this Haitian revolt, ignited by the 'contagion of equality' released by the French Revolution, James Walvin has argued, which had such a catalytic effect on the embryonic campaign against colonial slavery in Britain.[65] This volume of essays offers fresh perspectives on both the anti-slavery movement and the campaign for factory regulation which Oastler insisted was no less relevant to his Yorkshire contemporaries since 'victims of slavery' were evident 'even on the threshold of our homes'.

64. Driver, *Tory Radical*, passim; S.A. Weaver, 'Oastler, Richard (1789–1861)', *Oxford Dictionary of National Biography*; E.J. Evans, *Forging of the Modern State*, p. 287; *A-Z of Nineteenth and Twentieth Century British History*, (London: Hodder and Stoughton, 1998), p. 215.
65. J. Walvin, *Britain's Slave Empire*, (Stroud: Tempus, 2000), pp. 66, 68–70, 77–78, 127; D. Geggus, 'British Opinion and the Emergence of Haiti, 1791–1805' *Slavery and British Society, 1776–1846*, ed. by J. Walvin (London: Macmillan, 1982), pp. 123–49.

William Wilberforce, Yorkshire and the campaign to end transatlantic slavery, 1787–1838

JAMES WALVIN

2:1 Portrait of William Wilberforce by John Rising. The portrait, commissioned by Lord Muncaster and exhibited at the Royal Academy in 1790, shows the twenty-nine year old Wilberforce seated by a table strewn with papers and books, a scrolled document in his left hand and a quill pen in his right (Hull Museums).

THE STATUE OF William Wilberforce, which stands at the top of the 102-feet high Doric column in the centre of Kingston upon Hull, is altogether more aggressive and dominant than his tranquil pose in Westminster Abbey, where he rests next to the remains of his life-long friend, William Pitt the Younger. However different, both postures illustrate different aspects of the same remarkable man. It is fitting that Wilberforce dominates the skyline of Hull – or did until overshadowed by a modern building. In the late eighteenth century it was a city which thrived on its maritime trade, though not everyone liked the city's bustling commerce. Dorothy Wordsworth thought it a 'frightful, dirty, brick-housey, tradesman-like, rich, vulgar place'.[1]

Wilberforce was born into one of Hull's prosperous trading families, becoming MP for the city in 1780 at the age of twenty-one while still a student at Cambridge. From 1784 to 1812 he was MP for Yorkshire. But by 1812 the stress of travelling to and from Yorkshire – he was a diligent MP – and the burdens of representing the nation's biggest county, proved too much for the ageing and ailing Wilberforce so, reluctantly, he decided to step aside from Yorkshire and accepted the rotten borough of Bramber instead. Age and ill health forced his final retirement from Westminster in 1825.

Of all the issues that attracted his attention, and consumed his time (damaging his eye-sight in endless letter-writing), of the myriad topics he promoted in Parliament (not all of them progressive), Wilberforce is universally remembered for his work against the Atlantic slave trade,

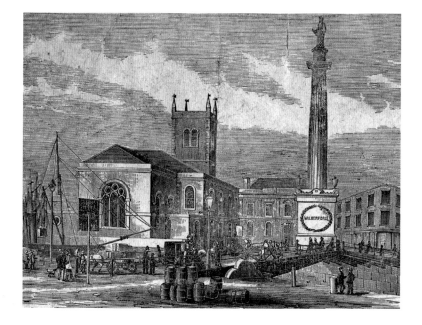

2:2 The Wilberforce Monument, comprising a twelve-feet high statue of Wilberforce, sculpted by Mr Feort of Dock Street, atop a ninety-feet high column, costing £1,200 and dedicated in November 1835. The foundation stone had been laid by Richard Bethel MP on 1 August 1834, the day on which slavery in the British colonies was abolished (Hull Museums).

1. Quoted in Ellen Gibson Wilson, 'The Great Yorkshire Election', p. 29, unpublished manuscript. I was kindly allowed access to this material by Mr H. S. Wilson and am much indebted to him for his generosity. Most of all, however, I am indebted to the late Ellen Wilson for her important and pioneering work in this area.

2:3 Wilberforce
statue, Hull
(Photograph:
E.A.H.Haigh).

2:4 Originally sited
by Princes Dock, the
monument was
moved to Queen's
Gardens in 1935, at
a cost of £1,500; the
dedication ceremony
was attended by Mrs
Arnold Reckitt,
William Wilberforce's
great granddaughter.
(Photograph:
E.A.H.Haigh).

and later slavery.[2] And it was when he was MP for Yorkshire that
Wilberforce laid the foundations for his work against the slave trade.
From that day to this, the links between Wilberforce, the abolitionist,
and his native county have remained strong. Fittingly, the most
important academic and civic initiative for the study of slavery and
abolition is located in Hull.[3]

At first glance it seems curious that Yorkshire provided the political
base for Wilberforce's drive against the slave trade, and was also the
scene for lively electoral campaigns dominated by the slave trade. The
county had no immediately obvious direct links to the slave trade: Hull
was not a slaving port, but drew its maritime commercial strength from
the North Sea, from trade to and from Europe and the Baltic. Equally,

2. There are many biographies of Wilberforce. The most recent is William Hague,
   William Wilberforce. The Life of the Great Anti-Slave Trade Campaigner (London:
   Harper Press, 2007).
3. www2.hull.ac.uk, The Wilberforce Institute for the Study of Slavery and
   Emancipation, at the University of Hull.

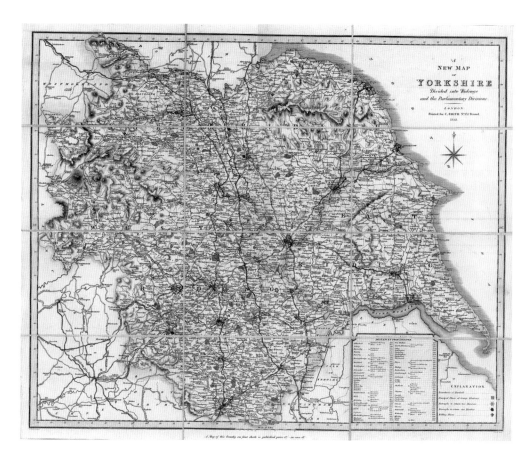

2:5 Smith's 1832
Map of Yorkshire
divided into Ridings
and Parliamentary
divisions.

the economic life of the county seemed far removed from that ebb and
flow of westward trade and commerce in the Atlantic that lay at the
heart of the slave trade. Yet first appearances can deceive. The links
between Yorkshire and slavery were more direct, and more important,
than first impressions might suggest.

The slave trade thrived on the export of goods to Africa and to the
American plantations from Britain's industrial hinterlands. Yorkshire
manufactures played an important part in the trade to West Africa.
The expanding canal systems of the mid- and late-eighteenth century,
linking Yorkshire and Lancashire, delivered textiles and metal goods
to the Liverpool ships bound for slave trading on the African coast.[4]

---

4. Kenneth Morgan, *Slavery and the British Empire*, (Oxford: Oxford University
    Press, 2007), p. 67: Joseph E. Inikori, *Africans and the Industrial Revolution in
    England* (Cambridge: Cambridge University Press, 2002).

Yorkshire was also the home, and ultimately the grand rural retreat, for one of Britain's most spectacular example of profits from slavery: the Lascelles family of Harewood House.[5] But the county's best-known link was of course the man who came to personify the campaign against the slave trade – William Wilberforce. Indeed Wilberforce has dominated and, to a degree, distorted the historiography of abolition. By personalizing the campaign against slavery, earlier historians have misrepresented the true nature of abolition itself. This process was initiated by his sons in their hagiographical study of their father published in 1838.[6]

From 1787, the abolitionist campaign, of which Wilberforce was the Parliamentary leader and spokesman, developed a new and highly-effective political *modus operandi* which was to influence the wider world of radical and reforming politics well into the nineteenth century. Indeed the structure and nature of abolitionist politics, devised and replicated across Britain after 1787, was adopted by subsequent reforming movements. Equally the vernacular of abolition, more especially the language and imagery of slavery, persisted long after British slavery had been fully abolished in 1838. In the process, slavery became a much-hated institution, and the word itself – slavery – came to describe anything that was hateful, sinful, morally bankrupting and inhuman.

Thus by the 1830s slavery was widely viewed in Britain as the most wicked of institutions. Subsequently, anything that looked wrong or morally suspect, anything that even smacked of slavery, could be dismissed in a word: 'slavery'. Here was a word, with its associated graphic images, which instantly condemned the object of attack. Merely to describe an institution as slavery was to condemn it utterly. Not surprisingly then, when the factory movement emerged in the wake of abolition, some of whose leaders had flexed their reforming muscles in the abolitionist campaigns, to speak of 'factory slavery' was instantly to seize the moral high ground in the political argument.

---

5. S. D. Smith, *Slavery, Family and Gentry Capitalism in the British Atlantic. The World of the Lascelles, 1645–1834* (Cambridge: Cambridge University Press, 2006).

6. *The Life of William Wilberforce*, by his sons, R.I. and S. Wilberforce, 5 vols (London: John Murray, 1838).

Who, in the 1830s and 1840s, could stand up and dispute the wickedness of slavery – in all its forms? Any institution that looked like slavery, or could be accused of being like it, was instantly damned.

Yet only fifty years earlier, slavery and its umbilical cord, the Atlantic slave trade, were economically vital and politically unchallenged. Within the space of two generations a remarkable change took place and slavery went from being commercially and politically unassailable to being an epithet of abuse and denigration: an economic and moral pariah. The story of that transformation is the history of the rise and triumph of abolition. It is a process that provides a remarkable insight into broader changes in Britain at large, and throughout Britain's localities and regions.

Although there had been earlier reforming campaigns – most recently the Yorkshire Association and the Society for Constitutional Information – the abolition campaign after 1787 established a political model and a vernacular, which were to have profound consequences on British reform long after the slave trade had been abolished.[7]

No one in 1787 could have predicted that the movement to end the slave trade would be successful. The campaign had modest, rather unpretentious origins. For a start, the slave trade itself had aroused relatively little opposition since time out of mind. By the time the British (more properly, in its early years, the English) became active in the Atlantic trade, others had pioneered the acquisition, loading and shipping of Africans on the protracted ocean voyage to the Americas.[8] The Portuguese and Spaniards used Africans as slaves in the Atlantic islands, in Spain and Portugal, and in their early settlements in the Americas. The entire story was transformed, however, by the

7. Caroline Robbins, *The Eighteenth Century Commonwealthman* (Cambridge, Mass.: Harvard University Press, 1958); E.C. Black, *The Association. British Extraparliamentary Political Organisations* (Cambridge, Mass.: Harvard University Press, 1963); Bernard Cook, ed., *The Consortium on Revolutionary Europe, 1750–1850* (Tallahassee: Florida State University, 1995). There is a need for caution about the effects of abolition: 2.5 million Africans were shipped to the Americas after 1808. This and all other data from the slave trade is derived from the remarkable slave data base master-minded by David Eltis, David Richardson and Stephen Behrendt: *The Trans Atlantic Slave Trade Database* at: www.slavevoyages.org (accessed 19 July 2011).
8. Seymour Drescher, *Abolition. A History of Slavery and Abolition* (Cambridge: Cambridge University Press, 2009), ch. 2.

2:6 The *Brookes* slave ship. The poster and ship model were based on an actual slave ship, built in Liverpool in 1780–1781, co-owned by Liverpool merchant Joseph Brookes and operating as a slave ship until 1804. Used by the London Committee in their abolition campaign, the poster was designed to highlight the horrors of the slave trade by depicting the amount of space allocated to the 451 slaves the ship was designed to carry, an image of overcrowding and cruelty designed to shock (Hull Museums).

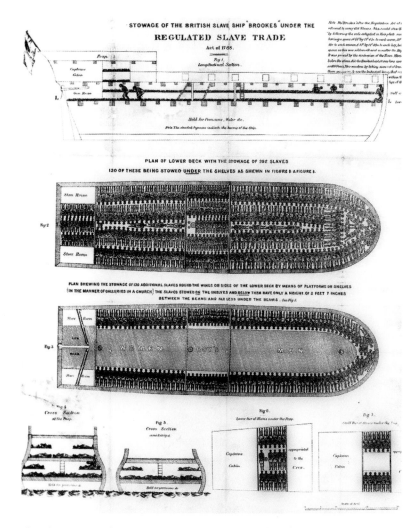

development of sugar plantations. Although African slavery was to spread to all corners of society across the Americas, from labour at the quaysides to work on the expanding frontiers, it was the sugar plantation that proved to be the engine behind the Atlantic slave trade. Over the entire history of Atlantic slavery, some 10.5 million Africans were loaded on to slave ships on the African coast, and over eight millions survived to landfall. Of those survivors, about seventy per cent were destined, initially, to work on sugar plantations. The whole process was linked to material consumption in the western world, as more and more people came to rely on slave-grown crops. The millions who took comfort and pleasure from these fruits of enslaved labour

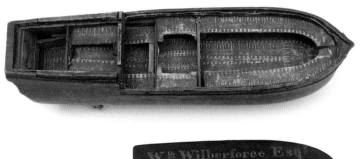

2:7 The model of the *Brookes* slave ship was shown to MPs by Wilberforce in his campaign against slavery. The paper diagram of enslaved Africans has been laid out on the decks and wooden partitions with hand written names for each section may be seen. 'William Wilberforce Esqr. To the House of Commons' is written in gold paint on the box lid (Hull Museums).

scarcely gave a thought to the Africans who made it possible. Caribbean sugar to sweeten tea from China and coffee from Arabia, sugar to add to the British passion for desserts: rum as meagre comfort for the wretchedness of life below decks on naval vessels – and, of course, slave-grown tobacco as part of a masculine culture everywhere. All was made possible by the efforts of African slaves on the plantations of the Americas.[9]

There had been some initial worries about the nature and morality of African slavery but the obvious benefits, which soon began to flow from the enslaved Americas and from the slave ships, simply drowned out such objections. The sound of profitable commerce effectively silenced ethical and religious scruples – Catholic and Protestant alike. Critical voices of people who witnessed the brute realities of the slave ships generally went unheeded. And as the slave trade grew, as slave ports flourished, spawning a thriving multitude of industries in their broader economic hinterlands, economics simply trumped morality. London, Bristol and then Liverpool flourished: by the late-eighteenth century, one African in five crossed the Atlantic in a ship from Liverpool. Though Liverpool dominated, ports around the country joined in. Ports from Lancaster to Poole were eager to join in the

---

9. Sidney Mintz, *Sweetness and Power* (London: Penguin Books, 1985); James Walvin, *Fruits of Empire* (London: Macmillan, 1997).

bonanza of the trade to and from West Africa. And the same was true elsewhere in Europe: in France for example, from Honfleur to Bordeaux.

The Atlantic slave trade was not a branch of commerce which simply grew of its own accord. It was carefully planned and directed, discussed and argued about in great political (and diplomatic) detail. First Royalty and then Parliament imposed their own distinct regulation on the trade. The British trade was initially allocated to the monopolistic Royal African Company. Later Parliament opened up the trade to wider competition. But everyone involved, from monarchs to parliamentary factions, argued not about the morality of slaving but about how best to organise the trade. The end result was that, from the 1670s onwards, Parliament passed dozens of Acts to control, regulate and license the slave trade. Parliament was, quite simply, a slaving legislature long before it undertook the political volte-face of staggering proportions and legislated to abolish the slave trade.[10]

The size of the Atlantic slave trade and its consequences for three continents were enormous. We know of 40,000 slave voyages. Some 12,000 of them were British, of which about one half originated in Liverpool. The financing and insuring of much of that trade came largely from London. Regional – sometimes distant and remote – industries dispatched their commodities to the nearest seaport for export to West Africa, there to be traded for African slaves, or to the American plantations where they fed, clothed and equipped the gangs of African slaves. Bulky products of West Yorkshire's textile industries and metal goods from Sheffield were transported to Liverpool's new docks and thence onto the slave ships.[11] The development of trade inside Africa (the growth of African consumption of British goods) was equally striking. Of course, this development of trade in the

---

10. William A. Pettigrew, 'Parliament and the Escalation of the Slave Trade, 1690–1714', in *The British Slave Trade: Abolition, Parliament and People*, eds, Stephen Farrell, Melanie Unwin and James Walvin. (Edinburgh: Edinburgh University Press for The Parliamentary History Yearbook Trust, 2007).

11. T. H. B. Oldfield, *An Entire and complete history, political and personal, of the boroughs of Great Britain*, 3 vols (London: G. Riley, 1792), I., pp. 343–44. See also Jane Langmore, 'Civic Liverpool, 1680–1800', chapter 3 in *Liverpool 800. Culture Character and History*, ed. by John Belchem (Liverpool: Liverpool University Press, 2006).

Atlantic was itself part of much wider development of British global commerce and colonial expansion. The Atlantic was integrated into a wider global commercial system. But what distinguished the Atlantic system itself was its reliance on the enslavement of Africans.

From the first, the slave system was shaped by brutality. Although it was a form of trade, with all sides striking commercial deals via exchanges of commodities, currency, bills of credit and precious items, all in return for African humanity, the slave ships could not function without violence. On the African coast and at sea, the ships became floating prisons, their African captives kept in place and dragooned throughout their seaborne ordeal for months on end by a brutal regime, which transformed Africans into prisoners and sailors into armed warders. Physical conditions on board a slave ship were, even under the best of circumstances, vile. At worst – in a storm, in navigational trouble or when beset by a slave uprising – one ship in ten experienced some form of revolts – conditions surpassed description.[12] Moreover those conditions were common knowledge in Britain itself. In addition to the tens of thousands of sailors who served on the Atlantic slave ships, periodic publications – travel accounts, commercial tracts, and personal memoirs – told the British reading public about the realities of the slave ships.

Yet for more than a century such terrible evidence did not become the stuff of public outrage, or the substance of political argument. From the first days of effective British commercial interest in slave trading in post-Restoration England, through to the American War in 1776, the slave trade was just that: a form of trade which was debated and disputed on commercial grounds. Thereafter, however, the politics of the slave trade changed – unexpectedly and quickly.

It is now recognised that the revolt of the American colonies had a seismic impact on the debate about slavery.[13] Throughout the eighteenth century there had been individual expressions of sympathy in Britain and in the colonies for slaves. Some, for example, objected

---

12. Eric Robert Taylor, *If we must die. Shipboard Insurrections in the Era of the Atlantic Slave Trade* (Baton Rouge: Louisiana State University Press, 2006).
13. For the best account of the origins of abolition, and of the American impact, *see* Christopher L. Brown, *Moral Capital. Foundations of British Abolitionism* (Chapel Hill: University of North Carolina Press, 2006).

to the way slave owners obstructed the spread of Christianity among the slaves. But these, and other objections to slavery, were mere personal views and there was no sustained effort to counter slavery or the slave trade by political action or by changing legislation. The one organisational exception to this rule was the Society of Friends (Quakers). But it was the breakaway of the American colonies in 1776 and the political debate which swirled around that Revolution on both sides of the Atlantic, that laid the foundations for the subsequent flowering of British abolition.

The Americans had many friends and supporters in Britain, some of whom had long shown sympathy towards the slaves. Among the profound political disagreements at the heart of the clash with the colonies was a dispute about the importation of African slaves to North America. A number of eminent Americans, most notably Thomas Jefferson, wanted to limit the imports of Africans: the enslaved population of North America was increasing of its own accord. Granville Sharp and others wanted to go even further and to end colonial slavery completely.[14] When hostilities broke out, the slaves became tactically and ideologically important. Some British officials, dangling offers of freedom, wanted to attract slaves to the British side for military and tactical reasons. Slaves who fled their owners to join the British ultimately found themselves on the losing side and the British now had the problem of what to do with them. Along with other loyalists, they had to be relocated: to Nova Scotia, to London and some of them, later, even to Sierra Leone.[15]

Behind these strategic issues there lay a much wider political discussion. American independence raised fundamental questions about political and social rights. It was a debate which easily spilled over into a debate about the morality of slavery. Few were better placed for that discussion than the Society of Friends, who had long wrestled with that issue. On a visit to Barbados in 1672, George Fox, had

---

14. See letter from Granville Sharp to Lord North, 1772, cited in Letter to Duke of Portland, 18 July 1783, in *Memoirs of Granville Sharp ... composed from his own manuscripts ... by Prince Hoare* (London: Henry Colburn & Co., 1820), p. 241.

15. For the most recent discussion of this topic, *see* Simon Schama, *Rough Crossings. Britain, The Slaves and the American Revolution* (London: BBC, 2005). But see also Cassandra Pybus, *Epic Journeys of Freedom* (Boston, Mass.: Beacon Press, 2006).

denounced slavery root and branch. North American Quakers were
particularly exposed to slavery at first hand, and in the course of the
eighteenth century often found their moral principles at odds with
their economic interests, as they sought good business in a world
permeated by slave-holding. Though hitherto renowned for their
quietist distancing from public politics, that had begun to change in
the 1760s. The American, John Woolman (who died and was buried
on a visit to York), and Anthony Benezet led the way in an increasingly
hostile attack on the slave trade in a string of tracts distributed
throughout the thirteen colonies, in London and thence across Britain.
Quaker opinion began to bend towards abolition. Benezet also
dispatched a string of letters about the slave trade to Quakers, and to
other sympathisers, in Britain, and by the late 1760s British Quakers
were well informed about the horrors and the ethics of the slave trade.
Prominent London Quakers conveyed their worries to other major
merchants, to ministers and even to the monarch. Thus, on the eve of
the American war, the seeds of doubt had been widely scattered by
Quakers in London and in North America.[16]

The American war created problems for the Quakers with their
well-known antipathy to warfare. British Quakers did not want to
appear to align themselves too closely to rebellious people, while
American Quakers could not afford to be accused of being unpatriotic
to the American cause. Equally, open support for abolition of the slave
trade could be damaging. It was entirely understandable that in the
run-up to the conflict, and during the war itself, Quakers tried to avoid
controversy by keeping their heads down. Yet this timidity masked a
number of important forces, which were to shape the course of
abolition in Britain after the war. First, a serious, lively debate about
the morality of slave trading had begun on both sides of the Atlantic,
a debate involving the exchange and reprinting of abolitionist literature,
all within the highly literate and remarkably efficient organisations of
the Society of Friends in North America and Britain. Here were groups
of people who conducted their religious organisations much as they
ran their individual constituent businesses: resourcefully, promptly and

---

16. For the Quakers, *see* Christopher Brown, *Moral Capital,* ch. 7; Judith Jennings,
The Business of Abolishing the British Slave Trade (London: Frank Cass, 1997).

with complete and open honesty. When the war ended, the time was
ripe to be more open about the slave trade.

The British defeat in 1783 was seen by many as a vengeful God
smiting the British for the wickedness of their ways. And what was
more self-evidently wicked than the slave trade and slavery? There was
a need for national redemption. And that meant an attack on slavery.
But the first step would be to end the slave trade. For years, a lonely
campaign had been led by Granville Sharp (1735–1813). He had long
been a fierce critic of British governments' handling of the American
colonies, and had established a reputation for his advocacy of black
legal freedom in England. In a series of slave cases in English courts,
Sharp had widened his arguments, stressing not merely the need to
secure black legal rights in England, but to see the entire slave system
brought to an end. Slavery was, he thought, a betrayal of traditional
English legal rights and a Christian outrage.[17] But Sharp was regarded
as a political eccentric, and despite the importance of his work for
individual black people in England, and notwithstanding his esteemed
status among British black people, many viewed him as little more
than a maverick gadfly.

After 1783, rumblings of discontent about the slave trade
converged from a number of angles. Writings from Scottish and French
Enlightenment thinkers were re-published, often in abbreviated form.
Quaker tracts were everywhere and were influential among Quakers
and non-Quakers. John Wesley (1703–1791), for example, was greatly
influenced by Benezet's writings, publishing his own highly derivative
attack on slavery in 1774.[18] Equally, he helped to swing his growing
band of followers against slavery thereafter. Throughout the subsequent
abolitionist campaigns (1787–1838), Methodists in Yorkshire were
notably fierce in their denunciation of slavery. The matter was stated
bluntly by Methodists in Barnsley. Slavery, they said, was 'repugnant
to our religion'.[19] Antagonism towards the slave trade took root in a
host of Nonconformist churches and chapels in the last quarter of the

---

17. Granville Sharp, *A Representation of the Injustice and Dangerous Tendency of
    Tolerating Slavery, or of Admitting the Least Claims of Private Property in the
    Persons of Men, in England* (London: 1769).
18. John Wesley, *Thoughts upon Slavery* (London: 1774).
19. *Journal of the House of Lords*, 63, p. 24.

eighteenth century, and provided a ready-made national network, which was used by the subsequent abolitionist movement. The key players and pioneers were, however, unquestionably the Quakers. Here, as in other areas of life – most notably contemporary commerce – the Society of Friends came to exercise an influence out of all proportion to their numbers.

2:8 Olaudah Equiano or Gustavus Vassa, the African, 1789 (Olaudo Equiano, self-published autobiography, 1789).

One critical figure in the rise of abolition was another of Benezet's contacts and sympathisers, Granville Sharp – best remembered, perhaps, for the 1772 Somerset case which challenged the legality of slavery in England. The outcome of that case (less clear in law than in public perception) spawned a wide debate about slavery itself – again, on both sides of the Atlantic. Ten years later, however, an even more staggering case took the British debate about slavery to a new level. Late in 1781, 132 Africans were killed when thrown from the Liverpool-registered ship, the *Zong*, as the vessel, running short of water, closed on Jamaica from Africa. In early summer 1783, the ship's owners claimed for the loss of the murdered Africans from their insurers. The following court cases, and the legal appeal, broadcast the scarcely-believable details: that Africans had been deliberately killed – murdered – by a British crew on a British ship, and yet the Liverpool owners had felt no qualms about publicly demanding compensation from the insurers. The court hearings, notably an appeal heard by Lord Chief Justice Mansfield, concentrated simply on technical questions of insurance. The matter of murder, mass murder, was ostensibly not at issue.[20]

The African, Olaudah Equiano, brought the story of the *Zong* to the attention of Granville Sharp who, outraged, instantly launched a campaign which quickly generated extensive public indignation.[21] But no one was brought to justice for the killings, even though Sharp named the men involved and gave their addresses to the Admiralty.[22] Yet the case exposed, admittedly in an extreme form, the violence and killings which were endemic in the slave trade. The case also revealed

---

20. See 'Symposium – The *Zong*: Legal, Social and Historical Dimensions', in *Journal of Legal History*, vol. 28, no. 3 (December, 2007).
21. *Memoirs of Granville Sharp*, p. 236.
22. National Maritime Museum Greenwich, REC/19, in Documents Relating to the Ship Zong, 1783, p. 99, letter from Granville Sharp to the Admiralty.

that insurance was commonly paid when Africans were killed, or
thrown overboard, in the course of suppressing a slave revolt. For all
its shortcomings, the *Zong* case had profound consequences. Time and
again after 1783, writers about the slave trade returned to the *Zong* as
a monstrous (and unpunished) example of the wickedness which lay
at the heart of slave trading. Though the case involved only one single
slave ship, it provided compelling evidence against the slave trade. The
data from the ships, the facts and figures about death and sickness, of
killings and revolts, proved to be the most potent evidence in
subsequent debates about the slave trade. What was needed, however,
was a system of publishing and disseminating that evidence so that the
British public could be informed about the realities of the slave ships.
Here, again, the Quakers were critical.

Quakers petitioned both Parliament and the American Continental
Congress against the slave trade in 1783. Quakers in London published
anti-slave trade tracts, and placed abolitionist pieces in various English
newspapers. Then, in 1786, they were joined by a young Cambridge
graduate, Thomas Clarkson (1760–1846), with his prize-winning
undergraduate essay against slavery. This too was published by the
Quakers. The essay proved instrumental in persuading Wilberforce to
adopt abolition. The two men agreed to collaborate: Wilberforce was
to agitate in Parliament, and Clarkson in the country at large. Then,
from May 1787, abolition was given formal structure by the founding
of the Abolition Society in London: most of the founding committee
were Quakers, with a sprinkling of Evangelical Anglicans like
Wilberforce.[23] Their aim was to discover more about the slave trade,
to disseminate that information as widely as possible, and to recruit
public support for a parliamentary campaign to end the slave trade. It
seemed hopelessly optimistic. They were to be amazed by the forces
they unleashed.

This small band of London Quakers unleashed a massive
propaganda campaign. Using Quakers across the country – Quaker
meetings, Quaker publishers and local sympathisers – tens of
thousands of tracts rained down on Britain's growing reading public.

23. The Society's full and formal name was *Society for Effecting the Abolition of the
Slave Trade*. Here, I abbreviate to *Abolition Society* throughout.

2:9 'Am I not a Man and a Brother'; ceramic cameo produced by the Wedgewood factory. Josiah Wedgwood, a leading Evangelical, was an original member of the abolition committee (Hull Museums).

The movement also adopted graphic images that quickly became a visual representation of abolition itself: the Wedgwood cameo of the supplicant slave, 'Am I not a man and a brother?' (Wedgwood was an original member of the abolition committee); and, from Quakers in Plymouth, the (now ubiquitous) cross-section and plan of the Liverpool slave ship the *Brookes*. Quakers up and down the land put their facilities, their know-how and their services – even their homes provided accommodation for travelling lecturers – at the disposal of abolition.

One of the basic instruments used to advance the cause was the voice of experience: they published and distributed tracts by men who had served on the slave ships and who bore witness to the horrors of seaborne slavery. Alongside this campaign, Thomas Clarkson undertook a series of massive nationwide lecture tours, covering 35,000 miles between 1787 and 1794. He spoke to packed audiences everywhere. He also trawled the docksides of the slave ports for sailors who could speak about the slave ships. Gradually he accumulated devastating evidence and detail about the ships, and about the damage they did to the sailors as well as to the Africans. The slave trade, far from nurturing future sailors for the British Navy, devoured them in horrifying numbers. Clarkson also carried with him a chest (now at the Wisbech Museum) which he filled with samples of crops, produce and commodities from Africa, displaying them to the public as proof that trade with Africa did not need to be solely in humanity.[24] There were

2:10 Thomas Clarkson, portrait by Carl Frederik von Breda (National Portrait Gallery).

24. 'Thomas Clarkson's African Box,' in *The British Slave Trade*, eds, Stephen Farrell *et al*, (Edinburgh: 2007), pp. 308–13.

great possibilities for normal commerce to be had from a re-configured trade to Africa. Thus Clarkson sought to side step the criticism of merchants and slave traders, that abolition would damage a profitable business. Clarkson, like Equiano in his autobiography, argued that normal trade with Africa would flourish, if only the slave trade could be ended.

All this evidence was carefully collected and assembled by Clarkson for submission to Parliament. At its core lay a simple reality: the sheer horror of the slave trade. It was violent, it was vicious and it caused death and suffering on an unimaginable scale. And all for what? For cheap luxuries, notably sugar, rum and tobacco. More and more people came to feel that such pleasures were hardly worth the cost. Might it not be possible, moreover, to cultivate those same crops without slave labour? Thus morality, religion and economics were woven together in an irrefutable denunciation of the slave trade. By 1789, abolition had seized the high moral ground, and was never to lose it, despite strenuous efforts by the slave lobby – planters, merchants – to deny what was said, and to stress the invaluable nature of the slave trade. Their argument was simple enough: without the Africans, the plantations could not survive. And where would Atlantic trade be

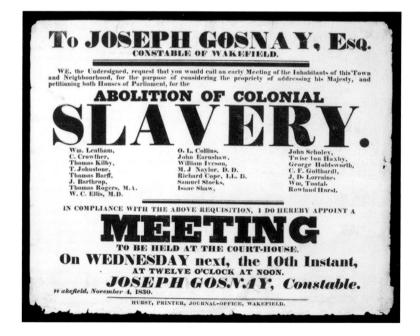

2:11 Poster advertising a meeting to be held on 4 November 1830, called by Joseph Gosnay, Constable of Wakefield, to discuss the abolition of colonial slavery (National Maritime Museum).

without the consumption of, and products from, the plantations of the Americas?

The abolitionists' ambition was to rally public support to put pressure on Parliament. They did this via the familiar means of petitions. The public response between 1787 and 1794 was astonishing. The Manchester petition of 1787 contained more than 10,000 names (from a population of 50,000). In 1788, 102 abolitionist petitions arrived at Parliament to support Wilberforce's motion to end the slave trade. By 1792 that had risen to 501 petitions. The process was clear from what happened in Yorkshire. Resolutions from a meeting in Leeds on 24 January 1788 were published 'in the Leeds and York papers, the *St James Chronicle* and the *London Packet*. It became a matter of civic pride to be seen to be taking an abolitionist stand. 'Clericas' told readers of the *Leeds Intelligencer* in 1788: 'Let us not, my friends, be backward in so laudable a business. This borough hath not been the last in other generous and human designs. Let us not on this occasion be said, that we want either religion or humanity'.[25]

Dissenting communities quickly rallied to the task, in Yorkshire and across the country. And, in a major political breakthrough, so too did local female activists. About fourteen per cent of subscribers to abolition in York in 1788 were women, and women signatories were notable in Leeds and Sheffield.[26] The *York Courant* of 21 February 1792 repeated a call first made in Manchester in 1787:

> It has been said that a Petition from the Ladies to Parliament, for an Abolition of the Slave-Trade, would have a good effect. The idea is certainly a proper one – for, as Female Misery is Included in the wretched allotment of the Africans, an appeal in their behalf from the same sex must carry great weight with it.

This female activity increased in later phases of the campaign. The *York Herald* noted in 1807, that 'The FAIR SEX, as the best canvassers

25. Quoted in J. R. Oldfield, *Popular Politics and British Anti-Slavery* (London: Frank Cass, 1998), p. 104.
26. Clare Midgley, *Women against Slavery. The British Campaigns, 1780–1870* (London: Routledge, 1992), pp. 18–19.

were distinguishable to a high degree'.[27] Public meetings called to denounce the slave trade were equally impressive: meeting halls, churches and chapels were packed to overflowing to hear speakers denounce the slave trade.

Though Wilberforce had made headway in Parliament, persuading Parliament to gather evidence and to debate his annual abolition motions, the initial rush of enthusiasm for abolition was, however, brought to an end by the darkening shadow cast by the French Revolution – in time, even Wilberforce was to be accused of being a Jacobin. After 1791, however, the volcanic slave uprising in St Domingue (Haiti) seemed to confirm the dire warnings of planters and slave traders: discuss abolition at your peril. Slaves were always poised to seize any opportunity to overthrow their masters, at sea or on the plantations. The failed British military effort to seize St Domingue – and the enormous loss of life involved – merely reinforced these cautions.

Through all this, Wilberforce, MP for Yorkshire, was the central parliamentary figure for abolition. He was well placed (and close to Pitt), eager to bend the ear of anyone – politician, minister, official – about the slave trade. His famous twelve propositions supporting abolition in May 1789 became the basis for the parliamentary campaign throughout. Wilberforce's persistence was astonishing, though sometimes his management of votes in Parliament was inadequate. And yet, year after unsuccessful year, the cause gathered ever more compelling evidence through parliamentary enquires. Defeated in 1791, Wilberforce's proposal passed the Commons in 1792 by 230 votes to 85, only to fall in the ever-resistant Lords – the resistance helped by the bullish Royal Princes. As slave upheaval flared across the Caribbean, and as Britain drifted into war with France, the abolitionist cause inevitably stuttered. But Wilberforce pressed on, though now on the back foot. Parliament repeatedly rejected his annual motions between 1794 and 1799, and after 1798 he decided to rest until circumstances changed. A short period of peace, and critical changes of government, revived his hope and in 1804 he renewed the parliamentary campaign. Again, the old tactics resurfaced: public

---

27. Midgley, *Women against Slavery,* p. 24.

agitation and lectures, a profusion of tracts, and careful parliamentary scrutiny. The broader campaign was now driven forward by Wilberforce's friends in the Clapham Sect, but again with Clarkson as the dogged, inexhaustible foot soldier.

The abolitionists' breakthrough came with the death of Pitt in January 1806. Pitt was committed to ending the slave trade to newly captured territories, which by then absorbed the great majority of British imports of Africans. But the new government of Fox-Grenville paved the parliamentary path for the Abolition Act, which was

2:12 Poster, published by Edward Baines, signed 'An Abolitionist', decrying Henry Lascelles for his family's connections with slavery and advocating a joint campaign between Wilberforce and fellow abolitionist Viscount Milton (West Yorkshire Archive Service, Kirklees KC174-17).

presented as a governmental measure. Full abolition was now inevitable, despite Fox's death in September 1806. The subsequent general election saw abolition as a critical electoral issue in constituencies across

2:13 Election poster published in Huddersfield by Brook and Lancashire, advocating 'No Milton-No Slavery' and pointing out Lord Milton's family's opposition to abolition (West Yorkshire Archive Service, Kirklees, KC174-16).

2:14 Election
poster 'A few Plain
Questions Answered'
printed by Smart of
Huddersfield and
outlining the
difference in attitude
of the Fitzwilliam
family (and Viscount
Milton) from the
Lascelles family
(West Yorkshire
Archive Service,
Kirklees, KC174-15).

2:15 1807 Election
Poster 'Lord H-
re---d's Address to
the Clothiers of
Yorkshire' Spoof
address from Lord
Harewood, father of
Henry Lascelles,
printed by Smart in
Huddersfield '…
Young Harries to the
end of time shall
represent the
County…' (West
Yorkshire Archive
Service, Kirklees).

the country. Potential MPs were pressed, and had to commit themselves, before the electorate to the slave trade or to abolition. The cacophony for abolition was deafening: 'Every measure that invention or artifice could devise to create a popular clamour was resorted to on this occasion. The Church, the theatre, and the press, had laboured to create a prejudice against the Slave Trade'.[28] With a totally new raft of MPs, many of whom had spoken out against the slave trade at the 1807 election, abolition was inevitable. It passed the Commons by 283 votes to 16. On 1 March 1807 it received the Royal Assent.

All the heady excitement of a fiercely contested election, with abolition at the heart of the arguments, was experienced at York in

---

28. Quoted in Jennings, *The Business of Abolishing the British Slave Trade,* p. 111.

1807. The Yorkshire county election that year was an extravagant
example of unreformed politics at work: vast expense, bribery, personal
vituperation – all the rough and tumble of contested politics. There
had not been a contested election in the seat for seventy-three years
and it was to be the last before 1832, but this one made up for lost
time and excitement. It was a noisy and costly fight in which three
issues dominated, quite apart from the personalities involved: the slave
trade, the 'Catholic' question, and the problems of the Yorkshire textile
industry. Wilberforce and two others candidates, Viscount Milton (heir
to the Wentworth-Fitzwilliam fortune) and Henry Lascelles (second
son of the Earl of Harewood), fought for the two seats in an election
which lasted fifteen days and cost an estimated £50 per vote cast
(23,007 men voted in what was the country's largest electorate).
Wilberforce could not call on aristocratic wealth for his campaign, but
was greatly helped by a national public subscription which raised more
than £64,000.

Though all three men were abolitionists, Lascelles' claims were
widely-doubted, largely because of his family's slave-owning wealth.
He had also deeply alienated the Yorkshire clothiers and had to cope
with their fierce attacks. Quakers in Sheffield declared that 'Mr
Lascelles, cannot be called either a friend to the abolition of the slave
trade, or to genuine religious liberty'. Another hostile poster declared:

WANTED
A HUNDRED
NEGRO
DRIVERS

To be employed in the Island of
Barbados

Apply at Har-w—d House.

2:16 Extract from
an election poster
(Papers of the late
Ellen Gibson
Wilson).

In both the 1806 and 1807 general elections, the Yorkshire
newspapers carried advertisements urging local voters to support only
those candidates who favoured abolition. In York, prominent Quakers

urged voters to support Wilberforce because of his dedication to the
'cause of the African race' over the past twenty years. Yorkshire Quakers
were joined by the county's Methodists in supporting Wilberforce.
Indeed Wilberforce had been attracted to Methodism in his youth, to
the great alarm of his parents. Now Methodists found him an attractive
figure for whom they were able to organise strong support via their
growing numbers in the county's industrial regions.[29]

The Yorkshire election of 1807 was marked by a remarkable degree
of personal abuse aimed at all three candidates. Even the godly
Wilberforce was attacked, much to his great distress, for what was seen
to be a secret alliance with Lascelles. Others disapproved of the public
subscription for his election expenses. Inevitably perhaps, his Tory
opponents took a swipe at his dissenting backers:

> How much it will shock
> The whole Methodist Flock
> To learn that the Saint they take pride in,
> To gain a few Votes
> His time now devotes
> To the VICE of the wicked West-Riding!

Wilberforce and Milton won – narrowly. The dispirited Tory *Leeds
Intelligencer* thought it a Whiggish victory, a 'triumph of Jacobinism
over the friends of King and Constitution'. They thought the result
'will long be remembered as the most disgraceful era in the history of
Yorkshire'.[30] Many others, however, rejoiced. After all, the slave trade
had been abolished. Moreover, the campaign over the past twenty years
to bring it to an end was to leave an impact on national popular,
electoral and parliamentary politics.

In passing the Abolition Act, the Commons decided that the slave
trade was 'contrary to the principles of humanity, justice and sound
policy'. Yet for much of the previous 150 years, these principles had
gone unnoticed. Throughout the past century the slave trade had been
accepted as the soundest of sound commercial policies, and justice and

---

29. Wilson, 'The Great Yorkshire Election', p. 75.
30. Wilson, 'The Great Yorkshire Election', pp. 276; 290.

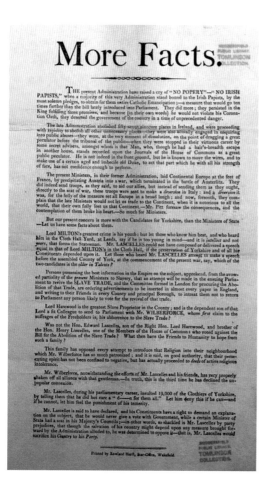

humanity had simply not entered the political equation. Now, in 1807, and within the space of a mere 30 years of a small band of Quakers and Evangelicals first meeting to plan its abolition, the British slave trade had gone: blown away by a mighty storm of public agitation. Moreover, it was widely accepted that Parliament lagged behind public feeling on the matter. Time and again, at critical points between 1787 and 1807, the British people had expressed a powerful revulsion against the slave trade, and Parliament had chosen to ignore their voice. By 1807 Parliament had come round to sharing the same view.

Despite the Abolition Act of 1807, there remained much to concern British abolitionists, notably the need to stop the 'illicit' trade and the desire to end colonial slavery itself. Each wave of subsequent abolitionist agitation revived the pattern of activity established in 1807.

2:17 Election poster 'More Facts', outlining opposition to Lascelles, printed by Hurst, Wakefield (West Yorkshire Archive Service, Kirklees KC 174-13).

2:18 1807 'Yorkshire Election Song' supporting Milton, to be sung to the tune of 'Rule Britannia', printed by Smart, Huddersfield (West Yorkshire Archive Service, Kirklees).

From the first, abolitionists had placed great emphasis on evidence – on facts: the data, the statistics, the personal voices – the hard, indisputable evidence about the slave ships and their human cargoes and crews. Port cities, sailors, former slave ship officers, all offered evidence which was tabulated, assembled, reprinted and published by abolitionists and then by Parliament. It was, in effect, a massive research exercise, the result of which was an unprecedented wave of data, which simply swamped the slave lobby's protestations that the slave trade was invaluable and indispensable.

The abolition campaign depended primarily upon cheap and free pamphlet literature. It also used the local press to good effect. In all this, it was greatly helped by local dissenting organisations. Meeting rooms, chapels and churches were ideal places to meet and listen. And it was no accident that substantial numbers of abolition petitions originated in religious organisations. Places of worship also offered a venue for itinerant abolitionist lectures. It was not simply that the slave trade came to be seen as an un-Christian outrage (though that is also true) but that the physical structures, the buildings of faith lent themselves to the development and progress of the abolition movement. All this was aided of course by the transformed nature of British life itself. Abolition thrived especially among urban people, not simply because it was an expression of religious outrage, but because it surged along the national networks of dissent. From the first, the pro-slave trade lobby of planters and slave merchants were caught totally by surprise, and failed to regain their poise. After the first impact of deeply shocking evidence about the slave ships in 1787–1788, the slave lobby found it impossible to catch or alter the public mood. They were no longer believed by an increasingly hostile British public.

With the slave trade outlawed, abolitionists did not have to wait long before confronted by another pressing issue. With the end of the Napoleonic Wars in 1814–1815, the slave trade became a diplomatic issue, as the British sought to press abolition on other European nations, notably the French. Thomas Clarkson now busied himself shuttling between European capitals, arguing for international abolition, greatly helped by Wellington allowing him the use of the diplomatic bags. The old abolition tactics were revived in 1814–1815: popular pressure generated by petitions, but this time to demand international abolition. Something like one and a half million people

signed up, from a population of twelve millions. Talleyrand, the French
Foreign Minister, bemused by what he saw, thought the British had
become fanatical about the issue.[31]

There remained, too, the survival of slavery in the colonies. It was
clear enough that ending the British slave trade would not, in itself,
end slavery in the colonies. Wilberforce later claimed that slaves should
be 'gradually transmuted into a free peasantry; but this the
ULTIMATE object, was to produce progressively by the operation of
multiplied, chiefly moral causes'.[32] The first step was to ensure that
abolition was being observed in the slave colonies. 'Slave Registration'–
a form of census – tried first in recently-acquired Trinidad in 1812,
was extended throughout the islands in 1819–1820 with the aim of
monitoring the enslaved population to see if illegal imports were taking
place. This raw demographic data was, henceforth, used in much the
same way as the data from the slave ships had been used: statistics
became the stuff of popular politics, though this time to bring slavery
to an end.

Predictably, all this was hated and resisted by the planters, who
continued to argue that external interference in their affairs merely
fuelled the slaves' innate rebelliousness. And the post-war years were
indeed marked by a string of slave rebellions: in Barbados 1816, in
Demerara 1822 and, most devastating of all, in Jamaica 1831–32.
Slave owners' fears were also heightened by the influence of newly
arrived British missionaries, notably Methodists and Baptists in the
Caribbean. Their success in establishing chapels and slave congregations,
in promoting slave preachers, and their effective use of the Bible,
transformed the slaves' social lives. It gave them a means of organising,
of expressing themselves and of challenging those around them. It is
significant, for example, that the Jamaican slave revolt of 1831–32 was
known as 'The Baptist War'.[33]

Missionaries dispatched to the slave colonies reported back to their
British congregations about the sufferings of the slaves. Methodists

---

31. J. Reich, 'The Slave Trade and the Congress of Vienna', *Journal of Negro History*,
    53 (1968).
32. Hague, *Wilberforce*, p. 148.
33. Michael Craton, *Testing the Chains. Resistance to Slavery in the British West
    Indies* (Ithaca, New York: Cornell University Press, 1982), ch. 22.

and Baptists in Britain learned of the persecution, not so much of slaves, but of co-religionists on the far side of the Atlantic. Once again hard facts, widely disseminated in lectures, sermons and in print, seeped across the face of Britain. Congregations across the land were appalled about what they learned of slave life in the Caribbean. When prompted, those congregations expressed themselves strongly for black freedom – sooner or later. In effect, the growth of British Nonconformist communities created large bodies of support for the slaves. By the 1820s, for example, there were a quarter of a million British Methodists. Baptist numbers were smaller, but nonetheless they also formed a large and vociferous body of support for the slaves. There were 15,000 dissenting places of worship across Britain, which again proved ideal meeting places, centres of information and *foci* for support for the slaves in the Caribbean. It would be wrong to claim that the growing British support for black freedom in the 1820s and 1830s was simply religious, for it was rooted in a much wider political and moral culture. Nonetheless, without the transformed face of British faith, without the structures and broad base for British Nonconformity, abolition in the 1820s and 1830s would have taken a very different course.

By 1824 abolitionists were divided by arguments about when the slaves should be freed. There was widespread agreement among Christians of all denominations that slaves should be freed. One parliamentary candidate in Yorkshire said in 1826: 'On the gradual abolition of Colonial Slavery, I am happy to believe there are not two opinions in the country'.[34] A candidate in Leeds was introduced with the preface: 'Mr. Willson is a Christian, he is a Protestant, he is a member of the Church of England: therefore he hates slavery both of mind and body.'[35] Anyone thought to be sympathetic to colonial slavery was ridiculed in print:

Freemen of York! Be firm to your great cause of
Liberty and Justice! Never let it be said that you
Have been represented by
A SLAVE DRIVER!

---

34. *Speeches and Addresses of the Candidates for the Representation of the County of York in the Year, 1826* (Leeds, 1826), pp. 26, 52, 55, 92–3, 125.
35. *Representation of the City of York* (York, 1826) – copy in City of York Reference Library.

Not surprisingly, the new economic attacks on slavery (that slave-grown sugar was maintained by artificial sugar duties) appealed to the industrialists of West Yorkshire. The Chamber of Commerce in Leeds joined others in 1827 in demanding both free trade and an end to slavery.[36] By then, there was a unity of objections: economic, ethical and religious.

In gathering anti-slavery petitions in the years 1824–1832, female abolitionists now got into their political stride. In Sheffield in 1831 two women were responsible for recruiting 187,000 names to the local abolitionist petition. With eighty members, the local women's anti-slavery society published and distributed thousands of tracts, published their own anti-slavery poetry and concentrated their efforts 'chiefly among the poor of this town'.[37] Everywhere, anti-slavery crowds were again enormous. In Bradford in 1830, despite the one shilling entrance fee, an abolition meeting was packed 'by numerous, respectable and attentive audiences'. In Leeds, an estimated 6,000 people filled the Coloured Cloth Hall.[38] At the general election of that year (Yorkshire now had four county members) all four MPs were abolitionists. One of them, Henry Brougham, wrote to Wilberforce that 'The elections turned very much on Slavery; your name was in every mouth, and your health the most enthusiastically received'.[39] Yorkshire was, by now, a major provincial centre for abolition, not surprisingly perhaps for an area with 1019 dissenting congregations, including the largest number of Quaker congregations of any county, in addition to the largest numbers of Methodists and Baptists.[40]

In this last phase, abolitionists were locked into a debate about the timing of emancipation: should it be immediate or gradual? But at each stage of the protracted argument, beginning effectively in 1824,

36. *Anti-Slavery Monthly Reporter*, no. 17 (October 1826), no. 22 (31 March 1827), no. 23 (30 April 1827).
37. *Report of the Sheffield Female Anti-Slavery Society*, (n.d.): M. A. Rawson, *The Bow in the Cloud* (Sheffield: Jackson & Walford, 1834); *Address to the Labouring Classes* (n.d.): R. Coupland, *The British Anti-Slavery Movement* (London: Thornton Butterworth, 1933), p. 137.
38. *Anti-Slavery Monthly Reporter* (October 1830), p. 405.
39. Robin Furneaux, *William Wilberforce* (London: Hamilton, 1974), p. 443.
40. E.F. Hurwitz, *Politics and the Public Conscience. Slave Emancipation and the Abolition Movement in Britain* (London: Allen & Unwin, 1973), pp. 82–3.

the abolitionists regularly called on its massive public backing to join
the argument: to rally to lectures in their tens of thousands, to sign
hundreds of petitions, and to press their local MP to take a stand on
the matter. Here was a reprise of the old tactics, but now, in the 1820s
and 1830s in a rapidly transforming Britain, increasingly urban, ever
more literate, and with a newly responsive population. MPs too had
changed. Now they were keen to curry favour with, and respond to,
their constituents. Moreover when the campaign to extend the
franchise took flight it became clear to MPs that they had to listen to
voters. Equally, voters became aware that they could hold their
representatives to account. Hence elections changed: MPs promised
to act according to the electorate's wishes. And one of those fiercely
expressed wishes, from the mid-1820s onwards, was an end to colonial
slavery.

All this was in the midst of bleak news from the West Indies.
Registration showed the slave population to be in decline, and periodic
outbursts of slave violence were met by savage reprisals from planters
and colonial authorities. The planters, fierce and unbending, seemed
utterly immune to argument. On the other hand, their slaves – more
and more of them Christian as the older Africans died out and newer
generations found comfort and strength in what the missionaries had
to offer – had little to show for their miseries. And hovering over the
entire scene was the spectre of violence, on a scale and of a kind which
was increasingly out of kilter with the changing sensibility of the
British people. At a time when cruelties of all kind (to animals or to
soldiers) raised increasing concern, the cruelties doled out to slaves
seemed unacceptable. Moreover, what was the point of all this: simply
to provide the British with sugar? Abolitionists began to point out that
sugar could be bought cheaper from other parts of the world where it
was cultivated by non-slave labour – hence the effective use of a sugar
boycott, advocated by female abolitionists in the 1820s and 1830s.

Slavery itself was now under sustained attack. From 1822
abolitionists had developed an economic critique of slavery, denouncing
the sugar duties, which protected the planters at the expense of British
consumers. In 1823 a new abolition campaign was launched, again
with the indefatigable Thomas Clarkson travelling the country. Within
a year 250 local abolition societies had been established, many of them
female. Organised by a London committee, the new campaign drew

upon the widespread ethical and religious outrage felt across the
country about slavery. The major difference from the campaigns of the
1780s and 1790s was that abolitionists now argued that slavery was
uneconomic. Once again planters found themselves faced by criticisms
they could not answer or cope with. Missionaries told of the planters'
recalcitrance in the face of Christian arguments, economists argued
the economic irrationality of slave-grown sugar. Slavery thus stood
condemned on moral, economic and political grounds. The main
debate among abolitionists and in Parliament henceforth was whether
freedom should be gradual or immediate. No one doubted however,
by the mid-1820s, that abolition, in the words of Thomas Clarkson,
'spoke the national voice'.

In 1823 the Commons resolved to press for gradual abolition,
hoping in the meantime that the slaves could be 'civilized'. The old
abolition tactics were again rolled out to exert pressure on Parliament.
Petitions, lectures, publications, with an increasingly religious tone –
not surprisingly, given that so many originated in churches. Women
were now a striking presence. Between 1823 and 1831 more than three
million tracts were published: half a million in 1831 alone. Yet the
cause stalled in Parliament. Wilberforce, old and sick, had retired from
Parliament in 1825, and the leadership had passed to Thomas Fowell
Buxton (1786–1845). By 1830, however, little progress had been
made, and emancipation seemed swamped in the wider push for
reform, most notably of course, the drive for parliamentary reform.
Then, in 1832 a new generation of younger abolitionists, tired of
waiting for black freedom, formed the Agency Committee to press for
immediate freedom. Quakers were, once again, at the forefront. All
this took place under the shadow of two horrifying events in 1831–
1832: the cholera epidemic which killed 32,000 people in Britain, and
the volcanic slave revolt – the Baptist War – in Jamaica: 60,000 slaves
were involved, fourteen whites were killed, and 540 slaves died in the
fighting or the repression. The slave leader, the Baptist preacher, Sam
Sharp, told his followers that he 'thought and learnt from the Bible,
that the whites had no more right to hold black people in slavery than
black people had to make the white people slaves'.[41]

---

41. Quoted in Michael Craton, *Testing the Chains*, p. 321.

The bloodshed in Jamaica caused an outcry in Britain, on the very eve of the debate about parliamentary reform. When a new election was called in August 1832, using the newly reformed franchise, abolitionists seized their moment. Candidates were pressed to declare their position on slavery, and the result was that some 200 MPs declared themselves for black freedom.

The reform of Parliament thus made black freedom inevitable. But even then there were hurdles to be cleared, notably the Lords, resistant, as they always had been, to tinkering with slavery. The Abolition of Slavery Bill in August 1833, inaugurating freedom twelve months hence, provided only limited freedom. Slaves under six were freed immediately but the rest became 'apprentices' for six years. They were to work for their former owners for most of the week, for free. Antigua and Bermuda opted for immediate freedom. Most striking of all about this arrangement, however, was the compensation agreed by Parliament: £20 million – the largest capital outlay outside of warfare made by Parliament up that point – was raised (via the Rothschilds) as compensation, not for the slaves, but for the planters. They were compensated on a per capita basis. Lord Harewood, for example, already fabulously wealthy through his family's holdings in the Caribbean, received £26,309 for the freedom of his 1,277 slaves on his West Indian plantations.[42] The whole system, and the astronomical sums involved, seemed to many to be the ultimate exercise in slave trading: freedom was being bought: each slave, yet again, had a price on his or her head. Moreover, they were only partly freed.

The 'apprenticeship' scheme was monitored by magistrates sent from Britain, and was designed to tie labour to the land until the planters found new means of replacing their former slaves. Planters feared that their labour force would simply vanish. But in some of the smaller islands, they had no alternative but to stay on the plantations. In Jamaica, with plenty of spare land available, many ex-slaves simply drifted off to a new life as squatters in the bush (often on Crown land), prompting a host of new social and legal problems. Throughout the period of apprenticeship, abolitionists kept up the pressure for total freedom. Once again they called on urban, and dissenting Britain to

---

42. Smith, *Slavery, Family and Gentry Capitalism*, pp. 251–52.

demand black freedom. By contrast, the pro-slave lobby tended for find support in small town, rural life and of course in the Lords. Slavery was clearly doomed. Finally, on 1 August 1838, full freedom was granted.

Whites feared the worst throughout the islands in 1838. There were wild rumours that freed slaves would seek revenge on their traditional persecutors. In the event, and after huge public celebrations, the ex-slaves celebrated in the new fashion – by going to church. It was a stunning transformation. A system, which was born in violence, and maintained by extraordinary levels of brutality, ended peacefully. Freedom was heralded by the sound of Christian worship among thousands of newly-converted Africans and their off-spring.

The abolitionists had triumphed and slavery was ended throughout the British Empire. But the abolition movement did not fade away in 1838. Thereafter the campaign against slavery became a major element in Britain's global politics: in naval and diplomatic activities in the Atlantic, in East Africa and the Indian Ocean, and even much further afield, notably in India. Indeed, the urge to abolish slavery world-wide became a dominant feature of a new form of British cultural imperialism. The irony was not lost on a number of contemporaries, notably the French who were reluctant to follow the British example. The nation which had dominated the Atlantic trade in the eighteenth century became the scourge of slave traders in the nineteenth century. Some thought that the British had lost their sense of their own historical past, or was it merely another example of British duplicity? The British no longer needed slavery, and henceforth urged others to follow their lead.

The roots and the nature of the British abolition movement are unquestionably complex, and historians continue to argue about them vigorously. An older school of historians who saw the abolition campaigns as evidence of a unique British morality at work – high-minded Christians seeking to end an ungodly institution – has been widely debunked. But the subsequent emphasis on economic self-interest, arguing that the slave trade and slavery were undermined by the shift in British economic interest, albeit one masquerading as high-minded Christianity, has tended to diminish and even delete the element of moral action and religious sensibility. Similarly, an older emphasis on the role of Wilberforce has, in recent years, been down played to the point that, in 2007 at the bi-centenary, he was in danger of being airbrushed from the story completely.[43] Today, it is possible to take an altogether different, closer look at the nature and structure of popular abolition. What now seems clear is that the campaign against the slave trade and slavery was a very different political phenomenon from the one described by earlier generations of historians. And therein lies its significance for the reforming campaigns that followed in the 1830s and 1840s.

Abolition was a new and unusually popular movement. Both Parliament and the West India lobby found it hard to cope with abolition because it emerged quickly, from new corners of British life. In addition, it operated in a fashion which offered a new kind of politics: a popular blend of moral and religious feeling which was rooted in the changing fabric of British urban and religious life. More than that, the voice of abolition, expressed in an unprecedented outpouring of print, public speeches and petitions, was based on irrefutable evidence. Abolitionists were assiduous researchers, doing their homework on the data from the slave ships in the 1780s and 1790s, and from the plantations in the 1820s and 1830s. Their political arguments were not simple assertions, outraged claims about right and wrong, about wickedness and good (though there was plenty of that), but were grounded in solid facts and arguments. Considering the abolitionist movement in the round, over the fifty years after its formation in 1787, is to become aware of a very modern-looking phenomenon in which empirical evidence was the key to success. The demography of Africans and of sailors, the tabulations of ships and goods, tables of sickness and death rates, shipping statistics ran alongside oral recollections. The words of contemporaries – of men who had served on the ships, of Africans who had suffered on those ships, of voices from the plantations – all were captured by the painstaking researches of the abolitionists, notably, of course, by Thomas Clarkson. This data was published by the ton, and distributed in all corners of the land. It was also accumulated, filtered and reprinted by Parliament itself (and thus provides the basic evidence which historians have trawled through for their own assessment.) The

---

43. The whole bicentenary was dismissed in some Caribbean quarters as a mere 'Wilberfest'.

abundance of such material is astonishing, but its sheer abundance is not the major point. It is the nature of that evidence, and the way it was used, which marks a remarkable shift in reforming politics.

The British people learned about the slave trade and slavery through the prodigious dissemination of such evidence. The printed and spoken word was used to great effect, in locations, most notably places of worship, which could house large groups. And the organisation of abolitionist politics was itself rooted in religious organisations, led of course by the pioneering Quakers. Moreover, this religious dimension to abolition was given greater significance by the conversion of ever more slaves by missionaries in the slave islands. British congregations learned that co-religionists (black and enslaved) were apparently being persecuted for their faith, or prevented from exercising that faith, by planters who seemed resistant to any form of change or argument.

In the last phase of the campaign, from 1825 onwards, the entanglement with the broader parliamentary reform movement is clear enough. Again, abolitionists made clever use of the coincidence, and ensured that the parliamentary reform agitation helped to nurture the abolition campaign. Forcing parliamentary candidates to declare their position on slavery ensured the return of abolitionists MPs. Once Parliament had been reformed – whatever the limitations of that reform – and once a new raft of MPs had taken their seats, it was clear that slavery was doomed. A reformed Parliament spelled the end of slavery. Thereafter, the arguments were about the precise timing of freedom, the interim arrangements – and the compensation to be offered. Even today, the sum finally agreed upon looks staggeringly generous, and provides a clear clue to the continuing sway the slave lobby could exercise over the British parliament and government.

The campaign to end the slave trade and slavery was not only exceptionally popular: it was successful. If those two mighty pillars of eighteenth-century trade and commerce, the slave trade and slavery, could be toppled by raising popular outrage, what else might give way to a campaign organised and managed as abolition had been? British reform was to owe a debt to abolition for pointing the way. From the factory movement through to Chartism, British politics learned from their abolitionist forebears. Indeed, there was, in places, an overlap of personnel and membership. Abolitionists became reformers with other aims: young abolitionists turned their attention to new reform movements in the 1830s and 1840s. No less a figure than Richard Oastler argued that the causes of anti-slavery and of Chartism were 'one and the same'.[44] Whether it was Parliamentary Reform, the Factory Acts, Chartism or the Poor Law, popular and parliamentary agitations were greatly influenced by the abolitionist movement that had gone before. And that was true right across the country. The ex-slaves in the Caribbean owed a debt of gratitude to the abolitionists: so too did British reformers who came after them.

44. Betty Fladeland, 'Our Cause being One and the Same': Abolitionists and Chartism', in *Slavery and British Society, 1776–1846* ed. by James Walvin, (London: Macmillan, 1982).

Richard Oastler: the Methodist background, 1789–1820

D. COLIN DEWS

CECIL DRIVER'S SUBSTANTIAL biography of Richard Oastler, *Tory Radical: the life of Richard Oastler*, published in 1946, makes reference to his Methodist background.[1] However, since 1946, other sources have become available which add to our knowledge of both Richard Oastler's Methodist upbringing and the Oastler family's Methodist roots, raising some interesting questions not addressed by Driver's otherwise detailed account.

The most important source is the Hobill Collection in The John Rylands University of Manchester Library. The origins of this collection derive mainly from the vast correspondence between Alexander Kilham and his contemporaries, which eventually passed into the hands of George Alexander Kilham Hobill, a member of Waverley Park Methodist New Connexion, London.[2] Along with his own collection of pamphlets and books, this collection, comprising, in total, some 771 items, was given to the Methodist New Connexion Conference in 1894, and in due course was deposited with the New

---

1. Cecil Driver, *Tory Radical: the life of Richard Oastler* (New York: Oxford University Press, 1946).
2. Revd Alexander Kilham (1762–1798), a pamphleteer advocating constitutional reforms, was expelled from the (Wesleyan) Methodist Connexion in 1796 after publishing *The Progress of Liberty* (1795) and established the Methodist New Connexion.

Connexion's ministerial training college at Ranmoor, Sheffield. However, Ranmoor College closed temporarily in the First World War (1914–1918), never to reopen. At this stage the collection was placed in storage in Nether Green Chapel, now Hallam Methodist Church, Sheffield, and its whereabouts was quickly forgotten. Just before the Second World War (1939–1945) the Hobill library was transferred to Hartley Victoria College, Manchester, but the manuscript material remained hidden in the basement at Nether Green; suffering from damp and decay, many papers were destroyed in 1939. However, some did survive and in 1965 this valuable collection was rediscovered and this has ensured its partial preservation, since regrettably, of the original 602 letters, only 161 now remain.[3]

The depositing of Richard Oastler's mother's Methodist New Connexion class books, formerly in the possession of the late Revd John Lawson, and other Leeds Methodist records at the West Yorkshire Archives Service's Leeds office, along with the survival of some early

3:1 Blue plaque commemorating the birthplace of Richard Oastler in St Peter's Square, Leeds (Ben Dalton http://openplaques. org/plaques/852).

3.   E.A. Rose, 'The Origins of the Methodist New Connexion: unpublished manuscripts', *Proceedings of the Wesley Historical Society* [*PWHS*] 35 (1965–6) pp. 94–97; 'The Methodist New Connexion in London', *PWHS* 38 (1971–2) p. 186.

G. Romney pinx.ᵗ   I. Spilsbury.

THE REVEREND IOHN WESLEY. M.A.

3:2 John Wesley
by George Romney
1789 (Wesley
Historical Society
Library, images
provided by
Oxford Centre for
Methodism and
Church History,
Oxford Brookes
University).

circuit preaching plans, further help with the reassessment of Richard
Oastler's Methodist family background.

Driver, drawing from John Ward's mid-nineteenth century history
of the Thirsk Circuit, sets in context the Oastler family's Methodist
background.[4] By the mid-eighteenth century, the family were yeoman
farmers at Kirby Wiske near Thirsk, where Richard's father Robert
was born in 1748. When Robert was about sixteen he joined the
Methodists but because of his father's opposition, he had to leave home
and went to Thirsk, where his two Oastler uncles had also joined the
Methodists; indeed, his Uncle John had in effect adopted him. His

4. J. Ward, *Methodism in the Thirsk Circuit* (Thirsk: David Peat, 1860).

uncles were instrumental in building the market town's first chapel in 1760 and a friendship developed between John Wesley and the family. Robert Oastler became a local preacher and remained in Thirsk for about twenty-five years.

In Thirsk, Robert Oastler had been a grocer but in 1789 he moved to Leeds – his wife Sarah, neé Scurr, came from the town – and went into business as a linen cloth merchant, with a house on the north side of St Peter's Square, at its rear being separated from the Old Boggard Chapel by a narrow street.[5]

Here Richard Oastler, the eighth and last child, was born on 20 December 1789. Sixteen months later Wesley made his last visit to Leeds when the Wesleyan Conference met at the Old Boggard chapel. According to Driver, Wesley stayed overnight with the Oastlers on Saturday 1 May 1790.[6] However, although Wesley's *Journal* is not precise on this point, it should be noted that on that day Wesley left Leeds by chaise at 10.00 am for Tadcaster and York; given that Wesley arrived in Leeds at 12.30 pm the previous day, this suggests that he stayed with the Oastlers on the Friday night.[7] By tradition, as a baby Richard Oastler sat on Wesley's knee and received his blessing.

Driver states that Robert Oastler in his early days had been a Tory but fails to develop the significance of this statement.[8] Oastler's change in political philosophy seems to have coincided with his move to Leeds, where he went on to become an 'advanced' Methodist, then a reformer and finally a 'Tom Painer', as the Methodist New Connexion secessionists were popularly known. Amongst his friends were Edward Baines (1774–1848), a Dissenter soon to become the proprietor of the radical *Leeds Mercury*, and around whom seems to have centred a loose group of similarly radically minded men.[9]

---

5. 'Biography of Mrs Sarah Oastler', *Methodist New Connexion Magazine* (1828) p. 354.

6. Driver, *Tory Radical*, p.13.

7. *The Journal of John Wesley* ed. by Nehemiah Curnock, 8 vols (London: Epworth Press, 1938), VIII p. 62.

8. Driver, *Tory Radical*, (1946) p.13.

9. [J.R. Stephens], *Sketch of the life and Opinions of Richard Oastler* (Leeds: J. Hobson, 1838), pp. 3–4. For Edward Baines and the *Leeds Mercury* see: David Thornton, *Mr Mercury: the Life of Edward Baines, 1774–1848* (Chesterfield: Merton Priory Press Ltd, 2009).

Although Cecil Driver correctly notes Richard Oastler's Methodist background, he fails to appreciate the extent of his father's religious radicalism, which indeed had emerged when he was still living in Thirsk. In 1784 John Wesley executed a Deed of Declaration, giving authority to the Legal Hundred, in reality the Methodist Conference, which would replace Wesley after his death. Another ninety-one preachers were omitted from the Legal Hundred and there was some concern within the Connexion whether in future all the preachers would have equal status. Richard Oastler in 1785 urged James Odie

3:3 Edward Baines MP (1774–1848) (From the book *The life of Edward Baines, late MP for the Borough of Leeds* by Edward Baines (junior) 1800–1890, Yorkshire Archaeological Society).

to circulate a petition expressing concern at the implications but Wesley, already recognising these concerns, wrote a general letter to the preachers in April 1785 to be read to the Conference following his death.[10] This was duly done when Conference met in July 1791, following John Wesley's death in March 1791, Wesley's letter emphasising that the preachers were all on an equal footing.[11]

With John Wesley's death in 1791, Methodism divided effectively into a pro-Church party, favouring the maintenance of Wesley's links with the Church of England and an increasingly vociferous group which wanted Methodism to go its own, separate way. Within the later group, the more radical elements supported Alexander Kilham and this would lead to the formation of the Methodist New Connexion in 1797. Oastler played an important and significant role both in giving

3:4 John Marshall MP (1765–1845) industrialist, educationalist, politician and owner of Marshall's Mill, Holbeck, Leeds (http://www.leodis.net).

3:5 Marshall's Mill, Holbeck, Leeds, where Richard Oastler's brother Robert tragically died on 13 February 1796 in a devastating fire on the site (Private Collection).

10. James Odie (d.1760, aet. 59) had both itinerated and continued in trade, this practice being forbidden by the Conference of 1768. This is possibly the cause of his superannuating in 1768 when he ceased to be one of the preachers. From 1784 he lived in Keighley and from 1769 to 1770 had been a supernumerary in the Yarm Circuit, which then included Thirsk, It seems probable that this is where Oastler first met him.

11. F. Baker, *John Wesley and the Church of England* (London: Epworth Press, 1970), p. 232; J. W. Laycock, *Methodist Heroes in the Great Haworth Round, 1734 to 1784* (Keighley: Wadsworth, 1909), pp. 360–369.

support to Kilham and in establishing the New Connexion in Leeds; some of Oastlers' correspondence survives in the Hobill Collection.

In the midst of all this, tragedy struck the family. James Dickinson, a Leeds family friend who at this stage seemed to be sympathetic to Kilham, wrote to him on 27 February 1796.[12] The letter begins with the impending charges against Kilham for publishing, in 1795, yet another tract, with the radical and revolutionary title *Progress of Liberty.* The letter then describes the consequences of a fire at Marshall's Holbeck Mills.

The origins of Holbeck Mills can be traced back to about 1785, the year in which John Marshall (1765–1845) entered into partnership as a flax spinner, leasing Scotland Mill, a water mill on Adel Beck, and began experimenting with machinery to be used for linen spinning. Then in 1791 he leased a site in Water Lane, Holbeck, a four storey-mill being erected by September 1791; by the close of 1792 further buildings had been added.

A second mill was built, in which spinning commenced in September 1795; five months later, on 13 February 1796, however, it was totally destroyed by fire. A wall collapsed reportedly killing seven and injuring twenty workers; the cost of the damage was assessed at £10,000.[13]

It is of this disastrous fire that Dickinson wrote to Alexander Kilham (1762–1798):

> On Saturday, 13th a most horrible fire broke out at … the manufactory of Messrs Marshall and Co. of this town which raged with unabating fury till it has consumed two immensely large buildings wherein was consumed by the dreadful conflagration machinery and flax to the amount to many thousands. It would have been well, and we should have been happy if it had ended here but, Alas! The scene most dreadful doth but now begin: about half after 12 o clock at noon. The rubbish was immediately removed, and six poor men taken out as dead, having their bones broken to pieces.

---

12. The John Rylands University of Manchester Library , Hobill Collection: James Dickinson (Leeds. 27 February 1796) to A. Kilham (Alnwick).
13. W.G. Rimmer, *Marshalls of Leeds: flax spinners, 1788–1886* (Cambridge: Cambridge University Press, 1960) pp. 22–45.

Young Mr Robt Oastler, a promising youth 12 years of age, was found on the Sunday morn buried in the ruins, broken to pieces and made the 7th Person kill dead on the spot and near 10 more very much, and

3:6 Revd Joseph Benson (1748–1821) *Methodist Magazine*, December 1802 (Wesley Historical Society Library, images provided by Oxford Centre for Methodism and Church History, Oxford Brookes University).

some dreadfully wounded, one of which is since died of his wounds in the Infirmary at this Place. We are not without hope of this apparent evil producing good effects towards the Methodists in this Town.[14]

Robert Oastler Junior's funeral became a *cause célèbre* as the Revd Joseph Benson (1748–1821), circuit superintendent, refused to conduct the burial in the Old Boggard Chapel graveyard, since being a supporter of the pro-Church party he believed that he should be interred in the parochial churchyard.[15] The letter continues:

You will no doubt be surprised when I inform on Wednesdays 17 Mr Oastler… was inter'd in the Ground at the back of our preaching House, being the first person who had been buried in it. I am very sorry to complain of the bad behaviour of Mr Benson on the occasion; his conduct was such at the Trustees Meeting, as would not be forgotten so long as he exists; no mean shuffle, did he scruple to be guilty of providing he could only accomplish his execrable design of preventing the interment in our ground, at the unfortunate youth. But fortunately for us one of the Church Party who was a Trustee had a conscience that would not suffer him to violate his word, which he had given to Mr Oastler, that he would stand his friend in the business. I have to observe that the Trustees made the majority and Mr Benson, after threatening what he would do, retired in disgust.[16]

Benson having refused to conduct the interment, it was taken by the Revd Thomas Langdon, a Particular Baptist minister in Leeds, who served as pastor of the newly built Baptist chapel in St Peter's Square, Leeds which opened in 1781 for forty-two years. This would have some impact on the family's future religious allegiances. Sarah Oastler would remain a member of the Methodist New Connexion until her

14. The John Rylands University of Manchester Library Hobill Collection: James Dickinson (Leeds. 27 February 1796) to A. Kilham (Alnwick).
15. Revd Joseph Benson (1748–1821) superintendent, Leeds Circuit, 1795–1797, and President of the Methodist Conference, 1798 and 1810. He was strongly opposed to Kilham's Radicalism.
16. The John Rylands University of Manchester Library Hobill Collection: James Dickinson (Leeds. 27 February 1796) to A. Kilham (Alnwick).

death but as a result of this incident it became her custom to worship with the Baptists on Sunday evenings.[17] In the 1820s she was a leader of a female class at Ebenezer MNC, their Leeds chapel until replaced by Woodhouse Lane in 1858.[18]

For a time Robert Oastler remained a local preacher in the Leeds Methodist New Connexion Circuit but at some point in the new century, and some years prior to his death in 1820, he returned to the Old Connexion. Although the reasons for this are not clear, it is known that he was persuaded to do this by a number of his friends. There is a possibility that it was for social and business reasons, possibly under the influence of the Dickinsons, a wool stapling family; certainly Richard Oastler was a close friend of Joseph Dickinson. By the end of the Napoleonic Wars in 1815, he and Richard, were active in the predominantly Wesleyan Leeds Strangers' Friend Society.[19]

Robert Oastler, on his return to the Old Connexion, does not seem to have retained his status as a local preacher. It was Richard Oastler, who had become a member of the Methodist society in Leeds in 1814, who in that same year now became a local preacher 'on trial' in the Leeds Circuit and was fully accredited as a local preacher after one quarter's preaching on the plan. By November 1820, his name no longer appeared on the plan, for in that year he left Leeds to become Steward of the Thornhills' Fixby Estate, near Huddersfield, ceasing to be a Methodist and later emerging as a Tory-Anglican factory reformer.[20]

----

17. Revd Thomas Langdon (1755–1824), Particular Baptist minister at the Stone Chapel, Leeds, from 1782 until his death. His daughter's biography, *A Brief Memoir of the Revd. Thomas Langdon, Baptist minister, of Leeds* (London: Simpkin, Marshall & Co; Leeds: Baines & Newsome, 1837) makes no mention of this incident. *See*: J. J . Scottorn, H.F. Weatherley, *A Short History Of South Parade Baptist Chapel, 1779–1979* (Leeds: The Church, 1979) pp. 7–10 for a more recent account of his ministry in Leeds.
18. West Yorkshire Archives Service, Leeds District Office, LCA 2466: Ebenezer Methodist New Connexion Society Class Book, 1820–1828.
19. Driver, *Tory Radical*, pp. 21–22.
20. Memorial sermon to William Smith by the Revd John Rattenbury, preached at Brunswick Wesleyan Chapel, Leeds, 1868 (undated newspaper cutting in the University of Huddersfield Special Collections, Wesley Historical Society (Yorkshire) Collection); Driver, *Tory Radical*, pp. 26-29; University of Huddersfield Special Collections, Wesley Historical Society (Yorkshire) Collection: Leeds Methodist Circuit preaching plan, November to April

However, perhaps worthy of further research are the connections surrounding the Oastler family, especially those linked to the Leeds Methodist community. When in October 1830 the *Leeds Mercury* finally published Oastler's letter on 'Slavery in Yorkshire', its proprietor, Edward Baines had been both a friend of his father and an early printer for the Methodist New Connexion. Another product of the Leeds Methodist community was Michael T. Sadler (1780–1835), who was the Tory Member of Parliament who moved the Ten Hour Bill in 1831.[21] Was it also a coincidence that Robert Oastler Junior, killed in the fire at Marshall's Mills, was the son of a Leeds linen merchant working in the flax mill of a pioneering manufacturer?

In conclusion, a consideration of Richard Oastler's Methodist family background raises significant issues not addressed by Driver, namely that his father, Robert, certainly by the 1790s, if not earlier, had developed radical political views which in religion took him, albeit temporarily, into the 'Tom Painite', Kilhamite, Methodist New Connexion; perhaps Richard inherited his political radicalism from his father.

Perhaps of greater importance is that Richard Oastler was just turned six years old, when his brother was killed in the fire at Marshall's Mills. Did the memory of that family tragedy set him on the path of reforming the factory system, for initially the campaign opposed the employment of child labour in the mills? Can the origins of Oastler's campaign as a factory reformer be traced back to that tragic day in February 1796?

1818–9; Thoresby Society, (Leeds) Vickers Papers: Leeds Methodist Circuit preaching plans: March to September 1813, May to October 1817, May to October 1818, November to May 1819–20, November to April 1820–21 It is possible that Robert Oastler may have ceased to be a local preacher when still as a member of the M(ethodist) N(ew) C(onnexion) but it is not possible to establish this as circuit plans for the Leeds MNC Circuit no longer exist for this period.

21. Michael Thomas Sadler (1780–1835), Member for Newark, 1829–30 and Aldborough, 1830–32. He came to Leeds circa 1800 and was in partnership with his brother Benjamin as a linen merchant; were there also business links with Robert Oastler, also a linen merchant? At this period Sadler was a Methodist but later, like Richard Oastler became an Anglican. It seems likely that for a time both Richard Oastler and Michael T. Sadler were connected with Albion Street Methodist Chapel, Leeds, and they were certainly friends. For Albion Street Chapel and the Oastler and Sadler connections: D. Colin Dews, *The Church with a Mission: Oxford Place Methodist Chapel, Leeds, 1835 to 2010* (Leeds: The Church, 2010) pp. 10–12.

The Huddersfield Short Time Committee and its radical associations, c.1820–1876

JOHN HALSTEAD

THE GENERAL HISTORY of the movement to limit the hours of employment of children in textile mills has long been available. It was only ten years from the passage of the Ten Hours Bill in 1847 before Samuel Kydd, himself a participant in the agitation, published the first comprehensive history, followed in 1888 by another closely involved, W. R. Croft. In the next century, at the end of the Second World War, the extensive research of Cecil Driver resulted in a thorough life of Richard Oastler, the most prominent leader of the movement. This biography was necessarily informative about more than just its principal character. Then in the post-war period, J. T. Ward produced a most detailed account, to be followed thirty-four years later by Robert Gray's intellectually more wide-ranging discussion. We are also fortunate to have biographies of John Fielden, W. B. Ferrand and G. S. Bull, to supplement that of Oastler. But this literature tends to deal with what might be termed the high politics of the movement; it quite understandably focuses on the parliamentary drama and the major events; the Short Time Committees and their members necessarily appear, but generally in an ancillary position, rather than as the central characters of the story.[1]

---

1. Samuel H.G. Kydd, *History of the Factory Movement from 1802 to the Enactment of the Ten Hours' Bill in 1847*, (New York: Kelley, 1966 reprint of 1857 edition); W.R. Croft, *The History of the Factory Movement: or, Oastler and his Times*,

This chapter brings the Huddersfield Short Time Committee (HSTC) more to centre stage. The Committee did not apparently leave any collection of papers, so information has to be gathered from a wide variety of sources and identification of many of the actors is not always certain. The chapter is principally concerned with the period 1820 to 1876, from the first known domicile of some prominent short time committee members in Huddersfield to the funeral of Joshua Hobson, one of the original members of the HSTC. It concentrates, however, on what might be termed the 'high period' of the HSTC, from the years before and around its formation to just beyond the passage of Althorp's Factory Act in 1833 to the Huddersfield by-election of January 1834, with selective forays into the period beyond. It identifies the original members, analysing the composition of the HSTC by age and occupation and outlines aspects of the Huddersfield district's radical and economic history relevant to the formative years of several committee members. It then takes the story from the despatch of the HSTC deputation to meet Richard Oastler on 19 June 1831 to the passage of the Act of 1833 and the divisions among the ranks of Tories and Radicals arising from the Huddersfield by-election of 1834. Finally, a concluding section briefly illustrates the continued involvement of the original HSTC members in the continuing campaign from 1834 to 1876 and provides a coda on people known to have joined the HSTC after its original formation.

The Huddersfield historian D.F.E. Sykes first provided the names of the original members of the HSTC and the list was reproduced with some variation of detail by Cecil Driver. Driver's list was presented as follows, the asterisk indicating those members selected for the deputation to meet Richard Oastler on 19 June 1831:

(Huddersfield: Geo. Whitehead, 1888); Cecil Driver, *Tory Radical: The Life of Richard Oastler*, (New York: Oxford University Press, 1946); John Towers Ward, *The Factory Movement, 1830–1855*, (London: Macmillan, 1962); Robert Gray, *The Factory Question and Industrial England, 1830–1860*, (Cambridge: Cambridge University Press, 1996); Stewart Angas Weaver, *John Fielden and the Politics of Popular Radicalism, 1832–1847*, (Oxford: Clarendon Press, 1987); John Towers Ward, *W.B. Ferrand: 'The Working Man's Friend', 1809–1889*, edited with an introduction by Norman Gash, (East Linton: Tuckwell Press, 2002); J.C. Gill, *The Ten Hours Parson: Christian social action during the eighteen-thirties*,(London: Society for Promoting Christian Knowledge, 1959).

Armitage, George (cloth finisher)
Armitage, William (cloth finisher)
Beaumont, George (weaver)
Bolland, Job (cloth finisher)
Brook, James (furniture dealer)*
Earnshaw, Charles (cloth finisher)
Glendinning, Samuel (cloth merchant)*
Hanson, John (fancy weaver)*
Hirst, John (co-operative store manager)
Hobson, Joshua (weaver)*
Holt, William (cotton twister)
Johnson, Thomas (weaver)
Kitson, William (cloth finisher)
Leech, John (general dealer)*
Pitkeithly, Lawrence (general dealer)*
Rawson, John (cotton spinner)
Rawson, William (cotton spinner).[2]

Mixed results were obtained from attempts to obtain more detail. We have no more information about Hirst, Holt, or Bolland. This leaves fourteen members for whom further information is available. A relatively unimportant group of six, of whom we have limited knowledge, comprised George and William Armitage, Earnshaw, Johnson, Kitson and William Rawson. This leaves eight more prominent figures. George Beaumont was very active up to 1834, but not thereafter; Brook and Glendinning were resident in Huddersfield and active throughout, like Leech. The most important, on a national rather than a simply local basis, were Hobson and Pitkethly. John Rawson was another significant figure within the factory movement though the degree of his activity within the HSTC is rather uncertain.

An analysis of the HSTC members' age distribution is clearly important in terms of obtaining some view of their likely mental

---

2. Driver, *Tory Radical*, p. 528; note to the text on p. 86. Driver's spelling of Pitkethly differs from the convention adopted in this chapter. There is considerable variation in the sources concerning the spelling of the surname. Lawrence himself wrote as Pitkethly and that is the form adopted here.

formation before 1831.[3] Six committee members appear to have been
born before 1800, including four who were prominent members: three
members of the deputation, James Brook (1798–1870), John Hanson
(1789–1877), and Lawrence Pitkethly (1789–1858) together with the
excluded George Beaumont (1794–1854+). Two others, George
Armitage (1788–1867) and Thomas Johnson (1794–1861+), whose
identification seems reasonably certain, were the less prominent
members of this group. These people had reached their adolescent years
by the time of the Luddite disturbances of 1812: James Brook was the
youngest, at fourteen; Johnson and Beaumont were eighteen; and
Hanson and Armitage were twenty-three and twenty-four respectively.
This puts John Hanson at exactly the same age as George Mellor of
the Longroyd Bridge cropping shop, when he was executed at York for
his part in the murder of William Horsfall.[4] Members of the group
were generally in their twenties, if not older, during the disturbed years
from 1817 and 1820; that is, at the time of the local risings of Folly
Hall and Grange Moor, or in 1819 at the time of Peterloo. There does
not seem to be a record of any direct impact of these events on these
particular people but their consciousness could hardly have escaped
being marked. The member of the HSTC to leave a record of the
impact of Peterloo was the youngest, then aged four. The shocked
reaction of his mother to the massacre in Manchester stayed with
William Armitage for many years.[5] By the time of the great political
excitement of the Reform Bill crisis of 1830–1832, the oldest veterans
were just over forty, while the rest ranged from thirty-two years of age
upwards.

The division of those born before and after 1800 is rather arbitrary,
but it separates people in their twenties from those who were still
adolescent in 1817, if not younger still. The elder post-1800 group,
born to 1806, comprises five persons who were all in their early to

---

3. Birth and terminal years are provided for HSTC members. A plus sign against
   the latter indicates our last trace and some uncertainty about the subject's year
   of demise.

4. Robert Reid, *The Land of Lost Content: The Luddite Revolt 1812*, (London:
   Cardinal, Sphere Books edition, 1988), p. 38, for the age of Mellor.

5. Alan J. Brooke, 'The Centre of Light and Knowledge: Thornton's Temperance
   Hotel 1854-1909' in *Aspects of Huddersfield: Discovering Local History 2*, ed. by
   Isobel Schofield (Barnsley: Wharncliffe, 1999), p. 38.

mid-teens by 1817: William Kitson (1801–1841+); Samuel Glendinning (1802–1883); John Leech (1803–1871); John Rawson (1804–1888); and Charles Earnshaw (1806–1851+). The younger group includes William Rawson (1808–1851+); Joshua Hobson (1810–1876); and William Armitage (1815–1893). William Armitage was only aged ten in 1825, about fifteen during the Reform Bill crisis and does not appear to have been a prominent figure during this period; Hobson, on the other hand, despite his relative youth in 1830, having just attained the age of twenty, was a key player.[6]

The deputation to Oastler therefore included members of the older group, Brook and Hanson, alongside the youngsters – by order of age – Pitkethly, Glendinning, Leech, and Hobson. A particular friendship was formed between Hanson, the oldest member here of the pre-1800 group, and Hobson, the youngest. There was a strong, general political affinity between the Owenite socialists, Hanson, Pitkethly, Leech and Hobson. Glendinning apparently did not share their politics and Brook's position is rather unclear. John Hanson and Joshua Hobson were politically close and undoubtedly shared an intellectual bond, being the most prolific writers of pamphlets and other published material from the group.[7] Hobson also worked closely and harmoniously in political alignment with Pitkethly; and Leech was said at one time to have been Pitkethly's business manager. Brook was the secretary to the HSTC at its formation and Leech was the chairman.[8]

As to their origins, not all were born within Huddersfield or its district. Pitkethly was a Scot, from Kinross. John and William Rawson were from the Halifax area and do not appear to have lived in Huddersfield at any time. Of course, Halifax, only seven miles north-north-west of Huddersfield town is no further distant than many places

---

6. This analysis is for fourteen original members of the HSTC, as we lack dates for John Hirst and William Holt and Bolland has been excluded since possible identification is untrustworthy. Hirst and Holt can be included however in our occupational analysis.
7. John Hanson produced four pamphlets in the period 1831 to 1839, two being in public controversy with Frederic Richard Lees for his attacks on Owenism. Joshua Hobson was the author of *Socialism as it is!* (Leeds: 1838); he published *The Poor Man's Companion* in 1842 and 1843, political almanacs compiled from parliamentary and other documents; and wrote a great deal for his speeches and material published anonymously during his career as a newspaper editor.
8. Ward, *Factory Movement*, p. 41.

included within conventional definition of the Huddersfield district –
such as Upperthong; nonetheless, that some members of the HSTC
were drawn from Halifax may appear surprising.[9] The explanation
seems to be that they developed links with the town from business
dealings in cotton warps. The STCs are said to have been 'very
informal affairs and in no sense exclusive', in which case any notion of
'membership' is loose and the term can be misleading.[10] Glendinning
was also born in Halifax and it may be true of Kitson, but unlike the
Rawson pair, Glendinning settled in Huddersfield and Kitson appears
to have been relatively close by at South Crosland, the village four miles
south of town. Pitkethly, from those born elsewhere, also came to live
in Huddersfield.

To these five committee members originating from outside of the
town, others may be added from villages and hamlets within the
district: Brook and Earnshaw were from Kirkheaton, two miles to the
east; Beaumont from Almondbury, nearly two miles east-south-east;
William Armitage from Honley, three miles to the south; and Hanson
from Holmfirth, a further three and a half miles in the same direction.
One member of the committee, Johnson, was from Netherton. It is
not clear whether this was the hamlet of Netherton within the
township of Sitlington, some four to six miles south of Dewsbury, or
the Netherton associated with South Crosland, though the latter may
be more likely. This leaves only three of those for whom we have
identifiable birth places, who were born in the town: Leech, Hobson
and George Armitage. In short, no fewer than around eight-seven per
cent of members of the HSTC were in-comers in one sense or another,
illustrating the point that in the first three decades of the nineteenth
century Huddersfield was a centre of rapid population growth; and
only seven (just over forty-one per cent) lived in the town centre.

Analysis of the occupational composition of the group reveals that
three were associated with cotton: Holt, about whom we have no
further information, was a cotton twister or spinner; like John and
William Rawson. Cotton warp and twist were employed within the
woollen trade and cotton spinning was in the van of factory employment.

---

9. The Huddersfield district is defined by the watersheds of the rivers which form
    its hinterland.
10. Driver, *Tory Radical*, p. 82.

Five were apparently in cloth finishing: George and William Armitage, Earnshaw, Bolland and Kitson. Finishing had long experience of machinery by 1831; it had been the industry branch most associated with trade unionism and it had generated the violent storm of machine breaking. This group of finishers no doubt had experience of factories or mills, though their employment in them in 1831 is uncertain. Samuel Glendinning stands out from those associated with textiles as the sole cloth merchant. He achieved some prosperity within the industry and cannot be termed an operative, though his career as an independent merchant still remained to be established in 1831. Four original members of the HSTC, according to Driver's list, were weavers: Beaumont, Hanson, Johnson, and Hobson. The information for Beaumont and Johnson seems to be the most reliable in this respect. Beaumont was a domestic hand loom weaver in the fancy or patterned cloth trade. Johnson was a woollen weaver, who was described in 1851 as a hand loom weaver and never as a power loom weaver, so we can safely assume that he was also employed domestically. In my view, the description of Hanson as a fancy weaver in 1831 is not trustworthy. It is more likely to be true of his early career in Holmfirth; and we have his own reliable evidence that he was spinning woollen weft in Huddersfield some time prior to 1832. While less relevant perhaps, it might also be noted that he held more than one occupation during his career. The characterisation of Hobson as a weaver is also very questionable, for there are reasons to suppose that he could have been working as a joiner in 1831. Nonetheless, at least twelve were apparently directly engaged in textiles when the HSTC was formed, or thirteen (76.47%) on the basis of the Sykes/Driver list. The numerically most important group within that is those from cloth finishing (9.41%) followed by cotton spinning and warp manufacture (17.65%).

The remaining members of the HSTC were engaged in retail dealing of one kind or another. Brook dealt in furniture; while Pitkethly, Leech, and Hirst were in general dealing, which would have included some textiles among other products. If we treat Glendinning also as a dealer since he was a merchant, the proportion rises to the relatively high figure of over twenty-nine per cent, almost one third. The interesting point about this data is that it is almost certainly different from that which might be compiled for the Leeds Short Time

Committee, which 'was composed almost entirely of representatives from each of the mills and workshops in the town'. Quite apart from the 'several small shopkeepers and the manager of the co-operative store' (Hirst), as Driver put it, and that any weavers were employed domestically rather than in mills or loom shops, around almost fifty-three per cent of the HSTC members were not directly involved in mill work.[11]

A similarly detailed examination of the membership of other Short Time Committees in Yorkshire and Lancashire could perhaps show that Huddersfield was not quite as different as it appears, but the composition of the HSTC requires some explanation. The answer is surely that Huddersfield was in 1830 still more of a marketing centre than a manufacturing one, even though much manufacturing took place nearby and was also on the increase inside the town.

The town's first market charter was received in 1671, from when it displaced Almondbury as the most important local market for cloth sold in the open-air around the churchyard. The indoor market, the Cloth Hall, was constructed in 1766 and enlarged in 1780, accommodating manufacturers both from the Huddersfield district and even from as far away as Saddleworth. In the nineteenth century, marketing spilled out of the Cloth Hall, extending to nearby inns and warehouses. The main driver here was the rise of the fancy trade; that is, patterned goods manufactured to the east and south east of the town. 102 fancy manufacturers were attending the market by 1822, with abode at inns and warehouses around the Cloth Hall; by 1830 the woollen manufacturers had also adopted the practice, and comprised half of the 255 firms listed.[12]

The biggest manufacturing establishment within close proximity of the town was Starkey's mills at Longroyd Bridge, but the continuously built-up area that formed the town and housed its centre was then upland, rather than down along the river Colne. The mills developed

---

11. Driver, *Tory Radical*, p. 82. The calculation about mill work assumes that all the cloth finishers were in mills, though that is not entirely certain, and it omits Hanson who had some experience of mill work prior to 1832 but who was not certainly employed there in June 1831.
12. W.B. Crump and Gertrude Ghorbal, *History of the Huddersfield Woollen Industry*, (Huddersfield: Tolson Memorial Museum Publications, 1935), p. 108.

4:1 Huddersfield Cloth Hall and the White Hart Inn. The Cloth Hall was built in 1766 and enlarged in 1780. The area outside the Cloth Hall and the White Hart was often used for public meetings (Kirklees Museums and Galleries).

by the Starkey brothers from 1819 onwards on the north bank of the Colne became a substantial establishment during the following decade. By 1834 the building of three factories and ancillary shops was virtually complete, while the firm employed three twenty-eight horsepower engines and 521 workers. A considerable amount of machinery for spinning, finishing and woollen power weaving was installed and insured in the next two years.[13] A second enterprise, established earlier and by 1816, was Fisher's silk spinning factory at Chapel Hill, also close to Longroyd Bridge.[14] Other establishments often mentioned as Huddersfield mills were at a greater distance from the town centre. The exception was Joshua Lockwood's mill at Upperhead Row. This occupied a central location in the town and is particularly relevant because of its connection with John Hanson. The mill may have been constructed in parallel with the Starkey investment at Longroyd Bridge; it was certainly in operation by 1825. The uninsured building

13. For full details on these mills see D.T. Jenkins, *The West Riding Wool Textile Industry 1770–1835: A Study of Fixed Capital Formation*, (Edington, Pasold, 1975), pp. 66, 166–168.
14. Jenkins, *Wool Textile Industry*, p. 226.

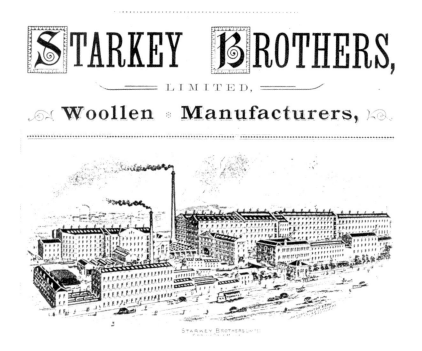

4:2 Starkey Brothers' headed notepaper showing the mill at Longroyd Bridge. The mills developed by the Starkey brothers from 1819 onwards on the north bank of the Colne became a substantial establishment during the following decade. By 1834 the building of three factories and ancillary shops was virtually complete, while the firm employed three twenty-eight horsepower engines and 521 workers (Kirklees Image Archive k021792).

collapsed in 1828 after a severe fire. It was rebuilt, however, and appears to have been operating power looms in 1833.[15] Despite these mills, it was said that in the early 1830s there were comparatively very few young male workers in the town of Huddersfield itself. Those in the town were apparently comprised of the best class of workmen in the woollen manufacture, rather than in the fancy trade, and there were few resident weavers.[16]

If this makes intelligible the occupational composition of the HSTC, what can be said about the formation of its members' politics? The committee was formed in a town that had already been for many years the centre of a district subject to deep economic and political turbulence. The original members of the HSTC would have come to it either with direct experience of earlier dramatic events or an acquaintance with other older people who had been associated with

15. Jenkins, *Wool Textile Industry*, p. 231; Vivienne Teasdale, *Huddersfield Mills: A Textile Heritage*, (Barnsley: Wharncliffe, 2004), p. 65; *Voice of the West Riding*, 17 August 1833.

16. William Stocks in evidence to the Select Committee on Handloom Weavers Petitions, 28 July 1833, [answers to questions 10021, 10023, 10025] British Parliamentary Papers.

them. In any case, the experience of the five-year period running up to the formation of the committee was, as a result of banking collapse and commercial panic, one of great economic distress, running in parallel with the reform crisis that engulfed the country and was coming to a climax in 1831–1832. Several strands or rivulets of experience were coming together at this time to create a strong stream of radicalism.

One of these strands was long-standing concern about the employment of children in mills or factories. Some inhabitants of Marsden complained before 1797 about the persistent physical abuse of pauper apprentices at Messrs Haigh's cotton enterprise. This belatedly prompted an inspection by parish officers of St Margaret and St John, Westminster, from whence the apprentices came.[17] Pauper apprentices do not appear to have been employed at other Huddersfield district mills, but the episode chimes with the recurrent national eighteenth-century interest in the fate of apprentice children and the move from the elder Sir Robert Peel of Bury to obtain a Health and Morals of Apprentices Act, which passed the House of Commons on 2 June 1802. Three years later, the Haigh enterprise at Marsden went bankrupt, and some of its apprentices were transferred elsewhere.[18] These events were too early to have a direct impact on HSTC members, but later developments were another matter.

The employment of local children in mills, not necessarily always alongside their parents, was undoubtedly growing in the district in subsequent years, if at an uncertain pace. The point was dramatically illustrated by the death of seventeen girls in a fire at Thomas Atkinson's Colne Bridge cotton mill on 14 February 1818. National debate about conditions of employment of children was already in progress, but this event further aroused public opinion. Previously, in January 1815, Robert Owen, the cotton manufacturer at New Lanark, had addressed

17. For full details see Katrina Honeyman, *Child Workers in England, 1780–1820: Parish Apprentices and the Making of the Early Industrial Labour Force,* (Aldershot: Ashgate, 2007).
18. According to Honeyman, *Child Workers in England* p. 196, after the failure of Haigh 'the remaining parish apprentices were distributed to other mills in the area', but this does not appear to mean within the Huddersfield district: the only example given, on p. 279, is of about thirty children who went to Merryweather and Whitaker, at Burley-in-Wharfedale.

Glasgow manufacturers, and while stating opposition to cotton import duties, also put forward a three-point Bill on factory employment. This was circulated to members of the Houses of Parliament. By June 1815, discussions with members of Parliament facilitated by the Tory Viscount Lascelles amended the Bill to apply to 'all cotton, woollen, flax, and other mills' employing twenty more people under the age of eighteen. No one under the age of ten should be employed; and none under eighteen should work over ten and a half hours. The age of those who perished at Colne Bridge included girls as young as nine and the fire broke out while they were doing night work. The shock to local public opinion is well illustrated by contemporary reports of the memorial service at Kirkheaton Parish Church. This service was attended inside and outside the church, by an estimated 4,000 people, since all could not be accommodated; and the vicar initiated that day, fundraising for the monument erected in Kirkheaton churchyard.[19]

This tragedy also attracted national attention and further aroused public opinion. Peel's Act of 1802 had been ineffective but because of it and his continued interest in the question, parliamentary leadership for Owen's Bill had settled on him. During the proceedings which eventually took place in the House of Commons, Peel alluded to the Colne Bridge tragedy. A weakened measure, again outlawing night work for children under sixteen, but restricting the labour of those under sixteen to twelve hours, rather than the ten and a half originally proposed, was eventually passed on 2 July 1819.[20] This episode illustrates, despite its legislative outcome, that the ten hours question was effectively already in the public domain before 1831 and would not have been ignored in the Huddersfield district. While the Haigh enterprise, when still operating at Marsden, was situated seven miles south west of Huddersfield town, the tragic event at the Atkinson mill,

---

19. According to Roy Brook, *The Story of Huddersfield*, (London: MacGibbon and Kee, 1968), p. 99, the girls, ranging from nine to eighteen years of age, had been 'locked in the mill, and the key mislaid', but no source is cited and the point is not confirmed by the detailed account in the *Hull Packet*, 24 Feb 1818. For the church service see *HP*, 3 March 1818.

20. For a full account of Owen in this respect, see J. T. Ward, 'Owen as a Factory Reformer', in *Robert Owen: Prince of Cotton Spinners*, ed. by John Butt (Newton Abbot: David and Charles, 1971), pp. 99-134.

4:3 Memorial to the seventeen victims of the devastating fire on 14 February 1818, at Thomas Atkinson's mill at Colne Bridge, in the churchyard of St John's Church, Kirkheaton (Photograph: E.A.H.Haigh).

located some three miles to the north east at Colne Bridge, in the township of Bradley, drew matters much closer. It is not possible to evince any direct causal relation between these events and the views of members of the HSTC, but that some four of these were Owenite socialists may strike one as curiously co-incidental.

The relatively high proportion of woollen cloth dressers or finishers among members of the HSTC is resonant of another strand of the district's history. The best paid men in woollens had been the hand shearers or cloth dressers in the finishing branch of the trade, yet their earnings and employment were under threat from the late-eighteenth century by the introduction of gig mills and mechanical shearing machines. The manufacturers of the Huddersfield district were more enterprising in their introduction at this time than the clothiers at Leeds and other parts of the Yorkshire textile districts. Gig mills, for artificially raising the nap of the cloth, were evidently in use at Bradley Mills, Dalton, in 1783, and 'the journeymen cloth dressers of Leeds and district' mounted a legal action against Richard Atkinson in 1787 in an attempt to stop them. This provoked trade union organisation, evident in 1799, and later in the guise of 'the Institution'.[21] When economic conditions deteriorated further and bargaining and petitioning failed, resort was had to machine breaking – 'collective bargaining by riot', in Eric Hobsbawm's memorable phrase. Huddersfield was its West Riding epicentre; men from the district formed the main body in the attack of 11 April 1812 on Cartwright's mill at Rawfolds, and croppers from Longroyd Bridge were convicted for William Horsfall's assassination at Crosland Moor on 28 April 1812 when riding home from the Huddersfield market. This was not the last episode of a desperate character, being followed in the disturbed conditions after the end of the Napoleonic Wars by the abortive risings locally at Folly Hall in 1817 and Grange Moor in 1820. The people involved this time came from a wider range of occupations than croppers.[22] The disappearance of such episodes as a consequence of the actions of the authorities and changing trade conditions was accompanied by more trade unionism. The weavers in the less well-remunerated branch of textiles, the fancy trade, successfully organized the West Riding Fancy Union from 1823 to 1825 in response to reductions in piece rates. The union failed

---

21. Alan J. Brooke, 'Labour Disputes and Trade Unions in the Industrial Revolution', in *Huddersfield, A Most Handsome Town; Aspects of the History and Culture of a West Yorkshire Town*, ed. by E.A. Hilary Haigh (Huddersfield: Kirklees Cultural Services, 1992), pp. 221–223.

22. John A. Hargreaves, 'A Metropolis of Discontent': Popular Protest in Huddersfield c.1780–c.1850', in Haigh (ed.), *Huddersfield, A Most Handsome Town*, pp. 189, 195–209. The machine-breaking quotation is from Eric J. Hobsbawm, *Labouring Men: Studies in the History of Labour*, (Weidenfeld & Nicolson, 1968 edition), p. 7.

when trade was severely hit by the West Riding banking collapse of December 1825.[23] One member of the HSTC is known to have had a strong trade union connection, but others were supportive of unionism at this time regardless of whether their employment was in a sometime unionised occupation. Sympathy for trade unionism was consistent with other common responses to economic circumstances, particularly criticism of ruinous competition in the textile trade and the advocacy of co-operation, a sentiment not necessarily confined to the Owenite socialists among HSTC members.

The public position of the Huddersfield Radicals by the early 1830s about strategy was that it should be 'peaceable and legal' and would employ 'moral and not physical force', though this did not exclude an element of popular intimidation at elections.[24] The great general question which formed, in a sense, a wrapper for grievances over living and working conditions, was Parliamentary Reform As the Huddersfield Political Union put it when seeking 'Equal Representation' in 1831, 'without which we are slaves, and while we declare that we respect the rights of every man, we also declare that we are determined not to neglect our own'. Representation, it was clearly implied, would be a remedy to then prevalent deafness of all parties 'to the cries of a degraded, insulted and starving population'.[25] It was not a new question. The relatively numerous independent freeholders of Yorkshire had long been accustomed to the journey to York Castle to vote for members in the West Riding elections; the County had been supportive of America against the British crown; and the Revd Christopher Wyvill had led a vigorous parliamentary reform movement in the county in the 1780s. The issue was live again in 1817. Radicals in the district had noted the

---

23. Brooke in Haigh (ed.), *Huddersfield, A Most Handsome Town*, pp. 223–225; see *Leeds Mercury*, 4 February 1826, for the Dobson failure.
24. The quotations about the way forward are taken from the first and third resolutions passed at the Huddersfield Political Union meeting of December 1831, reported in the *Poor Man's Guardian*, 10 December 1831. Exclusive dealing was resorted to during the elections of 1832 and 1834. The radical meeting of 26 June 1832 resolved that 'the labouring classes would deal with no butcher, barber, publican, shopkeeper, attorney, or medical man who should attempt to return a person in the Ramsden interest ... and that none should finger their earnings', *LM*, 30 June 1832.
25. See the first, second and fifth resolutions reported in the *PMG*, ibid.

letter of Godfrey Higgins, Esquire, of Skellow Grange, calling on the
Yorkshire gentry to lead for Parliamentary Reform, and his boldness
on that occasion was remembered during the reform crisis.[26] After the
Reform Bill passed in June 1832, the Political Unions of the West
Riding sought Higgins as their county Radical candidate before
eventually turning to Oastler.

So the HSTC came into being from within a long tradition of
economic, social and political struggle, which was again coming to the
boil from 1826 to 1832. Key members of the committee did not
confine themselves to the children's employment issue; and while that
was indeed a burning question, it formed part of a broader political
agenda. The HSTC was a product of discussions among those who
formed the Huddersfield Political Union and could have been, though
no direct evidence is available on the point, a subject of formal
consideration and resolution at one of its meetings. Before examining
the events of 1830–1831 however, it is necessary to trace what is
known of the earlier careers of Hanson and Pitkethly, then Beaumont
and Hobson.

John Hanson and Lawrence Pitkethly are two HSTC members
whose move into Huddersfield town can be dated.[27] Hanson's evidence
to a Parliamentary enquiry reveals that he moved to Huddersfield
around 1820, where employment was more plentiful and wages were
higher than in his native Holmfirth. The family had settled in a house
close to Lockwood's mill at Upperhead Row by 1832. By that time,
having been brought up originally in the domestic manufacture,
Hanson had experience of spinning woollen weft inside Lockwood's
mill. This was probably during the mid-1830s since it preceded work
'latterly, within these few years' for another person, 'a little manufacturer',
who took jobs in from both Huddersfield and Holmfirth. Hanson's

---

26. Godfrey Higgins, *Address to the Electors of the West Riding and the County of York*,
    Hackney, 1817, originally published in the *York Herald*, 25 January 1817.
    Higgins was invited and became an honorary member of the Huddersfield
    Political Union in November 1831, *VWR*, 31 August 1833.
27. This paragraph is based on John Hanson's evidence of 2 July 1832: BPP, *Report
    of the Committee on the Bill to Regulate the Labour of Children in the Mills and
    Factories of the United Kingdom*, answers to questions 9039, 9098, 9037, 9038,
    9043, 9102.

knowledge was also based on the experience of his children; two girls, who have not been identified, had been employed in various factories in Huddersfield and its neighbourhood over the previous four or five years, and one was currently employed at Lockwood's. It seems clear from this, and a comparison with the known family situations and record of other members of the HSTC, that Hanson was the most knowledgeable and qualified person to speak to the Factory Commissioners about factory employment. There does not appear to be any evidence, however, of Hanson's engagement in those aspects of radicalism which engaged some other members of the HSTC during the 1820s, despite his adoption of Owenite socialism.

Radicals in Huddersfield after the dramatic events of Peterloo and at Grange Moor were particularly focused on the free press struggle, the celebration of the radical exponent of the rights of man, Tom Paine, and support for Richard Carlile during his imprisonment in Dorchester gaol.[28] A group of these people is identifiable through correspondence with Carlile and the publication of their contributions to the 'victim' funds established for the support of his family. A key figure of 1822 is James Penny, 'Republican and Materialist' of Millbridge, to the north of Huddersfield in the vale of Heckmondwike. Penny sent funds from Dewsbury, Hightown and Millbridge, but also included money 'raised at a meeting of Huddersfield and Millbridge

---

28. There is a large literature on Peterloo. For the most detailed, but controversially revisionist account, see Robert Walmsley, *Peterloo: the Case Reopened*, (Manchester: Manchester University Press, 1969). Robert Reid, *The Peterloo Massacre*, (London: Heinemann, 1989), provides a very readable account. For an unusual and valuable focus on the events of 1819, see Michael L. Bush, *The Casualties of Peterloo*, (Lancaster: Carnegie, 2005). For 1820 as a 'radical war' and Grange Moor's connection with wider national events, the most valuable source is F.K. Donnelly, 'The General Rising of 1820: A Study of Conflict in the Industrial Revolution', University of Sheffield PhD thesis, 1975. On Carlile see Joel H. Wiener, *Radicalism and Freethought in Nineteenth Century Britain: the Life of Richard Carlile*, (Westport Connecticut: Greenwood, 1983).

29. *Republican*, 20 September 1822, for the meeting of Huddersfield and Millbridge 'friends' and Penny's representation of himself as a 'republican and materialist'; Penny forwarded funds from Huddersfield on other occasions, *Republican*, 1 November 1822. As a speaker toasting 'The immortal memory of Thomas Paine, the champion of Republicanism', at the meeting held on 29 January 1823 to celebrate Paine's birthday, see the *Republican*, 28 February 1823.

friends'.[29] One of these Huddersfield friends was Abel Hellawell,
a tinplate worker of Manchester Street, who also collected for Carlile
'as a materialist'. On one occasion Hellawell sent in thirty-nine
subscriptions from Huddersfield, eighteen from Marsden and nineteen
from Almondbury.[30] Penny was about to marry Hester Brooke of
Huddersfield in January 1824, and moved there by May to be Carlile's
agent and open a shop for his publications.[31] There was some
competition in the field, for if the later recollection of Christopher
Tinker's son Thomas is to be trusted, it was 'in the early 1820s' that
his father, a printer, 'ceased active work in his trade' in the town and
established a 'book and periodical shop, with a circulating library
attached'.[32] Tinker (1797–1844) was to be an important participant
in the events of 1830 to 1842 before he left Huddersfield for
Wisconsin on an Owenite mission, possibly at around the same time
as Lawrence Pitkethly's departure for America on 10 January.[33]

Lawrence Pitkethly, in many ways the key figure in Huddersfield
radicalism up to that point, seems to have arrived in the town at least
by the summer of 1824. He had given Mrs Carlile a 'swell black waist
coat piece for men' which Penny's wife, Hester, made up. Carlile wore
it through the winter of 1824–5. He had taken some of Carlile's
'books', which may mean editions of Thomas Paine rather than or in
addition to his journals, and would not sell them 'but take them to
Mann's of Leeds with whom he is very intimate'.[34] James Mann of

30. For the subscriptions, see the *Republican*, 9 April 1824. Hellawell had written
    to Carlile form Huddersfield on 18 January 1822, addressing him 'as the organ
    of a few Friends to Civil and Religious Liberty … We do not arrogate to
    ourselves infallibility, yet we know of no other mode of acquiring truth, but that
    of serious and fearless investigation … we have been ably supported by a few
    friends at Marsden … who are most hearty in your cause': *Republican*, 25
    January 1822.
31. Carlile to [W.V. Holmes], 7 January 1824. Richard Carlile Papers, Henry E.
    Huntingdon Library, California.
32. Letter of 31 March 1914 in the Thomas C. Tinker MSS, Wisconsin State
    Historical Society.
33. *Northern Star*, 29 April 1843.
34. Carlile to [W.V. Holmes], Dorchester Gaol [?]1825. Richard Carlile Papers,
    ibid. Evidence for Pitkethly at Huddersfield was previously based on his
    appearance in the list of subscribers to the Huddersfield Scientific and
    Mechanics' Institution.

Leeds was at the centre of West Riding radicalism to the end of the 1830s. He had been a cropper and was held by the authorities under the suspension of Habeas Corpus in 1817. His occupation raises the possibility that he was the Mann of Leeds involved in Luddism in April 1812.[35] But he was established by 1820 as the leading Leeds radical bookseller, sent to trial at York on a charge of selling a number of *Sherwin's Political Register* which contained the libellous remark that His Royal Highness, the Prince Regent, was 'an overgrown pauper'.[36]

Pitkethly's radical interests and involvement almost certainly started in Scotland. We know that until August 1811 he was mainly at Kinross, though he travelled to Perth and Glasgow to ply his trade as a 'wright'.[37] He lived afterwards – apart from a stay in Dalkeith during part of November and December 1813 for his marriage to Elizabeth Shaw – in St Cuthbert's parish, Lothian Road, Edinburgh; and information about the birth of his two children establishes his presence there until at least 1817.[38] There was no lack of radical sentiment in Scotland at this time, or of contact with other parts of the kingdom, and Pitkethly could have become an Owenite, like George Mudie, before leaving Edinburgh.[39] Perhaps Pitkethly's 'intimacy' with Mann indicates that he spent some time in Leeds before arriving in

---

35. E.P. Thompson, *The Making of the English Working Class*, 2nd edition, (Harmondsworth: Penguin, 1968), p. 645, n. 3. On the possibility of a connection between Mann of 1812 and Mann of 1817, we note that the latter's wife Alice was a widow aged 50 in the 1841 census. If we make the reasonable assumption that James could have been two years older than Alice, his birth would have been in 1789; that is, aged twenty-three in 1812.
36. *Republican,* 24 March 1820.
37. That is, an artificer or craftsman, possibly working in metal since his father was a 'smith'; WYAS:Kirklees KC/1040/1/1.
38. WYAS KC1040/1/2 indicates that Pitkethly may have left Edinburgh for Dalkeith on 3 November or immediately after; WYAS KC/1040/1/3 for the marriage; WYAS KC/1040/1/4 indicates tat he left Dalkeith on 10 December or soon after; Lawrence Pitkethly junior was born in 1815, his brother Robert S. Pitkethly in 1817. For evidence of the relationship see Laurence to Robert, 11 June 1879, WYAS KC1040/1/10.
39. Mudie was in Edinburgh until about 1820, as Pitkethly could have been. See the entry on Mudie in Joyce M. Bellamy and John Saville, *Dictionary of Labour Biography*, Volume 1, (London: Macmillan, 1972), 249–250 and Gregory Claeys, *Machinery, Money and the Millennium; From Moral Economy to Socialism, 1815–1860*, (Cambridge: Polity Press, 1987), Chapter 3, 'George Mudie: The Quest for Economic Socialism', pp. 67–89.

Huddersfield. There is some evidence that he may have visited America
after establishing a business in Huddersfield, before evidence records
his sending ten shillings and sixpence to the fund set up to support
the Revd Robert Taylor, who was imprisoned for blasphemy in 1828.[40]
He was almost certainly present at Taylor's meeting in the town when
he arrived on his 'Infidel Mission' with Carlile, following release from
prison in February 1829. Taylor's view of the visit in September was
that:

> we have been very successful, and have not only made our
> visit generally useful in the way of public excitement on the
> Infidel question; but we have made it peculiarly profitable to
> our mission, which is more than we can say for every place
> we visited.[41]

An unnamed correspondent from Huddersfield wrote to Carlile
the following month:

> your visit has taken effect with vengeance here. They cannot get
> done with it. The parsons were all alive and kicking last Sunday.
> Infidelity engrosses the whole conversation. *The Lion* has been
> in great demand by all parties.[42]

Arrangements were put in hand to erect a 'neat, plain and spacious'
Infidel Chapel. The intention was to erect the outer part of the
building at a cost of £500 and about 120 £1 shares had already been
taken by late October. The project was calculated to pay well as it
would be the only suitable place for lectures, exhibitions and theatrical
performances in the town.

It was intended to establish a good library a reading room, news
room and a school, but it is not clear what came of this project, which
foreshadowed the building of the Owenite Hall of Science a decade

---

40. *The Lion*, 17 July 1829. The evidence for a visit to America is in Lawrence
    Pitkethly to Robert S. Pitkethly, 20 November 1832, WYAS KC1040/1/5.
41. Revd Robert Taylor, Huddersfield, 13 September 1829, *Lion*, 18 September
    1829.
42. 'Friend at Huddersfield' to Carlile, 23 September 1829, *Lion*, 2 October 1829.
43. *Lion*, 23 October 1829.

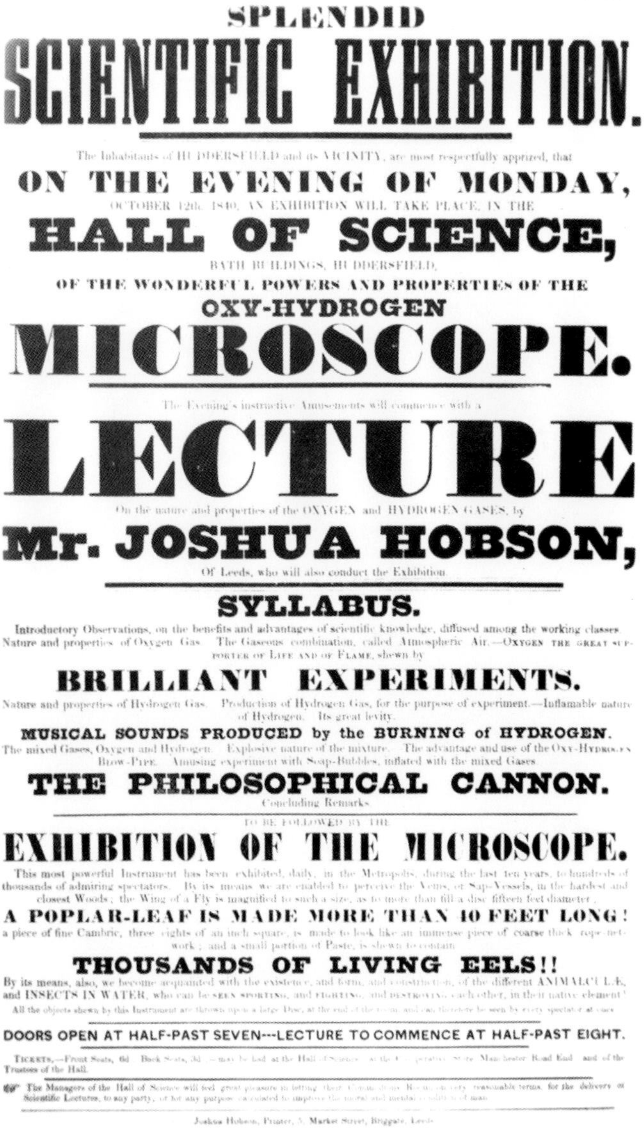

4:4 Poster advertising
a lecture by Joshua
Hobson at the
Huddersfield Hall
of Science (Tolson
Memorial Museum,
Huddersfield).

later.[43] Nonetheless, Taylor's visit stirred much controversy and conflict with Nonconformist local preachers. It is likely that all who later appeared as Owenite socialists would have been caught up in Taylor's visit if in the town. John Hanson is unlikely to have ignored the visit, nor Pitkethly or Joshua Hobson.

Before turning to Hobson, however, there is the problem of James

4:5 Former Hall
of Science, Bath
Street, Huddersfield
(Photograph: E.A.H.
Haigh).

Brook. There were several people named James Brook, so there are
difficulties in deciding whether the various sources naming James
Brook actually refer to the same individual. For example, was the James
Brook the 'Christian but a hater of persecution' who subscribed to the
Carlile victim fund, the Brook of the HSTC? [44] And could it also be
the same James Brook, the 'Huddersfield district preacher', challenged

44. *Republican*, 4 October 1822.

by Taylor and Carlile to discuss theological questions while on their
infidel mission to Huddersfield?[45] Linkage here may seem improbable,
but 'district preacher' may also be 'lay preacher' and the question
calls for further investigation. It seems clear however that James Brook
of the HSTC was also the James Brook who was active in the
Huddersfield Vestry during 1837, in complaints of tyranny in the
administration of the workhouse, in the anti-Poor Law movement and

4:6 Joshua Hobson
(1810–1876) portrait
by Richard Waller
(1810–1882),
1874, oil on canvas
(Kirklees Museums
and Galleries).

45. *Lion*, 18 September 1829.
46. Huddersfield Vestry Minutes, 30 March 1837; *NS*, 3 February 1838, 24 March
    1838; 21 April 1838, 20 October 1838.

elections to the Board of Guardians.[46] There is a clear link between the Brook active on poor law questions and the Brook active during the dispute over the Ramsden Estate Leasing Bill, who was self-taught and went to work in a cotton factory when little turned six years of age.[47] His birth at 'Kirkheaton', as the 1851 census enumerator recorded it, is not necessarily incompatible with the statement that he was resident in a village which had no Sunday school or that his forefathers on his mother's side were farmers on Pilkington's estate at Bradley for 400 years. He evidently worked in the cotton factory until he was fifteen years of age. This strongly points to Brook having been employed by the Atkinson's at Bradley Mills. There is some inconsistency between this and the notion that he arrived in Huddersfield at a the very young age of two, which is one implication of the statement in 1858 that he had lived in Huddersfield for 'nearly sixty years', but a generous allowance should no doubt be made for imprecision of memory, or information taken second-hand. He was almost certainly in Huddersfield by 1813 or 1818 when he joined a building club.[48] This interpretation of Brook's early life, if accurate, clearly illuminates his role on the factory movement.

Joshua Hobson was nineteen years of age in 1829. He was born the youngest of four children, according to his obituary, in November 1810, on what was then called the Green Side, later becoming 38-40, West Parade. The family house was built by his father, who died leaving his mother a widow when the children were of 'tender years'. After a few weeks in a dame school he was educated, 'when old enough', at Seedhill School in a class taught by James Campsey Laycock, for whom he had a high regard. He was 'scarcely in his teens' when, unknown to his mother, he absconded to Oldham and became a handloom weaver, where he was reputed to have published 'revolutionary effusions' in the Lancashire press. He was apprenticed to Thomas Flockton, joiner, in Back Green, on returning to Huddersfield. It might be supposed that Hobson left Huddersfield sometime between 1810 and 1812, as this would be consistent with the obituary and ten to twelve was not an uncommon age at that time for workmen to go 'on the tramp'.

---

47. *NS*, 19 January 1839, 27 January 1839, 2 February 1839; *Huddersfield Chronicle*, 31 July 1858.
48. *NS*, 2 February 1839; *HC*, 31 July 1858.

Hobson's return may have been prompted by a desire to assist the
family, which could have been in difficulties during the commercial
crisis that gathered way during 1826. He had certainly returned by
1829, since his obituary suggests he became associated with the town's
reformers when 'still in his teens'.[49]

In parallel with the excitement of Taylor's mission, there was great
concern about trade conditions. One response was the founding of the
Huddersfield Co-operative Trading Association in April 1829; its first
President, Amos Cowgill, had occupied the same position in the West
Riding Fancy Weavers Union of 1824–1826.[50] Co-operation, and the
establishment of co-operative communities, was an Owenite project.
There is early evidence of support for co-operative communities by
people from the Huddersfield district and Pitkethly was aware of
Owen's communitarian experiment at New Harmony, Indiana.[51]
Owen's activity on this project often took him from England during
1824 to 1829 and as previously noted Pitkethly visited America before
1832, perhaps during 1826–1828 and calling at New Harmony.[52] The
early co-operators were essentially community builders; and George
Mudie brought a group together soon after his arrival in London from
Edinburgh on 23 January 1821, to discuss the establishment of a
community.[53] In Owen's absence, co-operators in England began to

---

49. *Huddersfield Weekly News,* 13 and 20 May 1876. The information about his
    'revolutionary effusions', as yet untraced, is from D.F.E Sykes, *The History of
    Huddersfield and its Vicinity,* (Huddersfield: Advertiser Press, 1898), p. 301.
    Sykes is not always reliable: see Cyril Pearce, 'The Local Historian as Activist:
    Some belated thoughts on the life and times of D.F.E. Sykes,' *Huddersfield Local
    History Society Journal,* 11, winter 2001. Hobson is the only member of the
    HSTC so far to have an entry – by Simon Cordery – in Joyce M. Bellamy and
    John Saville, *Dictionary of Labour Biography,* VIII, (London: Macmillan, 1987),
    pp. 113–114.
50. Thornes in Haigh (ed.), *Huddersfield, A Most Handsome Town,* p. 172; Brooke
    in Haigh, pp. 223–225.
51. On early support see T. Leavitt (ed.), *The Hollingworth Letters: Technical Change
    in the Textile Industry, 1826–1836,* Society for the History of Technology and
    MIT Press, 1969. I owe this reference to Alan J. Brooke; on Pitkethly's visit see
    note 40 above and WYAS KC1040/1/5.
52. W.H.G. Armytage, 'Owen and America', in Sidney Pollard and John Salt (eds)
    Robert Owen: Prophet of the Poor, (London: Macmillan, 1971), pp. 214–222.
    Evidence of Pitkethly's having visited America is in WYAS KC/1040/1/5.
53. See n. 39 above.

work towards creating communities at home, but ran into difficulties in attempting to raise funds for the necessary investment. The debate that ensued prompted William Bryan, a Brighton co-operator, to write to the *Co-operative Magazine* in March 1827, proposing that co-operative households do their own retailing to accumulate profits. The profits from trade would first be used to finance manufacturing goods for the society, then when capital was sufficiently accumulated in the purchase of land for living on it as a community.[54]

The Huddersfield Co-operative Trading Association did get to the stage of producing its own goods, engaging Samuel Glendinning to represent 'for a short time the woollen manufacturing department of the Co-operative Society in Westgate', as well as appointing John Hirst to manage the store. The strength of this pair's ideological attachment at this time, to the social philosophy firmly established by Robert Owen and well-publicised in 1817 and 1821, is unclear, unlike that of Pitkethly.[55] Their association with co-operation may have been largely pragmatic, dictated by current economic circumstances. This is almost certainly likely for Glendinning, who in his youth attached himself to the Primitive Methodists, became a local lay preacher with them and continued his attachment to the last. He is said to have 'always held feelings of strong antagonism to (the) doctrines and principles' of the town's leading socialists, secularists and freethinkers, despite his coming into their society through his 'advanced politics'.[56]

Another response to the commercial crisis was the establishment of a Huddersfield subscription for the relief of the unemployed in 1826, but the money raised in London and by the more 'respectable' people of the district was not adequate; distress remained acute in the fancy trade, despite some improvements in woollens and worsteds. The focus of a different approach was at Almondbury, a centre of the fancy trade. A series of public meetings was held on Almondbury Bank from 6 June to 6 July 1829. These involved George Beaumont, the putative

54. Sidney Pollard, 'Nineteenth-century Co-operation: From Community Building to Shopkeeping', in Asa Briggs and John Saville (eds) *Essays in Labour History*, 2nd revised edition, (London: Macmillan, 1967), pp. 77–82.
55. Robert Owen, *A New View of Society*, 1817; *Report to the County of Lanark*, Glasgow, 1821.
56. Obituary in *HWN*, 14 July 1883.

4:7 Rose and Crown Inn, Kirkgate, Huddersfield (Huddersfield Local Studies Library).

member of the HSTC, who moved the resolution that, in the opinion of the meeting, the employment of machinery and the reduction in wages had been the great cause of a vast increase in pauperism and crime. One resolution of particular interest in the light of Robert Taylor's visit and the 'infidel' excitement at Huddersfield in September, called for an inquiry into the great wealth consumed by the clergy; and sought the application of any surplus over and above what was required for 'decent support' to be applied to the reduction of taxes pressing most exclusively on the labouring part of the community.[57] The eventual outcome was a meeting of operatives and masters at the Rose and Crown Inn, Huddersfield, on 21 July, which unanimously agreed

57. *LM*, 12 July 1829. The resolution is also of interest in relation to the fusion of radicalism and Owenite thought discussed in Gregory Claeys, *Citizens and Saints: Politics and anti-politics in early British socialism*, (Cambridge: Cambridge University Press, 1989), p. 178.

to the conduct of an inquiry into living conditions. This was concluded by September, finding that in the townships most occupied in the fancy business some 13,000 had not more than two and a half pence a day to live on, before meeting any expense occasioned by the wear and tear of looms.[58]

The July meeting of the operatives' representatives and the principal manufacturers was chaired by William Stocks (1783–1851). Stocks, formerly a linen draper who had turned to dealing in cotton warps, was secretary of a Sunday School from about 1815 and noticed that class teachers frequently marked against names, 'no clothes', 'no shoes', and so on, as excuses for non-attendance. He started to investigate by home visits in about 1817 or 1818, and was astonished by the state in which poor people were found. His part in the investigations of 1829 therefore expressed a long-held commitment.[59]

Concern about social and economic conditions in the district was felt and expressed then among a broad section of the population, and had resulted in various actions – through trade unionism, co-operation and petitioning Parliament – when Oastler's letter on Yorkshire Slavery appeared in the *Leeds Mercury* on 16 October 1830, followed by a second at the end of the month. The local Radicals responded by publishing the letters as a broadside; and held a meeting on 2 November which issued to him their congratulations. It is clear therefore that the factory issue was alive in radical minds well before the formation of the HSTC.

This was all running in parallel to the increased political activity associated with Parliamentary reform. The first Political Union in the Huddersfield district was formed at Almondbury in April 1830 – George Beaumont was one of those involved – to be followed by Kirkheaton later in the summer; and Huddersfield in December. The Huddersfield body, being based in the main marketing centre, became the more important, absorbing key figures from those involved at Kirkheaton and Almondbury. The Almondbury Union wrote to Henry Hunt respectfully requesting him to become a leader and

---

58. Letter originally published in the *Leeds Mercury: Morning Chronicle*, 21 September 1829.
59. William Stocks evidence, 28 July 1833, Select Committee on Handloom Weavers Petitions, BPP, questions 10012, 10013, 10021, 10028.

adviser, but it does not appear to have lasted beyond the summer and George Beaumont was among those who formed the Huddersfield Union. The Kirkheaton Union was formed in August by Thomas Leadbeater of Mirfield, a young solicitor, but he was called to chair the first Huddersfield Union meeting.

The founders of the Huddersfield Union included Thomas Vevers, James Brook, Samuel Dickinson, John Hanson, Charles Littlewood and John Heaton.[60] Dickinson, like Beaumont, was one who spoke at the Almondbury meetings of 1829. In addition to Brook, Hanson and Beaumont, definite evidence of Political Union membership includes Hobson, Pitkethly, and Leech; that is, the overlap of membership between the two bodies included at least five of the six appointed to the HSTC deputation to meet Oastler. Hobson, despite his youth, was in a leadership position in November 1831 when he issued, with Hanson and Leech as joint secretaries of the Huddersfield General Committee of the Political Union and Operatives, a handbill which took the initiative in calling for a general meeting of delegates at Manchester 'to arrange a plan and frame general resolutions for a grand meeting all over Britain and Ireland, on the same day and hour'.[61] The Political Union was still in existence in 1833, if not later, and became a forum for a broad swathe of radical opinion in the town and district during that period.[62] Membership can be inferred even when evidence is not directly available and all members of the HSTC were probably in attendance at its meetings at one time or another.

---

60. Nancy D. LoPatin, *Political Unions, Popular Politics and the Great Reform Act 1832*, (Basingstoke: Macmillan, 1999), pp. 45, 47, 60; John A. Hargreaves, 'A Metropolis of Discontent': Popular Protest in Huddersfield c.1780–c.1850' in Haigh (ed.) *Huddersfield, A Most Handsome Town*, pp. 205-09.

61. HO 52/15, f. 544; John Belchem, *'Orator' Hunt: Henry Hunt and English Working-Class Radicalism*, (Oxford: Clarendon, 1985), p. 250; John Halstead, '*The Voice of the West Riding*': Promoters and Supporters of a Provincial Unstamped Newspaper, 1833–34', in *On the Move: Essays in Labour and Transport History Presented to Philip Bagwell*, ed. by Chris Wrigley and John Shepherd, (London ; Rio Grande, Ohio : Hambledon Press, 1991), p. 28, n. 18. I am grateful to Dr John A. Hargreaves for the important information that Hobson was a joint signatory with Hanson and Leech.

62. It met on 10 June 1833, when it was addressed by John Cleave, *VWR*, 15 June 1833 and Huddersfield Radicals were involved in founding Political Unions at Holt Head and Penistone in July and August 1833, *VWR* 20 July and 10 August 1833. LoPatin mistakenly places its demise in December 1832.

Alongside the factory question, the Political Union was concerned with two other issues during this period. The first was the Reform Bill and the representation of the borough after a seat had been gained under the new Act, which became particularly entwined in the factory issue at the time of a by-election in 1834. The second was the issue of a free press; more specifically, the creation of a local radical organ, which could ventilate views on factory matters as well as other radical concerns. Pitkethly and others had been supporters of Carlile and unstamped radical journals had been circulating in the town since the end of the wars with Napoleon, but the unstamped press issue became a very live one between 1830 and 1836, with the launch of several hundred titles and increased prosecutions.[63] The Huddersfield reformers held their own meeting in support of the unstamped on 19 August 1831, when the speakers included Abel Hellawell and Thomas Vevers. But the Political Union also decided to launch its own penny paper, *The Voice of the West Riding*.

4:8 Swan Yard, across Kirkgate from the Swan Inn, Huddersfield. Joshua Hobson's printing press was situated in Swan Yard and it was from here that the *Voice of the West Riding* was first published (Kirklees Image Archive, k015538).

---

63. Patricia Hollis, *The Pauper Press: A Study in Working-Class Radicalism of the 1830's*, (Oxford: Oxford University Press, 1970). See also Joel H. Wiener, *The War of the Unstamped: the Movement to Repeal the British Newspaper Tax, 1830–1836*, (Ithaca: Cornell University Press, 1969), though, in my view, his interpretations are not always as reliable as those of Hollis.

It is clear that the establishment of a printing press was a Union project since it was in operation at least six months before the paper, producing handbills, broadsides and posters for the HSTC and the Political Union under the rubric 'Union Free Press'. It operated from Swan Yard, across Kirkgate from the Swan Inn and the adjoining Pack Horse Hotel, where the Union Rooms were located. The frame for this press had been built by the joiner Hobson, but a prospectus was issued to solicit funds. The projected newspaper certainly required working capital; and it is possible that when the prospectus was issued, the capital cost of the press had not been completely discharged.

It is unfortunate that copies do not appear to have survived, since the prospectus would have listed the names of original subscribers; but we have some knowledge of it from Joshua Hobson. The prospectus was addressed to 'Friends and Advocates of the Rights of Man'. The promoters sought to correct a situation in which:

> we have long been compelled to submit to the capricious and dictatorial monopolists of the press, who have hitherto abetted the claims of wealth against poverty, of power in preference to right, of institutions rather than persons; by whom faction and legitimacy have been eulogized to the expense of liberty and justice.

It had not been possible to publish anything 'emanating from the working classes, setting forth their wrongs and vindicating their rights'. The choice had been either to undergo 'petty and arbitrary censorship', or engage a printer at Manchester or some other place, incurring expense, trouble and risk. [64]

Hobson made pointed reference to the *Leeds Mercury* when he asserted that their press would 'vindicate the working classes from the calumnies and misrepresentations of ... parasitical scribes who figure in the provincial newspapers'. The language of the prospectus suggests that it came from Hobson's pen and he seems to have been the prime mover in the venture, but he did have a managing committee comprising two fellow Owenite socialists, George Brook and Read Holliday, alongside John Wood and William Wilson.

---

64. Halstead in Wrigley and Shepherd, *On the Move*, pp. 22–57.

The *Voice* first appeared on 1 June 1833 and within a month was taking up issues of ill treatment of children in factories. One of these occurred in the mill of Norris and Sykes, signatories two years previous to the petition by Huddersfield master manufacturers, against Hobhouse's Factory Employment Bill.[65] There at New Town Mill, Joseph Firth of Cowcliffe, aged thirteen, was badly beaten by an overlooker, Robert Clay. Firth had evidently been singled out from a group of boys working at the mill who had 'bah'd' a mason working on the premises for having been a black sheep. A further incentive for reporting the case was, no doubt, that the *Voice* believed the firm had discharged men and boys following the West Riding Ten Hour meeting of 1 July at Wibsey Moor, and it appealed for information.[66] A week later it carried a report on the hearing of Firth's case before the Huddersfield magistrates; Clay was ordered to pay two shillings to the surgeon, a week's wage to the boy and £1 to the Infirmary. We understand, the paper commented bitterly, that the law awards damages for injuries to persons, property and character, but in this instance the *person* was lost sight of – the magistrates declined to look at the sufferer's wounds – and pain and bodily injury amounted to no more than loss of labour![67]

It is not clear whether the prosecution of Hobson initiated by the Stamp Office in August was related to this reporting, though Hobson alleged that their action was prompted by a letter signed by William Moore from Huddersfield.[68] The charge under the clause in the Six Acts of 1819, defining what constituted a stamped newspaper, was laid by Joseph Brook, the local agent for the London Stamp Office, in the guise of its Sub-Distributor of Stamps. Hobson conducted his own defence in a spirited manner. He tried to show that the summons should be quashed on a technicality. In his examination Brook sought to expose the hand of the Stamp Office in bringing the prosecution; the partiality of proceeding against himself and the Voice while ignoring *The Witness*, an unstamped printed by William Moore; finally noting that the politics and principles of the paper were the cause of

---

65. *PMG*, 17 September 1831.
66. *VWR*, 6 July 1833.
67. *VWR*, 13 July 1833.
68. *VWR*, 25 January 1834.

the prosecution, before defiantly remarking that the paper would not be put down, 'as long as I can find the Public to support me'. 'I defy the law. I did not consent to the tax. I seek full penalty or acquittal. If you wish to enter the lists fairly with me and the people, *convict*'. Sir John Kaye, sitting with four other magistrates, announced the conviction of a £20 fine or six months at the Wakefield House of Correction, informing the defendant that if he found sufficient sureties he might appeal to the quarter sessions. Hobson replied: 'No, of what use is me sinning all my life, and then applying to the devil for absolution'. According to the *Voice*, 'the court was crowded to excess, vast numbers were unable to get inside, and great excitement pervaded the whole town'. The proceedings had ended, following Hobson's final sally, with great cheering. The crowd included people who had travelled up to ten miles to attend.[69]

Hobson's imprisonment attracted national attention. He was placed with common felons at Wakefield, had his hair cut, was made to wear prison uniform and was unable to receive assistance from his friends outside. The case was raised in Parliament by Colonel Evans and William Cobbett; Thomas Rawson, a subscriber to the victim fund set up to assist Hobson, chaired a meeting of town inhabitants, whose petition reached the Commons on 19 August; others flowed in from the Political Unions at Wakefield and Nottingham, two individuals – Bready and Lawrence – at Sheffield, the inhabitants of the parish of St Mary-le-Bow, as well as from the Society of Free Inquirers in another London parish, Mary-le-Bone.[70] These protests may have led to an amelioration of conditions, but at the end of October Hobson was still contrasting his treatment at Wakefield with that of unstamped paper vendors arrested in London; and there was no release before his term expired in January 1834.[71]

Production problems at the *Voice* were solved during Hobson's absence by the employment of John Francis Bray and the assistance of

---

69. *VWR*, 10 August 1833.
70. *House of Commons Journals,* 19, 23, 28 and 29 August 1833. P.T. Bready at Sheffield opened reading rooms and was an agent for the unstamped. Hollis, *Pauper Press*, pp. 113–114.
71. *VWR*, 2 November 1833; *VWR*, 25 January 1834.

William Rider.[72] An editorial soon noted that the prosecution was 'in some sort welcome', since it probably rescued the paper 'from oblivion ... our bitter enemies in the excess of their hostility, have not only lent us crutches, but stilts, and we travel with wonderful celerity.'[73] The maintenance of a northern radical press became a central objective. Hobson attempted to solve the problem by taking over the *Demagogue*, renaming it the *Argus and Demagogue* in August 1834, after the failure of the *Voice* in June; but this also expired after four issues and Hobson decided to move his printing and unstamped selling activities, that autumn, to the more populous Leeds, where he was again prosecuted.[74] A group Leeds Radicals including Hobson and William Hill, had formed a committee and issued a few shares to promote a further newspaper venture before May 1837.[75] While the evidence for this is not cited, it is certain that discussions about the creation of a journal were taking place prior to the crucial development, Feargus O'Connor's conversation with Hobson at the Peep Green anti-Poor Law meeting. There, Feargus expressed an intention to start a newspaper in the north and sought Hobson's advice about Leeds as the locale. They subsequently entered on the project 'as a matter of business'; Hobson as publisher, his old Huddersfield friend and Swedenborgian minister, the Revd William Hill, as editor, for what became Britain's most successful newspaper the *Northern Star and Leeds*

---

72. Bray, the author of *Labour's Wrongs and Labour's Remedies*, (Leeds: 1839), was a printer who took charge of the office and remained unmolested. William Rider contributed regular articles from Leeds.
73. *VWR*, 17 August 1833.
74. *The Demagogue* was edited by William Rider and only appeared in two issues, 28 June and 5 July 1834. It attacked Edward Baines senior, of the *Leeds Mercury*, for his parliamentary opposition to factory reform. Its printer was Alice Mann, widow of James Mann. For the conviction in Leeds on 16 January 1836 see the *Caledonian Mercury* of 21 January 1836 and the *Ipswich Journal* of 23 January 1836. Information was again laid against Hobson at Leeds on 4 March 1840; this time for publishing the Owenite *New Moral World*. Robert Owen appeared on Hobson's behalf, but sixty-nine issues had already appeared and Hobson said his enquiry at the Stamp Office before publication elicited the view that *NMW* was not a newspaper. The magistrates decided not to convict. *NS*, 7 March 1840.
75. Driver, *Tory Radical*, p. 371.

General Advertiser.[76] This new radical organ now outsold the London *Times* in what must have seemed from Hobson's point of view a dramatic reversal of the previous relation between his *Voice* and the *Mercury*. In all Hobson's journalistic ventures and his ancillary printing business, space and support was available for Oastler and the rest of the Factory Movement. His contribution therefore, like that of Pitkethly of Huddersfield, who was also brought into the discussions about founding the *Star*, was immense.

George Beaumont was evidently very active until 1834; in addition to his role in founding the Political Unions at Almondbury and then Huddersfield, he was a member of the Operatives Committee in which Hobson, Hanson and Leech played prominent parts.[77] He supported the unstamped and moved the 'grand national holiday' or general strike resolution at the Huddersfield Political Union in December 1831.[78] His participation in the Almondbury meetings of 1829 on distress in the fancy trade and his part in the subsequent survey of households was followed by his petition – with Thomas Vevers and Christopher Tinker as co-signatories – to Parliament in 1833.[79] He was also – perhaps somewhat curiously – actively promoting trade unionism outside his own trade, since there is evidence crediting him with founding a Journeyman Steam Engine and Machine Makers and Mechanics' Union in 1831. Nonetheless, during January 1834 he came into conflict with a trades union over its handling of a strike involving

---

76. Ibid.; James Epstein, *The Lion of Freedom: Feargus O'Connor and the Chartist Movement, 1832–1842*, (London: Croom Helm, 1982), pp. 61-68. The quotation is from Hobson's own account in *Joshua Hobson's letters on O'Connor and his Land Scheme, Manchester Examiner, November 1847*, Goldsmith's Library, University of London, A847. William Hill was a school teacher at the National School, Seed Hill, Huddersfield in the early 1830s and appears to have spent some time in Leeds before being in Bradford by April 1835 where he established a Swedenborgian Church, *The Intellectual Repository and New Jerusalem Magazine*, XXXVI, November 1835, pp. 671, 673; and XLIII, January 1837, p. 377.
77. According to J.R. Sanders, 'Joshua Hobson: 'One of Freedom's Boys', 1829–1836', unpublished Manchester BA dissertation, 1973, p. 102, Beaumont was also a secretary, but see note 61 above.
78. *PMG*, 11 September 1831; *PMG*, 10 December 1831.
79. *Cobbett's Weekly Political Register*, 6 April 1833; John Fielden, in presenting this petition also provided information collected by Captain Joseph Wood at Scammonden in 1832 to William Stocks' evidence from the survey of 1829.

his own employer, which led to a dispute with Captain Joseph Wood's election committee.[80] There is only limited record of factory movement activity apart from his initial membership of the HSTC, but he may have played some kind of organising role until at least 1834. He appears to have been assaulted on 10 February 1833 when walking home to Almondbury from Huddersfield, but when it transpired that his assailant, G. Stancliff of Dalton, had a wife and ten children, Beaumont requested of the magistrates that the warrant be dismissed.[81]

The HSTC was formed when the terms of the Bill that James Cam Hobhouse intended to introduce into the House of Commons were announced. Hobhouse, the Radical MP for Westminster, had been responsible for factory bills since the elder Peel's Act of 1819 and now had the Acts of 1825 and 1829 to his credit. Yet this legislation was ineffective, like its predecessors. As the terms of his new effort became public in February 1831, the reformers who had previously publicised

4:9 Fixby Hall; the Oastler family's living quarters were in the far wing (Photograph: E.A.H.Haigh).

---

80. See Brooke in Haigh (ed.), p. 227.
81. *LM*, 14 March 1833.

Oastler's intervention now mobilised within the HSTC to gather evidence.

The next key event was the Fixby Hall Compact meeting of 19 June followed by the development of a plan of campaign of mass meetings. Before this plan could be put into effect, Hobhouse had introduced his bill on 4 July, only to desert it on 28 September; the campaign was now in support of Oastler's friend, M. T. Sadler of Leeds, who had taken over the parliamentary leadership. The first meeting was held in Huddersfield on 26 December 1831. The HSTC was responsible for the advertising and organisation and the six members of its Fixby Hall deputation were on the platform. Three of these moved or seconded resolutions: James Brook, secretary to the HSTC from its inception to at least 1834, moved that the limitation of factory hours would protect benevolent masters and extend and equalize labour, which John Hanson seconded; Pitkethly moved that the resolutions be sent to Sadler. Other HSTC members also participated; Beaumont seconded Pitkethly and Charles Earnshaw seconded Richard Brook's resolution that ten hours a day was sufficient labour for children.[82]

The campaign continued with meetings at Bradford on the following day, at Leeds on 7 January 1832, Keighley on 30 January, Dewsbury on 6 February, culminating at Halifax on 6 March prior to the presentation of Sadler's Bill to the House of Commons. HSTC members do not appear to have been present at Dewsbury, but this cannot be certain since 'Oastler's Own' evidently constituted a bodyguard on occasion and probably not just at Huddersfield. HSTC members were present at the other meetings; Brook was at Bradford, seconding Oastler's resolution in favour of Ten Hours after an abortive attempt to prevent him from speaking on the grounds that local people

---

82. *LM*, 31 December 1831. For James Brook as secretary of the HSTC see Ward, *Factory Movement*, p. 41, referring to March to June 1831; Driver, *Tory Radical*, p. 195, referring to the Fixby Park meeting of 22 August 1832; *Working Man's Friend*, 29 June 1833 in HO 64/19, *VWR*, 19 October 1833; signatory as secretary of the HSTC for its presentation of the Bible to the Revd G. S. Bull to take place on Monday, 20 October 1834 at the Ebenezer Chapel, Spring Street, Huddersfield, University of London Library, Goldsmith's-Kress Library of Economic Literature no. 28740; also on 20 September 1834, Goldsmith's-Kress Library of Economic Literature no. 28741.

4:10 Poster advertising the 'pilgrimage' to York at Easter 1832 (West Yorkshire Archive Service, Bradford, DB27/C1/48/2).

were 'fully competent to discuss the question without being addressed, or amused, or instructed by persons from a distance'; he was also at Keighley; Pitkethly was at Leeds, and Hanson and Law Stoney of Huddersfield with Abraham Whitehead of Holmfirth, at Halifax.[83]

83. For Bradford, *LM*, 31 December 1831; Leeds, *LM*, 14 January 1832; Keighley, *LM*, 4 February 1832: Dewsbury, LM, 11 February 1832; Halifax, *LM*, 10 March 1832. Law Stoney, not an HSTC member, was living in Halifax in 1851, employed as a Methodist New Connexion Minister. Abraham Whitehead, a clothier or woollen weaver, can be more precisely placed at Paris in the township of Fulstone, close to Scholes, near Holmfirth.

Sadler's Bill was proposed in the House in March, but was immediately sent to Committee which commenced sitting on 12 April. The preceding series of successful Yorkshire meetings had concluded with the formation of a Central Committee for the Yorkshire STCs, based in Leeds, with a similar body for Lancashire and Cheshire at Manchester. Samuel Glendinning of the HSTC was the Yorkshire secretary in 1833 and may have occupied the position from inception. It was from this central body that witnesses were organized to present evidence to the committee on Sadler's Bill.[84] There is no evidence that Abraham Whitehead was a member of the HSTC, but he was to present evidence on the Committee's first day.[85] Hanson was a member

4:11 Huddersfield Market Place, showing the Market Cross, with the George Inn, in its original location, in the background (Kirklees Image Archive km01674).

84. William Osburn was Chairman of the Short Time Committee at Leeds from 6 March 1832 and he examined most of the witnesses before they went to London. For Glendinning as Secretary of the Central Committee see an *Address to the Friends of Justice and Humanity in the West Riding of York* issued when the delegates met at the Yew Tree Inn, Birstall, on 28 October 1833, reprinted in *The Factory Act of 1833; Eight Pamphlets 1833–1834*, New York, Arno Press.

85. Minutes of Evidence, Select Committee on the Bill to Regulate the Labour of Children in the Mills and Factories of the UK. Ward, in writing about Whitehead's contribution to the Halifax meeting of 6 March, says he was a 'Ten Hours organiser', *Factory Movement*, p. 50; and also notes, p. 113, that he spoke at the fifth Co-operative Congress at Huddersfield during Easter week, 1833.

of the Central STC as well as the HSTC, though his membership
received no mention in evidence when he appeared later on 2 July, and
he was to lose two months employment for his pains.[86] Apart from
marshalling witnesses, it was decided on a yet greater demonstration
of public opinion: a monster county meeting at York at Easter,
24 April.

The idea of the York 'pilgrimage' for a meeting in the old Castle
Yard – site of the Revd Christopher Wyvill's great parliamentary reform
campaign meeting of 1780 – came originally from Oastler, was discussed
with Sadler and Wood at Bradford, then adopted enthusiastically by
the Short Time Committees. The Central Committee made a general
plan; each district Committee devolved responsibilities to factory and
village sub-committees.

On the Easter Monday of the march contingents from smaller
places were to converge on the larger; at Huddersfield, Oastler's
Own division assembled in the market place at five o'clock to await
others from the districts. The whole assembled and set off at six,
led by Oastler, Leech, Pitkethly, Glendinning and Hanson. The
organisational effort for this immense demonstration was huge and
would have involved all HSTC members as well as other activists.
William Armitage, for example:

> was not a platform orator. He mainly confined himself to going
> and begging for the cause, to distributing literature, and to quiet,
> unobtrusive but caustic advocacy.

In addition, he was almost certainly one of those who 'marshalled'
Huddersfield reformers on the day, as later in 1838 at a great West
Riding Chartist meeting on Peep Green.[87] Barns and warehouses were
taken over at different points; straw was got in; inns were notified and
sustenance arranged for each contingent; lists of marchers were drawn
up and food tickets issued.

The tributaries of contingents streamed into Leeds during the day
and made rendezvous at the White Cloth Hall Yard, where they were

---

86. William Osburn, in evidence taken by Drinkwater, 1833 (450), *Factories
    Inquiry Commission: First Report of the Central Board*.
87. Sykes, *Huddersfield and its Vicinity*, pp. 302-303.

refreshed and assigned warehouse billets for a few hours rest before starting the all-night march to York. Heavy rain was falling by the time they set off just before midnight and it continued to drench them until near dawn. The bread and cheese ordered was missing when they reached the race course outside York and resentment developed that threatened a riot. Oastler had gone on into the city and had to be summoned by one of the Huddersfield men while Pitkethly tried to appease the vast crowd. The day was saved when Pitkethly saw him coming and shouted, 'the King, the King!' The crowd cleared a path, Oastler's oratory steadied them, brought them back to bedraggled good humour, and remounting his horse, he led them with bands, bodyguard and banners to Castle Yard, where the meeting lasted five hours. Captain Joseph Wood of Sandal, soon to enter Huddersfield as its Radical candidate for the 1832 general election, was among those who addressed the crowd of 12,000 in the yard and as many outside. Hanson proposed a vote of thanks to Sadler. The return started just before dusk. The contingents left Tadcaster early on a bright Wednesday day, were refreshed in Leeds, and shortly set off for their respective towns. Thousands lined the streets in Leeds to watch their coming and Huddersfield Market Place was thronged when the district's contingents arrived there. Oastler had walked with the contingents and had to get to Fixby; others still had another two or three hours to home.[88] The responsibility for sending the petitions adopted at the meeting on the following Saturday to the two county members in the Commons, Lord Morpeth and George Strickland, and to the Duke of Sussex, for the House of Lords, fell to an 'indefatigable member of the Central Short Time Committee', John Hanson.[89] Shortly after, Hanson went with Oastler, William Osburn of Leeds and other members of the Central Committee, to give evidence to the Factories Inquiry Commission and an audience with Sussex and others.[90]

---

88. This account of the 'pilgrimage' follows Driver, *Tory Radical*. Oastler had acquired the soubriquet 'the Factory King' as a result of *Leeds Mercury* sarcasm about his alleged pretensions to 'grandeur' in conceiving the march. The *Mercury*'s attack had an unintended effect.
89. *PMG*, 30 June 1832.
90. Kydd, *Factory Movement*, pp. 321–322; Ward, *Factory Movement*, p. 67.

Soon after the Ten Hours contingents were back home and while Sadler's Committee was sitting, progress on the Parliamentary Reform Bill entered a critical phase. Lord Grey's administration failed to bring in a bill when Lyndhurst's postponing motion was passed on 7 May. The Huddersfield inhabitants assembled on 12 May in the large room at the George Inn. The Constable, James Booth was called to the chair on the motion of William Moore, in favour of Grey's measure. John Sutcliffe moved the first motion that the virtual defeat of the Reform Bill by the hostility of the House of Lords had excited in the meeting 'an inexpressible feeling of consternation and dismay'.[91] Pitkethly attempted to move an amendment calling upon the whole community to refuse to petition Tory or Whig, or any form of government, until they were put in full possession of their rights, universal suffrage and vote by ballot. The Huddersfield Radicals had of course additionally declared themselves for annual parliaments and no property qualification, whether for voters or candidates, at their previous meeting. Nonetheless, when the chair pointed out that the amendment fell outside the terms of the requisition and could not be put to the meeting, which Pitkethly accepted, confusion reigned. Samuel Dickinson and Christopher Wood, the latter specifically identified as a member of the HPU, intervened helpfully and calm was restored. George Beaumont was involved, as was Thomas Vevers. The most cogent remarks, from the point of view of the majority at the meeting, came from William Willans, leader of the middle-class liberal element, Congregationalist of the Ramsden Street Chapel and relative of Baines at Leeds. His own sentiment was that there was no one who contributed to the support of government, unless incapacitated by crime, who did not deserve the elective franchise, but they were not to consider the matter as an abstract right, rather whether they should exert themselves to the utmost to secure the Reform Bill and for that he strongly urged the necessity of union among all classes in support

---

91. The source for this paragraph is *LM*, 15 May 1832. The report does not always provide first names, as in the case of Sutcliffe, but we are confident this is John Sutcliffe (1776–1858), wool stapler of Chapel Hill, later a town magistrate, who gave evidence to the Lords Committee on the State of the British Wool Trade, 13 June 1828.

of the meeting's second resolution that all supplies of public money be stopped until the Reform Bill shall have passed.

The town Radicals, like Oastler, did not expect any great change if the Reform Bill were passed. Ten days previously Pitkethly had put pen to paper on behalf of the Political Union. He wrote to Francis Place on the instruction of the Political Union to convey its thanks for his 'handsomest and kind present of Books' commenting that:

> the state of the country is desperate, the poor are to a great extent destitute of education, information, comfort or the necessaries of life, their situation is dreadful, their energies are wasted by over-working and starvation, they are without hope of any relief from the legislative enactments, they have sufficient discernment to prove that Whigs require as large an amount of revenue to support the state as the Tories and that all pretensions to economy when out of place are lost when in place and their only hope is a general stand against oppression and without relief is afforded and very soon I fear that order cannot be supported…within this neighbourhood many families are existing in the most wretched state, even upon *three halfpence* or less per day and working 15 and 16 hours; they are nearly naked without furniture of any kind and whole families sleeping on one piece of straw without covering….

Pitkethly concluded:

> I feel much astonished that the factory question has not engaged the attention of the press and of philanthropists much more of late. Humanity demands that they should and justice cannot be enforced without this principle … be established – the inhumanity exercised on helpless innocent children is without parallel in the history of the world and if you, Sir, witnessed the barbarities of one day in our mill you would never again be happy.[92]

---

92. Pitkethly to Francis Place, 2 May 1832, BM Add. MSS 35, 149 Folio 168. The text of this letter is of interest in relation to William Thomson, *The Age of Harmony, or a new system of social economy eminently calculated to improve the circumstances of the oppressed, enslaved and impoverished portion of the people of*

A more important meeting than the Reform meeting at
Huddersfield was held in Leeds two days later, on 14 May. Pitkethly
was present there too, moving that the resolutions be transmitted to
the three papers in Leeds. The Reform Bill passed and received the
Royal Assent on 7 June.

Pitkethly appears to have had the central position in town's
Radicalism at this point. We have seen that he was strongly connected
to Radicals in Leeds and even more widely. His inclusion on the
platform at York during the Easter pilgrimage was testimony to his
importance, but some contemporaries found his presence in that role
less than commanding.[93] His talent seems to have been organisational
and his unswerving hard commitment. Oastler joked about Pitkethly's
ultra-Radicalism as compared to his own ultra-Toryism, a point he was
to make in slightly different terms about Hobson about a year later.[94]
Pitkethly was an assiduous correspondent and already had premises at
Walker Street, Salford, as well as in Huddersfield. [95] He travelled
extensively on business, but paid careful attention to all local issues,
frequently attending the local Vestry.

The Sadler Committee, still in session, held its last sitting on
7 August. Attention had already turned to the question of election,
Huddersfield having been enfranchised for the first time as a
Parliamentary Borough. Captain Joseph Wood had entered the town

---

Great Britain and Ireland, which, as Ward notes, *Factory Movement*, p. 113, was
dedicated to Pitkethly. Unfortunately, Ward renders Thomson as Thompson,
inviting confusion with the Irish William Thompson (1773–1833), author of
An Inquiry into the Distribution of Wealth Most Conducive to Human Happiness,
1824, and *Labour Rewarded: The Claims of Labour and Capital Conciliated*,
1827, rather than the Scottish William Thomson, who was a member of the
Parkhead and Westmuir Economical Society of Glasgow and subsequently
edited the *Chartist Circular*. The copies of his *Age of Harmony* held at the
London School of Economics and the University of London Library are of the
second edition, Glasgow, 1834. Attempts to trace a first edition to place an
earlier date on Pitkethly and Thomson's acquaintance have been unsuccessful.

93. Lloyd Jones, *Newcastle Weekly Chronicle*, 16 August 1879; Robert Gammage,
History of the Chartist Movement, 1837–1854, originally published in 1854,
revised 1897 edition, reprinted 1969, (Merlin Press), p. 64.

94. *Working Man's Friend*, 29 June 1833, HO 64/19; *Argus and Demagogue*, 23
August 1834.

95. Lawrence Pitkethly to Robert Pitkethly, 20 November 1832, WYAS
KC1040/1/5.

for the first time as a Radical candidate on 25 June and he was back again for the conclusion of the Sadler Committee sittings. The Whigs were alarmed by Oastler's support for Wood, a Ten Hours man, and summoned John Charles Ramsden to the constituency. Their putative candidate, the son of Sir John Ramsden, Huddersfield's Lord of the Manor, had already been a Member for the West Riding for some seventeen years.[96] His father owned Almondbury and at Huddersfield the whole of the ground on which the town stood, apart from that under one house.[97] Resentment in the town over Sir John's 'peculation' in failing to revise Ramsden canal dues in accordance with the terms of the Act, which was to come to a head two years later, was already simmering. Richard Oastler's sarcastic appellation for John Charles, put to the public in 1832, was 'Mr Soke'; his motive was profit, and the family failed to keep the clauses of the Ramsden Canal Act. On the factory question, Oastler claimed to have it in writing that his son was in favour of twelve hours, rather than ten a day.[98] The hostility of the non-electors compelled him to 'retire precipitately from the town', inducing the Whigs to adopt Captain Lewis Fenton as their new, eventually successful candidate.[99]

At Leeds, Sadler, the promoter of the Ten Hours Bill, was defeated in the general election on 12 December 1832. Victory went to John Marshall, the town's linen manufacturer, and Macaulay, like Fenton at Huddersfield, opponents of the Ten Hours Bill.[100] The committee report on Sadler's Bill came out early in 1833 and the short time committee delegates gathered at Bradford on 11 January. There was more support for Ten Hours among prominent manufacturers at Bradford as compared to the hostility of the greatest at Leeds, so the

---

96. Ramsden informed a meeting at Sheffield on 27 April 1831 that he had then been in Parliament for sixteen years, or since 1815, *MC*, 30 April 1831.

97. Ramsden's comment on remarks of Lord Milton in the House of Commons during the Reform Bill debate on the representation of Huddersfield, 5 March 1832: *LM*, 10 March 1832.

98. *PMG*, 7 July 1832, for Oastler's speech at Leeds; *Poor Man's Advocate*, 28 July 1832, for his speech at Huddersfield on 10 July.

99. The words in quotation are from Joshua Hobson's obituary, *HWN*, 13 and 20 May 1876.

100. See W.G. Rimmer, *Marshall's of Leeds: Flax Spinners 1788–1886*, (Cambridge: Cambridge University Press, 1960).

THE

MEMORIAL

OF THE

Physicians and Surgeons,

OF BRADFORD,

IN FAVOUR OF THE

TEN-HOUR-BILL,

Addressed to the House of Commons, July 13th, 1833.

"**We, the Undersigned Physicians and Surgeons of Bradford, have** viewed with Concern the Proposal made by Lord Althorp for limiting the Time of Labour for Children in Factories to a Period of Eight Hours daily, conceiving as we do that, if such a Measure were adopted, it would fail to afford that Protection to their Health which is now generally admitted to be absolutely necessary.

"**It is our deliberate Opinion that a Limitation of Children's** Labour in Factories to Eight Hours a Day will occasion the Employment of Two Sets of Hands, by which those serious Evils resulting from *early* and *late* Hours of working would be continued in their most baneful form, especially injurious in the Winter Season.

"**We see too much Reason to fear that, for the sake of obtaining** Double Wages, the same Children would be employed in more Establishments than one, particularly in densely populated Manufacturing Districts.

"**We are also of Opinion that the foregoing Evils may be pre-** vented by a Bill limiting the Period of Labour to Ten Hours a Day, which, under a proper and efficient System of Senatory Regulations, presents the greatest Proba- bilities of securing those Advantages which are contemplated by the present Legis- lative Interference.

SIGNED.

JOHN OUTHWAITE, M.D., Physician to the Dispensary.
WILLIAM MACTURK, M.D., Physician to the Dispensary.
WILLIAM SHARP, Consulting Surgeon to the Dispensary.
THOMAS LISTER, Surgeon to the Dispensary.
WILLIAM SHARP, Jun. Surgeon to the Dispensary.
JON. A. ILLINGWORTH, Surgeon.
THOMAS BEAUMONT, Surgeon.
JOHN CLAYTON COOPER, Surgeon to the Dispensary.
ALEXANDER MUIR, Surgeon.
JAMES DOUGLAS, Surgeon.
JOHN WALKER ROBERTS, Surgeon.
WILLSON CRYER, M.D.
EDWIN CASSON, Surgeon.
HENRY N. SETTLE, House Surgeon to the Bradford Dispensary.

BRADFORD, March 2d, 1835.

HENRY WARDMAN, PRINTER, CHAPEL-LANE, BRADFORD.

4:12 Memorial of the physicians and surgeons of Bradford in favour of the Ten Hour Bill (West Yorkshire Archive Service, Bradford, 9DB27/C1/97/5).

seat of the West Riding Central Committee now moved there. In October of 1833 Samuel Glendinning of the HSTC was secretary to the Central Committee, but by 1842 Matthew Balme of Bradford occupied that position and Glendinning had moved to the Chair.[101]

---

101. For Glendinning as secretary see, *Address to the Friends of Justice and Humanity* issued by the Meeting of Delegates assembled at the Yew Tree Inn, Birstall, 28 October 1833. Text reprinted in *The Factory Act of 1833: Eight Pamphlets 1833–1834*, (New York: Arno Press, 1972). For 'Glendening' with Balme see them as signatories of a letter on behalf of the meeting of Delegates from the Short-Time Committees to Rt Hon. Lord Ashley, acknowledging his Lordship's letter of 2nd inst. intimating that 'Sir Robert Peel had signified his opposition to the Ten Hours' Bill', Bradford, 9 February 1842, reprinted in *The Fleet Papers*, II, pp., 19, 146–147. For Balme see article by John A. Hargreaves, *Oxford Dictionary of National Biography*, 2004.

As Sadler was now out of the House a new champion had to be found and that was Ashley. Ashley first became aware of the factory question on publication of the Sadler committee report, and wrote to Sadler offering his support; but nothing followed until after a Tory colleague, Sir Andrew Agnew, facilitated a meeting with Parson Bull of Bradford.[102] Bull had to exercise some persuasion. He was looking for someone who could take a lead in the country as well as in Parliament and had already called upon a number of Members with an introduction and advice from Sadler without success. His mission was undoubtedly undertaken with the STC Central Committee's knowledge, as well as that of Oastler and others, for he wrote immediately on the day after receiving Ashley's assent to all the secretaries of the West Riding committees. Ashley, then 31 years old and with an evangelical background not dissimilar from Oastler's, gave notice on 5 February of his intention to reintroduce Sadler's Bill. It took effect on 5 March.

Delegates from six STCs had been elected to assist Ashley and the movement as a whole started a second campaign of meetings to support the Bill on 19 February. Ashley's move scuppered the plans of Lord Morpeth to introduce an employer sponsored Bill for eleven hours, but Patten adopted an employer's demand for a further enquiry

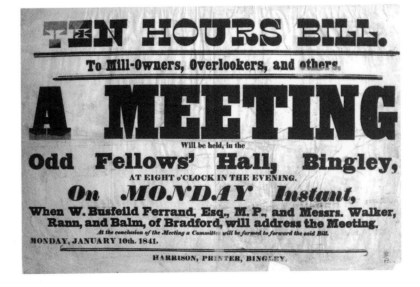

4:13 Poster advertising a meeting about the Ten Hours Bill in Bingley (West Yorkshire Archive Service, Bradford, DB27/C1/66/1).

---

102. G.F.A. Best, *Shaftesbury*, (London: Batsford, 1964), p. 82.

into factory employment. The proposal to set up a Factory Commission
was debated and carried in the House on 3 April. The first report of
the Factory Commissioners was available and published on 25 June
while Ashley's Bill was proceeding to its eventual rejection on 18 July.
Althorp had been Ashley's main critic in debate on 5 July and he
introduced his successful alternative on 9 August, receiving its Royal
Assent on 29 August.

The main focus of the Yorkshire meetings during this period was
to hinder the enquiries of the Factory Commissioners. A rough
reception was prepared for them when they visited Bradford and as
Oastler reported to the Huddersfield meeting of 18 June, chaired by
Pitkethly, STC men kept a good look out for them, followed them on
horseback, and engaged them in conversation over breakfast at an inn
in Doncaster, from where they scuttled back to London. The
conversation revealed that their expressed intention to visit Keighley
and Huddersfield had been frustrated by fear of their reception. The
tone of the resolutions adopted at the Huddersfield meeting well
conveys the hostility they could have expected. The first, noting that
'the factory system can no longer be endured' and that 'the evils' it
inflicted were 'unspeakably grievous to the working classes and their
children' added that 'the enemies of the poor have added treason and
insult to injury by abusing the prerogatives of the Crown …
appointing a set of worthless Commissioners to perpetuate infant
murder'. The second resolution was 'at a loss for words to express …
disgust and indignation, having been threatened with a visit from an
inquisitorial itinerant tribunal to enquire whether our children shall
be worked more than ten hours a day'. The meeting was unanimously
determined 'once and for all … that they should not'.

Events now moved on apace. In November, Oastler's friend John
Wood at Bradford unilaterally instituted a ten-hour day in his own
mills and Captain Fenton died of a fall from the upper storey of his
Huddersfield home on 27 November. The latter precipitated a by-
election of 8 January 1834, which put the Whig candidate, John
Blackburne, a barrister of the Middle Temple, into the House. The
election campaign created a split amongst the Ten Hours supporters.
Was Wood to stand again, or should there be an alternative? Just as
the unity between liberals of a Whig party stamp, largely middle class,
and Radical liberals of a no-party variety, largely working class, had

fractured as the Reform crisis came to a head, now unity between mainly middle-class Tory proponents of Ten Hours, and its more working class radical supporters, broke down.[103] The problem was that Wood, the Radical candidate of 1832, hesitated when invited to stand by William Stocks. He had since turned Roman Catholic and despite the passage of emancipation there were obvious problems in winning all Protestant votes. He suggested that Sadler, without a seat, but a fellow Ten Hours man, should be run as the popular anti-Whig candidate. But this proposal split the anti-Whig forces. Tories warmly welcomed the idea and issued placards on Sadler's behalf immediately, but others had their doubts. As Pitkethly put it,

> the Radicals are resting on their oars until Fenton is buried: Captain Wood is the favourite with people though 'some object to his turning Catholic' and General Johnson most likely for us at present.[104]

Wood's late announcement only a week before the poll that he would stand after all did not completely remove the confusion; and at the election, the opposition of 255 split into 147 for Sadler, 108 for Wood, while Blackburne triumphed on 234. The position of the HSTC men in this business is not entirely clear. Lawrence Pitkethly, who appears to have been the only member with a vote, cast for Wood.[105] Hobson, Pitkethly's close collaborator, would have been a Wood supporter, like Christopher Tinker, who was a principal subscriber to the expenses of his election committee.[106] James Brook, Glendinning

---

103. For differences among the Huddersfield supporters of reform see the report of the meeting of 12 May 1832 in *LM*, 15 May 1832. This was followed by a less respectable gathering on 2 June which passed a resolution condemning 'the conduct of 'those men who had formerly advocated vote by Ballot, shorter Parliaments and Universal Suffrage, who now wished to make Huddersfield a closed borough in the hands of Mr Ramsden', *LM*, 30 June 1832. The turncoat particularly in these Radical sights was William Moore, (1795–1882), bookseller, bookbinder and stationer, who was also shortly to become the postmaster.
104. Lawrence Pitkethly to Robert Owen, 3 December 1833, Co-operative Union Library, Press Mark 607.
105. *VWR*, 11 January 1834.
106. *VWR*, 18 January 1834.

and Leech, to take the more prominent and evidently eventually the
more prosperous members of the HSTC, did not have a vote at this
stage. There is some support for the idea that Brook had Tory
sympathies at this stage and would have been inclined to support
Sadler,[107] like William Stocks, who did have the vote and perhaps wrote
to Wood inviting his candidacy more from his position as Chief
Constable, rather than as a radical.[108] Voters identifiable as 'co-
operators', such as Thomas Dickinson and Christopher Wood
plumped for Wood, and it may be true of HSTC member John
Hirst.[109] The frictions of this period were associated with George
Beaumont's fall from Radical favour and disappearance from the
factory movement.

Lack of space precludes either discussion of the distraction from
the Ten Hours movement caused by Robert Owen's promotion of eight
hours from 25 November 1833 or the enthusiasm for Regeneration,
which also touched Huddersfield, until the collapse of the movement
on 7 June 1834.[110] Nor can the fuse which was constructed by the
passage of the Poor Law Amendment Act into law on 4 August 1834
and the explosion of opposition consequent on its lighting by the Poor
Law Commissioners' decision to move into the north in January 1837
be fully explored. As a historian of the anti-Poor Law movement noted,
in only one Poor Law Union can it be said with any certainty that there
was extensive co-operation between Radicals and Tories over the
boycott of Guardian elections in 1837 and that was the work of the
HSTC.[111] Suffice to say, several Huddersfield HSTC members were

---

107. See Brook's support at the Huddersfield public meeting of 21 November 1832
     for the defeated Tory resolution, *MC*, 24 November 1832.
108. Stocks voted for Sadler, like his father. The description of Stocks as a radical is
     usually linked to a mention of his position as Chief Constable. He did say in
     his speech at Fixby on 22 August 1832, however, that he had differed with
     Sadler 'on some political topics' and he was then Chairman of the Huddersfield
     Political Union. *Leeds Intelligencer*, 30 August 1832, in Volume 6 of Oastler's
     tracts on White Slavery, Goldsmiths' Library, University of London.
109. It is difficult to identify Hirst in the sources with any confidence, but it is
     possible that he had established himself as the independent provision store
     keeper of Sheepridge who voted for Wood, *VWR*, 11 January 1834.
110. A regeneration 'missionary' visited the town and a committee was formed.
     Lawrence Pitkethly to Robert Owen, 26 February 1834, Co-operative Union
     Library, press mark 677.
111. Nicholas C. Edsall, *The anti-Poor Law movement, 1834–1844*, (Manchester:
     Manchester University Press, 1971), pp. 86-87.

heavily engaged in the struggle, as they were in the Chartist campaign, from the launch of the *Northern Star* on 18 November 1837 to 1842. Pitkethly was the most important actor in Chartism, during the National Convention of 1839 and in correspondence with Chartist prisoners and saving the life of John Frost, but Hobson, Hanson, Leech, William Armitage and others were all engaged.[112] Glendinning does not appear to have been involved and as noted above Brook seems to have been particularly concerned with the new Poor Law question. Space constraints also require that the polemics between Oastler and the Dissenters in Huddersfield during 1835 are set aside. This reflected the support of Anglican ministers at Ten Hours' movement meetings and the absence of dissenting clergy, about which Glendinning – himself a New Connexion lay preacher – commented sharply.[113] Similarly insufficient space precludes examination of Parliamentary developments, including manoeuvres over factory legislation after Althorp's Act – the Poulett Thomson Bill of 1836; the Fox Maule Bill of 1839; and Ashley and Hindley's move for a Select Committee to enquire into the operation of Althorp's Act up to the successful passage of Ten Hours Bill into law on 8 June 1847.

Hobson was resident in Leeds from August 1834 until he returned to his home town in 1846. Weekly meetings of the HSTC would not have been held regularly throughout this period, but that he kept in close contact with the affairs of the town is evident from columns in the *Northern Star*. He purchased Christopher Tinker's business in Market Walk in 1842 and was nominated from that address to the General Council of the National Charter Association in 1842.[114]. Attendance at Huddersfield by the Halifax members was no doubt intermittent and John Rawson moved from Halifax to Bradford in 1841. He became active there and served on the Central Committee,

---

112. The general starting point for the history of Chartism is now Malcolm Chase, *Chartism: A New History*, (Manchester: Manchester University Press, 2007), but for Pitkethly to James Duffy, 5 September 1840, a Chartist prisoner in Northallerton gaol, see Fred Singleton, *Industrial Revolution in Yorkshire*, (Clapham via Lancaster: Dalesman, 1970), pp. 182-184. For Pitkethly's central role in the Frost Committee see *NS*, 31 October 1840, 9 January 1841, 1 May 1841 and 15 May 1841.

113. Ward, *Factory Movement*, p. 294.

114. *NS*, 17 December 1842.

but his important career will have to be treated in another place. With the government's defeat on the no confidence motion of 4 June 1841 and the revival of the movement during the autumn, Hobson and Leech were despatched by the Yorkshire STCs with George A. Fleming, Crabtree and Titus Brooke, on a deputation to Sir Robert Peel. This reported back to a Leeds meeting, on 18 January 1842. Hobson, secretary of the Leeds STC at the time, was placed in the chair and the report was read by Fleming. Leech obviously represented the HSTC in the deputation, since Crabtree and Brooke were from Bradford. A published version was printed by Hobson and widely circulated. It also appeared in Oastler's *Fleet Papers*. Oastler remained in prison initially at the Fleet and subsequently at the Queen's prisons from 9 December 1840 until 12 February 1844. The treasurer of the Liberty Fund set up at Roberttown on 15 November 1843 to raise funds to pay off Oastler's debts and secure his release was Pitkethly. STC members were active organising collections and participating in the celebrations following his release. Pitkethly left Huddersfield for America on 10 January 1842 to scout out communities for emigration.[115] A report on the visit refers to his being with his friend Charles Earnshaw, who could be the HSTC member.[116] It also refers to being with Mr Howarth, who was a business associate from Manchester.[117] Pitkethly left Huddersfield for Marble Street, Manchester, at an unknown date, but probably in the late 1840s, where he died on 2 June 1858.[118]

The last record of HSTC members comes from reports of the funerals of Oastler and Hobson. Oastler died of a heart attack at Harrogate on 22 August 1861. John Leech was a pall bearer for Oastler representing the operatives of Yorkshire. His burden was shared by Abraham North, who also assisted, with another ten unnamed individuals, representing the operatives. Joshua Hobson represented the HSTC along with James Gledhill and George Whiteley and other unnamed persons.

115. *NS*, 29 April 1843.
116. *NS*, 6 May 1843. Charles Earnshaw is found in the 1851 census at Paddock Foot, but not in the census for 1841.
117. NS, 24 June 1843.
118. West Yorkshire Archive Service, Kirklees KC1040/1/7; *HC*, 5 June 1858.

The occupations of North and Gledhill are not quite what one might expect of representatives of the 'operatives'.[119] North was a 'Bill Poster' or a 'Bill Poster and Watchman'. The watchman implies some employment prior to 1848 by the Vestry or the Improvement Commission.[120] The former would have brought him into contact with town Radicals and the bill posting activity undoubtedly involved publicity for town meetings or other events to mobilise popular feeling. Indeed, he was a witness in 1865 in a case brought by Edward Clayton against James Brook, for posting a bill that failed to carry the name of the printer. The election was a contest for a seat on the Board of Guardians and the legislation under which the offence was committed had originally been designed to catch seditious and treasonable publications. The magistrates imposed a penalty of one farthing on Brook; that is, finding him guilty of the offence but clearly treating the prosecution as vexatious.[121]

James Gledhill was born at Low Moor but living during the 1830s – from at least 1833 and up to some time in 1842 – at Lowerhouses in Almondbury parish, working as a fancy weaver. He contributed to Hobson's victim fund in August and September 1833, and moved a resolution at a Lowerhouses and Longley Chartist meeting of 1839 to protest against the arrest of the Revd Joseph Rayner Stephens.[122] His move to Huddersfield brought a new occupation, however – that of police constable! His house in 1851 was in Albion Street, next door to that of an HSTC member, George Armitage. Whiteley, however, appears to fit more neatly into the notion of an 'operatives' representative. If correctly identified, George Whiteley was born in the Soyland township of Halifax parish and was in the Huddersfield district at Almondbury by 1832. No definite trace has been found for 1841, but he was employed as a cotton twister or spinner at Paddock Foot in 1851 and in spinning silk in Huddersfield in 1861.

---

119. The noun 'operative' can usually be taken to imply the addition of 'textile' as a silent adjective.
120. North attempted to obtain employment as a police constable but was not selected. *Bradford Observer and Halifax, Huddersfield and Keighley Reporter*, 1 May 1845.
121. *Huddersfield Chronicle and West Yorkshire Advertiser*, 27 May 1865.
122. *VWR*, 24 August and 7 September 1833; *NS*, 9 February 1839.

Abraham North appeared at Hobson's funeral on 11 May 1876 as
an HSTC representative with Gledhill and James Gartside.[123]
Necessarily absent were those old comrades who had died such as
Lawrence Pitkethly in 1858, followed by George Armitage on 11
March 1867;[124] James Brook on 14 April 1870;[125] and John Leech on
4 January 1871.[126] A number of unnamed HSTC representatives were
present. The newspaper reporter's silence suggests that this did not
include the movement's surviving prominent veterans – William
Armitage, who survived to December 1893; Samuel Glendinning, to
9 July 1883, and John Hanson 26 December 1877. The absence of
Hanson could easily be explained by age and domicile, since he was
probably living with his daughter, a Mrs Tinker, out of town at Shepley
Green, six and a half miles to the south-south-east of town, though
now connected by railway.[127] Samuel Glendinning might have been
inhibited from attendance by political differences. He was a committed
Liberal voter and unlike Brook may have sided with the *Huddersfield
Examiner* and the Ramsden estate in the struggle with Hobson and
the *Huddersfield Chronicle* over the tenant-right issue.[128] In any case,
Hobson's funeral appears to mark the last reference to the meeting of
a substantial number of HSTC members.

123. *HWN*, 13 and 20 May 1876. Unfortunately, unlike North and Gledhill, we
     have been unable to identify Gartside in other sources.
124. Interred on 15 March 1867, Edgerton Burial Register.
125. *Huddersfield Observer*, 23 April 1870.
126. *HO*, 7 January 1871.
127. Obituary notice in *HWN*, 5 January 1878.
128. It seems clear from poll book and directory data – though some inference is
     required – that Glendinning voted for William Willans in 1852, Richard
     Cobden in 1857, stayed neutral in 1865, and voted for Leatham in 1868.

Press and People: Oastler's Yorkshire Slavery campaign in 1830–32

EDWARD ROYLE

RICHARD OASTLER IS best known for his leadership of the Ten Hours movement in the West Riding in the early 1830s. His involvement began with his famous letter headed 'Slavery in Yorkshire', published in the *Leeds Mercury* on 16 October 1830, and the press remained central to his efforts over the next two years, not only printing his letters but, even more importantly, reporting the meetings by which large numbers of working people across the county were drawn into the agitation to end child labour in textile mills. The purpose of this chapter is to explore Oastler's relationship with the Leeds newspapers and to set it against the background of the nature and development of the provincial press as well as contemporary events in national and local politics, in particular the agitation for parliamentary reform.

As was indicated by the headline under which Oastler's letter appeared, the immediate context was provided by the campaign to end black chattel slavery in the British Empire, following upon the successful abolition of the Slave Trade in 1807. Yorkshire was William Wilberforce's own county, and as such it was at the forefront of the anti-slavery campaign. The factory movement sought to capitalise on this by association, copying both the methods and language of anti-slavery. However, there were significant differences, the implications of which will be explored in this chapter.

Just as when, with the abolition of slavery campaign, the importance of the role of the slaves themselves is acknowledged, so with factory reform it is recognised that success was not solely something handed down by campaigners like Peel, Owen, Wood, Oastler, Fielden and Ashley from the middle and political classes.[1] Victory was achieved by the people themselves in a continuing struggle throughout the 1830s and 1840s. The difference was that the victims of the factory system lived not in the distant West Indies but in the crowded streets of Bradford, Leeds, Halifax, Huddersfield and the other textile towns of the West Riding, where they were ready to participate in the theatre of popular politics, to sign petitions and to give evidence to parliamentary enquiries. This made the factory movement more threatening and immediate than anti-slavery, and its consequences more divisive. Whereas the anti-slavery movement enjoyed much cross-party support, the Ten Hours movement stirred party rivalries. With anti-slavery, a common evangelical humanitarianism among Methodists, Nonconformists and members of the Established Church in Yorkshire – personified by Wilberforce – created a moral consensus shared by most Tories and Whigs alike in a broadly-based agitation for abolition.[2] This was not the case with the campaign for factory reform. Here evangelical views diverged between a form of Christian moral economy, shared with some traditional Tories, which stressed welfare paternalism to protect the weak, and the free-market ideas of the new 'classical' political economy, which found favour with Whig politicians and leaders of the industrial economy.[3] Many Wesleyan Methodist mill-owner employers, for example, who were among the strongest supporters of anti-slavery, found their belief in a free market for labour, which undermined the economic case for slavery, reinforced their evangelical humanitarianism; but these same people could also argue

1. Michael Craton, 'Slave Culture, Resistance and the Achievement of Emancipation in the British West Indies, 1783–1838' in *Slavery and British Society, 1776–1846*, ed. by James Walvin , (London: Macmillan, 1982), pp. 100–22.
2. By the 1826 election support for abolition was politically almost universal: James Walvin, 'The Public Campaign in England against Slavery, 1787-1834', in *The Americas*, ed. by David Eltis and James Walvin, (Madison: University of Wisconsin Press, 1981), pp. 63–79 (pp. 70–1).
3. Boyd Hilton, *The Age of Atonement: The Influence of Evangelicalism on Social and Economic Thought 1795–1865* (Oxford: Clarendon Press, 1988), pp. 91–8, 212–13.

that a free market for labour meant there should be no legislative interference with their own rights as employers. At most, some conceded that an exception might possibly be made for children, because they were not legally responsible adults, which is why the factory reformers emphasised the need to limit the hours worked by children even though their final aim was Ten Hours for all. These differences over political economy created turbulent waters in Leeds politics in the early 1830s as the agitation for parliamentary reform, broadly supported by the Whigs and opposed by the Tories, gained momentum. In these circumstances Oastler sought to use the local newspapers to further his own cause but soon became embroiled in bitter local strife as the newspapers in turn exploited that cause for their own party ends.

The cruelties of slavery and of the slave trade were widely recognised by the early nineteenth century, thanks to the long and ultimately successful campaign against the Slave Trade. Richard Oastler was but one of many people from an evangelical and pietistic background who had grown up with the language of anti-slavery and the moral commitment to end the abuse of man by fellow man. But although Oastler himself seems, perhaps strangely, to have discovered the cause of the factory children as late as 1830, other reformers had already committed themselves to ending child labour and were drawing parallels between what was happening in the textile mills of Britain and on plantations in the West Indies.

A work of propaganda published in 1828 by the Radical, Richard Carlile, deliberately drew on existing outrage against the slave trade and the enslavement of Africans to make the case for ending child labour in the textile factories of Britain. This was John Brown's *A Memoir of Robert Blincoe, an Orphan Boy; sent from the workhouse of St Pancras, London, at seven years of age, to endure the Horrors of a Cotton-Mill, through his infancy and youth, with a minute detail of his sufferings*.[4]

---

4. The *Memoir of Robert Blincoe* was first published by Richard Carlile in the *Lion* (25 January to 22 February 1828) and issued as a pamphlet in a second edition by John Doherty (Manchester, 1832). The quotation is taken from the reprint of the 1832 edition (Firle, Sussex: Caliban, 1997), pp. 41–2.

As the narrator of Blincoe's story exclaimed:

> May this exposition of crimes and sufferings inflicted upon the
> friendless, the orphan, the widow's son, induce honest and upright
> men, senators and legislators, effectually to curb the barbarous
> propensities of hard-hearted masters and rescue their nation from a
> worse stain, than even the African Slave Trade, horrible as was that
> odious traffic, ever inflicted.

The language of this propagandist work was both graphic and
effective, and could, with very little alteration, have been used to
describe a slave market in the colonies:

> The greater part of the children were much exhausted, and not a few
> of them seriously indisposed, before they arrived at Nottingham.
> When the waggons drew up near the dwelling and warehouse of their
> future master, a crowd gathered to see the livestock that was just
> imported from the metropolis, who were pitied, admired, and
> compared to lambs, led by butchers to slaughter. [...] After being well
> refreshed, the whole of the boys and girls were drawn up in rows, to
> be reviewed by their masters, their friends and neighbours. [...] They
> looked over the children and finding them all right, according to the
> invoice, exhorted them to behave with proper humility and decorum.[5]

This powerful work was re-issued in 1832, and in the same year,
on 23 August, Richard Oastler and other leaders of the ten-hour
movement attended a procession in Manchester headed by a banner
bearing the representation of a deformed man and the words 'White
Slavery' and 'Am I not a man and a brother', in conscious imitation of
the anti-black slavery campaign.[6]

---

5. *Memoir of Robert Blincoe*, pp. 20–1.
6. Alfred Kydd, *The History of the Factory Movement from the year 1802 to the
   enactment of the Ten Hours Bill in 1847*, 2 vols (London, 1857; reprinted NY:
   Burt Franklin, n.d.), I, pp. 254–55; and R. G. Kirby and A. E. Musson, *The
   Voice of the People. John Doherty, 1798–1854. Trade unionist, radical and factory
   reformer* (Manchester: Manchester University Press, 1975), p. 376.

5:1 'Am I not a Man and a Brother' depicted on the Skelmanthorpe banner (Tolson Memorial Museum, Huddersfield).

The parallel and place were highly relevant. Lancashire owed much to slavery and the exploitation of labour. Liverpool's prosperity in the eighteenth century rested mainly on slave-grown sugar, but from the later eighteenth century cotton was increasingly imported into Britain from the United States and so a new slave-grown product added further to its wealth.[7] The trade in cotton depended upon a form of slavery at both ends: black slavery in the cotton fields of the American South; child slavery in the cotton mills of Lancashire. This symmetry was exploited in the campaign for parliamentary legislation to curb the excesses of exploitation in Britain, and in 1833, the year that the Act for the Abolition of Slavery in the British Empire was carried, the first effective Factory Act was also placed on the statute book – though, like the Slavery Abolition Act, it was regarded as an unsatisfactory compromise by those who had agitated for it.

---

7.   The cotton crop in the United States rose from 2 million lbs in 1791 to 182 million lbs in 1821, and Liverpool replaced London as the chief port. See S. D. Chapman, *The Cotton Industry in the Industrial Revolution* (London: Macmillan, 1972), pp. 43–52.

5:2 Robert Owen's New Lanark Mills, Scotland (Photograph: E.A.H. Haigh).

There had been earlier attempts at factory legislation. In 1802 the Health and Morals of Apprentices Act was introduced by the largest cotton spinner in Lancashire, Robert Peel of Bury, to control the conditions under which pauper children like Blincoe worked. The fact that Blincoe's apprenticeship was from 1799 to 1813 shows the Act's limitations. Peel tried again in 1819 with a more general act to protect young children, and there were further Acts introduced by the Radical MP, John Cam Hobhouse, in 1825 and 1831, but such legislation was resisted by many employers and emasculated by the House of Commons. It protected only children and young people, there was no mechanism for enforcement, and it applied only to cotton factories.[8]

These attempts to secure legislation illustrate the naïve optimism of some of the reformers. Peel may well have been experienced enough

8. For a summary of the background and early movement for reform, see J. T. Ward, *The Factory Movement* (London: Macmillan, 1962), pp. 13–31; and Ursula R. Q. Henriques, *Before the Welfare State. Social administration in early industrial Britain* (London: Longman, 1979), pp. 68–72 and *The Early Factory Acts and their Enforcement* (London: Historical Association, 1971), pp. 1–4.

to expect the rebuffs he received, but this was not the case with Robert Owen, who from 1799 was the effective master of New Lanark, the largest cotton spinning complex in Scotland. Reform of factory labour conditions seemed to Owen a straightforward, necessary and humane reform. At New Lanark he felt he had demonstrated that shorter hours and improved living conditions were both humane and profitable. He had made New Lanark a showpiece of the industrial revolution and expected that 'those who have influence in the affairs of men', once convinced of the truth of his message, would use their political authority to create those better social circumstances that would in turn create better and happier people.[9] In 1815 he published his *Observations on the Effects of the Manufacturing System*, in which he attacked the unfettered drive for wealth which caused the oppression of workers who were reduced to a bare subsistence.[10] Owen now

5:3 'Woman spinning' in George Walker's *Costume of Yorkshire* (Yorkshire Archaeological Society).

---

9. The phrase quoted is from the opening of Owen's *First Essay on the Formation of Character* (1813). The original dedication of this *Essay* was to William Wilberforce. See Robert Owen, *The Life of Robert Owen*, vols I and IA (London: Effingham Wilson, 1857–58; reprinted London: Cass, 1967), I, Appendix B, pp. 257–8 and 265.

10. *Life of Robert Owen*, IA, Appendix H.

5:4 View of Huddersfield from Woodhouse by Henry Warren, engraved by S. Bradshaw, n.d. (Private collection).

brought to the attention of government the need to extend to all children the protection given to orphans by Peel's Act of 1802, since parents in their struggle to survive had become the willing exploiters of their own offspring. The cause was taken up once more by Peel, who brought a Bill before Parliament, and Owen lobbied hard, writing open letters addressed both to the Prime Minister and to British master manufacturers, but the measure eventually carried in 1819 was only a shadow of what Owen had originally hoped for.[11] This inability to convince people of what was to him blindingly obvious pushed Owen into more extreme language. Richard Oastler was to demonstrate a similar impatience when economic and political expediency cut across his own moral certainty in the 1830s.

By the beginning of the nineteenth century the technology for the mechanised spinning of cotton was being applied to the worsted industry in the West Riding, centred on Halifax and, increasingly,

11. *Life of Robert Owen*, IA, Appendices M and N.
12. John James, *The History of the Worsted Manufacture in England* (1857, reprinted London: Cass, 1968), pp. 604–7; E. Lipson, *The History of the Woollen and Worsted Industries* (London: Black, 1921), pp. 183–5.

Bradford. The new steam-driven spinning frames, located in factories which relied heavily on the labour of women and children, produced a transformation in the industry and the communities which served it. In 1810 Bradford borough had five small spinning mills; twenty years later there were thirty-one.[12] This was the setting for Richard Oastler's dramatic entry into the agitation for factory reform.

The local newspaper press, to which Oastler turned in 1830, had its origins in the previous century. The first newspapers to be published in the provinces were the *Bristol Post Boy* and the *Norwich Post*, both begun around 1701 or 1702. By 1712 there were about a dozen. The number had doubled by 1723, including the *Leeds Mercury* of 1718. By 1760 there was at least one weekly newspaper established in every provincial town of significance: about forty in all.[13] These early newspapers were, in the main, advertising sheets. Each issue was in practice restricted in size by the Newspaper Stamp Duty to one sheet of paper (one sheet folded once would give a four page folio newspaper) and was also limited by the slow technology of production. Newspapers therefore came out only weekly and were printed on hand presses throughout the week, so that only the last page to go to press was able to carry anything that might be called 'new' news. Initially such papers avoided partisanship, since their main aim was to attract advertisers from all quarters. This began to change towards the end of the century, especially in the 1790s when news of revolutionary events in France increased the public appetite for news and also polarised opinion in Britain between loyalist conservatives and radical reformers.[14]

One of the first provincial newspaper editors to use a strongly political editorial – that is, overtly partisan comment as opposed to reporting the news – was Joseph Gales of the *Sheffield Register*. Gales wrote editorials in which he attacked the government of William Pitt for the war with France as he sought to 'rescue my Countrymen from the darkness of Ignorance and to awaken Them to a just sense of their

---

13. The extensive literature on the early press has been summarised by Jeremy Black, *The English Press 1621–1861* (Stroud: Sutton, 2001).
14. Donald Read, *Press and People 1790–1850: opinion in three English cities* (London: Arnold, 1961), pp. 61–5, 69. Read's three cities were Leeds, Manchester and Sheffield.

Privileges as Human beings'. In June 1794, he was indicted for conspiracy and fled to the United States.[15] But the pressures for the development of an independent, campaigning provincial press were too strong to be snuffed out, despite a series of increases in taxation which raised the price of the newspaper stamp from 1½d. a sheet in 1776 to 4d. in 1815. By the latter date, the effect of this level of duty, combined with further duty on advertisements and on paper itself, was that a four-page newspaper cost at least 7d. or the equivalent of over £2.00 to-day.[16]

The nineteenth century can be called the golden age of the press, when it was the unchallenged and unrivalled medium for news, but there were marked differences between the London and provincial newspapers. The latter were more numerous and less subject to government influence, but they had much smaller circulations. In an age when provincial economies were local, a provincial paper could not attract enough national advertising to rival the London press. Books and patent medicines were among the few products with a national market and hence were long to be the staple of national advertisements in the provincial press. For most of the advertisements, on which their finances depended, the newspapers were dependent on local advertisers and the great provincial papers of the early nineteenth century were consequently based in the local or at best regional economies of county towns such as York or Norwich, and rapidly-growing commercial and industrial centres such as Bristol, Liverpool, Sheffield, Leeds, Birmingham, Newcastle and Manchester.

The leading paper in Leeds was the *Leeds Intelligencer*, started in 1754 and quickly replacing the *Mercury* which closed the following year but was revived in 1767. Both the *Intelligencer* and *Mercury* in the 1790s were loyalist, until in 1801 Edward Baines, a young printer, took the *Mercury* over with financial backing from a group of wealthy manufacturers and merchants, nearly all of whom were religious Dissenters. Baines succeeded in building up the circulation of the paper to make it first, the leading newspaper of the Whig-Liberal-Dissenting

---

15. Read, *Press and People*, pp. 69–70.
16. *Ibid*, pp. 66–7. The calculation of the modern cost is based on the relative prices of wheat bread in 1815 and 2010. In terms of a labourer's wage the comparative price would have been at least three times as much.

manufacturers of the West Riding, and then, after 1817, the leading provincial newspaper in England. This was achieved by identifying the paper with those new economic forces which were transforming provincial England and giving voice to the needs of those who in commerce and industry were still unrepresented in parliament and ignored in the making of government policy.[17]

The *Mercury's* anti-government stance proved highly popular during the depression which followed the ending of the French Wars in 1815, especially when, in 1817, Baines investigated and exposed the role of 'Oliver the Spy' as *agent provocateur* in the unrest and armed risings of that year. This was an early example of what was to become an important feature of the nineteenth-century press: not simply reporting the news or reacting to it, but actually making it. In 1821 a similar paper was begun in Manchester by John Taylor and a group of liberal Unitarian manufacturers: the *Manchester Guardian*. Papers such as these in the major provincial centres, representing the views of the rising class of manufacturers who were Liberal in politics and Dissenting in religion, were to play an important part in the agitation which reached a crescendo in 1830–32 to secure a reform of the parliamentary franchise and open up the political system to the new social forces.[18]

Newspapers like the *Leeds Mercury* and *Manchester Guardian*, however, did not remain unchallenged, for in most major provincial towns by 1830 there were at least two papers and sometimes more. Unlike the London press, which continued to be influenced by the favours or otherwise of politicians and national party opinion, the provincial papers were the organs of local factions, usually Tory and Anglican on the one hand and Liberal and Dissenting on the other. In Leeds, opposed to the *Leeds Mercury* was its old rival, the *Leeds Intelligencer*. There was also the *Leeds Patriot*, started as a Tory paper in 1824 but taken over in 1828 by John Foster as a Radical paper appealing to the working classes. It failed in 1833, the same year that a new middle-class Radical paper, the *Leeds Times*, appeared whose most famous editor from 1839 to 1842 was Samuel Smiles.[19]

---

17. Read, *Press and People*, pp. 60–1, 74–9.
18. Read, *Press and People*, pp. 113, 79–84.
19. Read, *Press and People*, pp. 93–5, 103–04.

As one might expect, in the early 1830s Edward Baines's *Leeds Mercury* was a strong supporter of Lord Grey's Whig government, formed in 1830 to introduce parliamentary reform. This measure, carried in 1832, gave Leeds separate representation in the House of Commons with two seats, one of which was to be to be occupied by Edward Baines himself between 1834 and 1841. Not surprisingly, the Tory *Leeds Intelligencer*, under its editor, Robert Perring, took the opposite line. Perring, who became editor in 1829, was, like Baines, both editor and co-proprietor of his paper and was personally identified with it. The issue, though, was not a straight fight between pro- and anti-reform papers for, if the *Mercury* championed the cause of political reform, advocated even more radically in Foster's *Leeds Patriot*, Perring's *Intelligencer* supported the equally strong demand for factory reform, also advocated by the *Patriot*. So when Oastler turned to the press to highlight the need for factory reform he became rapidly caught up in the wider struggle between the political factions in Leeds and their respective newspapers. Both Whig/Liberal and Tory papers laid claim to be the true friends of the working-classes through their support for parliamentary or factory reform respectively. And far from merely reporting the two causes, both Baines and Perring became deeply involved in the campaigns themselves. A cynic – or a supporter of the *Patriot* – might observe that neither the middle-class Tories and Anglicans who, broadly speaking, represented the older cloth-merchant elite of Leeds, nor the middle-class Liberals and Dissenters who, broadly speaking, represented the newer manufacturing elite, had much genuine concern for the working classes. The latter were simply bystanders in a local struggle for power, though that might be to judge too harshly the humanitarian paternalism of the Tories and the genuine belief of the Liberals in the importance of extending political rights.

In 1822, the rotten borough of Grampound had been deprived of its two parliamentary seats. These would probably have been transferred to Leeds if there had been any agreed basis for the urban franchise, but in the absence of the latter they were added instead to the representation for Yorkshire, giving the largest county in England four MPs instead of the usual two. The two new seats were understood, however, to be for the manufacturing and urban interest in the county. In 1826, the Holbeck flax manufacturer and close friend of Baines, John Marshall, took one of these new Yorkshire seats in partnership with Lord Milton, the Earl of Fitzwilliam's heir, in an uncontested election. Marshall decided not to stand in the 1830 election and Baines was concerned to ensure that a second Whig-Liberal candidate would contest a seat alongside the Whig, Lord Morpeth, heir to the Earl of Carlisle of Castle Howard. An editorial in the *Mercury* of 17 July 1830 recommended to the freeholders of Yorkshire the name of Henry Brougham, MP for Knaresborough, a man who was a prominent Radical-Whig who had achieved fame as legal advisor to Queen Caroline against George IV in 1820 and who was also well-known as a champion of the anti-slavery cause. But he held no land in the county of Yorkshire (his estates were in Westmorland) and so he was clearly being put forward as an outsider in the interest of the Leeds-dominated 'Bainesocracy'.[20] The *Intelligencer* was quick to respond, having the advantage of being published on a Thursday, five days after the *Mercury*: 'In last Saturday's number of that journal [the *Mercury*] we find a long and laboured article, the object of which is to persuade the Freeholders to call upon Mr Brougham to represent Yorkshire.' Perring went on, with heavy sarcasm, typical of editorial style at that time:

> Our contemporary's modest diffidence of his own powers is well-known; we wonder, indeed, how he contrived to screw himself up to the pitch which inspired the article alluded to. We can only account for it on this principle. He put Mr Marshall in for the County [...] he probably thought he had an undoubted right to name Mr Marshall's successor [...]

And at the conclusion to the editorial, Perring expressed the hope that 'the siren voice of the charmer who charms neither wisely nor well in the *Mercury* [...] will find the really independent freeholders made of stuff which is not to be moulded to the arrogant dictum of a newspaper writer.[21]

---

20. N. Gash, 'Brougham and the Yorkshire Election of 1830', in *Pillars of Government and Other Essays on State and Society, c.1770–c.1880* (London: Arnold, 1986), pp. 77–92.
21. *Leeds Intelligencer* [*LI*], 22 July 1830.

Two days later, the *Mercury* was able to report in jubilant tones that Brougham had indeed been nominated alongside Morpeth as Whig candidate for Yorkshire.[22] Five days after that, the *Intelligencer* was left to deplore 'That the Whig Aristocracy of the great County of York have been compelled to succumb to the Bainesocracy of Leeds', which it defined as 'Mr Baines of the *Leeds Mercury*, aided by a small train of Unitarian and Presbyterian Dissenters, and the stray sheep of the Radical interest'.[23] Since the fifth candidate, whose emergence ultimately forced a poll, received virtually no support, Brougham was subsequently one of the four Members elected. It is probable that his known opposition to slavery was one reason for his success in a Yorkshire election in which the slavery issue was made as prominent as parliamentary reform.

The *Mercury*, though, was not to have everything its own way, largely because of Oastler's famous letter and the events which followed. Oastler's father was a Leeds linen merchant and, like many

5:5 The Moravian settlement at Fulneck with the school attended by Richard Oastler, where he imbibed a strong sense of moral justice (Photograph: E.A.H. Haigh).

22. *Leeds Mercury* [*LM*], 24 July 1830.
23. *LI*, 29 July 1830.

of them, a Tory. He was also a prominent Wesleyan Methodist and indeed was John Wesley's host on his last visit to Leeds in 1790. But in 1797 he was a leader of the Methodist New Connexion secession, which took place in Leeds, and thereafter he supported the New Connexion not only in the Leeds area but elsewhere in the county.[24] Young Richard was educated among the Moravians at Fulneck and imbibed from his upbringing a mixture of Toryism, pietism and a strong sense of moral justice. Like many Methodists he was also a vigorous supporter of civic philanthropy and the anti-slavery cause. His friendships in Leeds included Michael Thomas Sadler (1780-1835), also a linen merchant and a Tory Anglican with pietistic Methodist sympathies who devoted much of his time to philanthropy and was a friend and keen supporter of William Wilberforce whose election campaign he managed at the 1807 Yorkshire county election. In 1800 Robert Oastler gave up the linen trade to become land steward on the Fixby estate belonging to the absentee Thomas Thornhill, who resided in Norfolk. On Robert Oastler's death in 1820 Richard succeeded to the post and from 1821 lived on the estate, acquiring the outlook of a paternalistic Tory squire, expressed not least in his adherence to the Church of England and his strongly Protestant antipathy to Roman Catholicism.[25]

In the last week of September 1830 Oastler paid a visit to Horton Hall, residence of his friend John Wood, an Evangelical and prominent Bradford worsted spinner who, like Peel and Owen in the cotton industry, was deeply concerned about working conditions in the mills. He had, however, failed to persuade most of his fellow employers that to require children to work in excess of ten hours a day was more than was either reasonable or humane. He put the problem to Oastler: 'You are [...] very enthusiastic against slavery in the West Indies; and, I

24. See University of York, Borthwick Institute, Faculty Book III, p. 212, registering for Dissenting worship a chapel in Grape Lane and Coffee Yard, St Michael le Belfrey parish, York, 17 November 1798, the property of (among others) Robert Oastler.

25. See the entries in *ODNB* on Sadler and Oastler (by Stewart A. Weaver); also Cecil Driver, *Tory Radical: the life of Richard Oastler* (NY: Oxford University Press, 1946, reprinted NY: Octagon Books, 1970), pp. 13–35.

assure you, there are cruelties daily practised in our mills on little children, which, if you knew, I am sure you would strive to prevent'.[26] What followed was like a conversion experience and the next day Oastler set out to enlighten others as he had been enlightened. Once people knew, they too would want to reform working conditions. Methodists and others who were prominent manufacturers and sincere opponents of slavery overseas could not fail to reform at home once they had realised there was a form of slavery also going on in front of their unseeing eyes. And so Oastler turned to the press.

Next day, on 29 September 1830, Oastler composed a letter to the *Leeds Mercury* which he handed to Edward Baines in person. But it was not published for another two weeks, appearing in the *Mercury* on 16 October under the heading, 'Slavery in Yorkshire'. In this famous letter, Oastler wrote that

> Thousands of little children, both male and female, *but principally female*, from SEVEN to fourteen years of age, are daily *compelled* to labour from six o'clock in the morning to seven in the evening, with only – Britons blush while you read it! – *with only thirty minutes allowed for eating and recreation!* – Poor infants! Ye are indeed sacrificed at the shrine of avarice, *without even the solace of the negro slave: –* ye are no more than he is, *free agents*.

Baines must have been in something of a quandary when he received this letter and seems to have agonised for several days over whether to publish it. On the one hand, this was a communication from the son of an old associate of his. He had visited Robert Owen's model factory village at New Lanark with Robert Oastler in 1819.[27] On the other hand, the tone of the letter, accusing the manufacturers of avarice and inhumanity, was not likely to be acceptable to readers of the *Mercury*. If Baines did not publish the letter, he would be accused of censoring free discussion; if he did publish it, he would

---

26. As quoted by Kydd, I, p. 96.
27. Driver, p. 24, states that it was Edward Baines junior who went with Oastler to New Lanark in 1819, but Owen recalled that it was Baines senior – *Life of Robert Owen*, vol. 1, p. 203; see also their *Report*, published in August 1819, reprinted in vol. 1A, Appendix R.

offend the very constituency on whom his circulation and the prosperity of the paper depended. So he hesitated and then, when he did finally publish, he added an editorial in which he deplored the tone of the letter but encouraged a debate on the necessity for legislation to curb the free market when it caused employers and parents to exploit children. In this way he managed to support reform of a kind without imputing any moral blame to the employers. Predictably, a correspondence followed, including further and ever longer letters from Oastler. Finally, when Oastler sent a letter to the *Mercury* 'of unmerciful length' on the debate in Parliament on Hobhouse's Factory Bill in early 1831, Edward Baines junior, in his father's absence in London, decided to print only extracts. These appeared on 19 March 1831, with this justification:

> He applies to the worsted spinners every epithet in the language connected with the bottomless pit – 'fiendish,' 'diabolical,' 'infernal,' 'hellish,' &c, besides the milder and more soothing appellatives of 'tyrants,' 'monsters,' 'freebooters,' &c, &c. Really this brimstone rhetoric is not to be endured.

On the same day that this rebuke appeared, Oastler penned a letter to the editor of the *Leeds Intelligencer*:

> Knowing, as I do, that your constitutional principles assure your readers all your correspondents shall have 'fair play,' and having to day been treated rather cavalierly by the Junior Editor of the *Leeds Mercury*, I have to request you will do me the justice to insert in your highly respectable paper, the whole of my 'unmerciful' letter, on a most 'unmerciful' subject, which has been most 'unmercifully' treated by my 'unmerciful' friend above alluded to.

Delighted at this, Perring gladly inserted the whole letter.[28] Thereafter, the cause of factory reform was his, just as the Baineses were the champions of parliamentary reform.

---

28. *LI*, 24 March 1831.

This propaganda gift came just in time for the Tories. On 1 March 1831, Lord John Russell had introduced the Whig Reform Bill into the House of Commons and in the same issue of the *Intelligencer* that printed Oastler's letter came reports that the Bill was having difficulties on its second reading as former supporters defected to the opposition. The Bill passed narrowly, but Grey then asked the King to dissolve Parliament and in the subsequent election secured a large majority which in September 1831 carried a new Bill through the Commons, only for the House of Lords to reject it.

The two movements for factory and parliamentary reform now entered a new and tense stage. In the Commons, Michael Sadler, now MP for the rotten borough of Aldborough in the North Riding, took over the parliamentary leadership from Hobhouse and secured a Select Committee to enquire into the need for effective factory legislation. 'Short Time Committees' of working men were organised to give evidence to the Committee, urging the need for reform.[29] Meanwhile, aware that his seat would be abolished when the Reform Bill was carried, Sadler began to nurse the prospective new constituency of Leeds in the Tory interest. Thus factory reform became an election issue and a means by which the Tories could respond to their impending defeat over parliamentary reform. The two newspapers returned to attack each other with renewed venom. The *Mercury* sought to discredit Sadler and his campaign; the *Intelligencer* did all it could to undermine Baines and his proposed candidates for Leeds, John Marshall junior and Thomas Babbington Macaulay, the writer and son of one of the foremost anti-slavery campaigners.[30]

Each side was jockeying for electoral advantage. The *Intelligencer* declared that, if the old constitution were to be destroyed, rather than put power in the hands of shopkeepers with property worth £10 to £15 a year, there should be a popular element in the voting. The *Mercury* countered this bid for popular support by sarcastically congratulating the Tory editor on his conversion to Universal Suffrage.

---

29. Sadler was MP for Newark (1829 and 1830) and Aldborough (1831), both seats controlled by the Duke of Newcastle. For the Short Time Committees, see chapter 4.
30. See entry in *ODNB* (by William Thomas). His father was Zachary Macaulay (1768-1838).

The *Mercury* also vigorously criticised the Tory *Yorkshire Gazette* for its support of Sadler for the West Riding nomination.[31] These issues were aired at a meeting on Factory Reform, addressed by the various candidates in the Cloth Hall Yard, Leeds, on 9 January 1832. The *Intelligencer* described this as 'one of the most gratifying and glorious manifestations of public feeling ever manifested in the town of Leeds' and went on:

> We will begin our sketch of the history of this most important meeting by noticing the pitiful conduct of our contemporaries of the *Mercury*. They felt, from the beginning, that if they had lent themselves to those who oppose the reasonable wishes of the people, they had neither part nor lot in the matter; that if they appeared as friends they would be despised; if as foes, defeated; they therefore adopted their usual course in an extremity – a quibble.[32]

The *Mercury* opened the year 1832 with the boast that its circulation was now 'higher by many hundreds than that of any other provincial journal, and we believe it is *five* or *six times* the average circulation of country newspapers'. Such, it implied, was the relative insignificance of the *Intelligencer* and the *Yorkshire Gazette*. It did not choose to dwell on the Monday meeting on Factory Reform, where the Liberals were clearly discomfited, but instead commented on a meeting on the Thursday (the day of publication of the *Intelligencer*) on the subject of a Poor Law for Ireland, at which Sadler came off the worse when Baines diverted the meeting to a discussion of Irish Tithes and the shortcomings of the Church. Sadler had long been interested in the problem of the poor in Ireland and in 1829 had published an anti-Malthusian essay on *Ireland: its evils and their remedies*, which condemned child labour on strongly moral and religious grounds.[33]

---

31. *LM*, 7 January 1832.
32. *LI*, 12 January 1832.
33. For an extract from the 1829 work, condemning child labour, see Kydd, I, pp. 125–6. A further attack on Malthusian economics followed in 1830, entitled *The Law of Population: a Treatise in Six Books, in Disproof of the Superfecundity of Human Beings, and developing the real Principle of their increase*. It was savagely dismissed by Macaulay in the *Edinburgh Review*: see vol. 51:102 (July 1830), pp. 297–321; see also the review of Sadler's speech on 'The State and Prospects of the Country, delivered at Whitby', in which he attacked the political economists: *Edinburgh Review*, 50:100 (January 1830), pp. 344–63; also Ward, p. 30.

Though the actual speeches at both the factory reform and poor law meetings were reported at length in both papers, they were carefully supplemented by editorials to help their readers assess and interpret events in line with their common prejudices.[34]

The climax to this journalistic contest came at Easter 1832, when the operatives campaigning for factory reform in the West Riding made a great pilgrimage on foot to York, culminating on Easter Tuesday in a county meeting on the Knavesmire. They were accompanied on this protest march from the industrial districts to the county town by Robert Perring, editor of the *Intelligencer*, but not by his rival of the *Mercury*. The *Intelligencer* of 26 April 1832 devoted six and a half columns of tiny print to an account of the meeting and the speeches, and a further half column to leading editorial comment of a largely favourable nature. The *Mercury*, whose editorial concern was primarily the need for the King to create new peers to see the Reform Bill through the House of Lords, devoted only its fourth editorial on 28 April to the county meeting:

> We cannot look upon the County Meeting held at York last Tuesday, without regret at the nature of the attendance on the hustings, and the character of the speeches delivered. The colour of the very few respectable persons who were present on the hustings was of the deepest *blue* [that is, Tory].

The partisan nature of the campaign, it argued, and Oastler's violent language, had repelled moderate men such as, presumably, Baines and his readers of the *Mercury*. In the actual report of the meeting, which occupied half the space allotted by the *Intelligencer*, the meeting was belittled:

> Many of those who set out never reached the place of their destination, being overpowered with fatigue and hunger: and hundreds who arrived at York, took shelter in the public houses, and did not attend the meeting.

---

34. *LM*, 7, 14 and 21 January 1832; *LI*, 19 January 1832.

The report concluded with a mixture of slander and cynical casuistry:

> The return of the several parties to their homes was a truly pitiable scene, owing to their hunger, exhaustion, the effects of the weather, and in many cases the still worse effects of liquor. Yet a great number supported their sufferings with uncommon spirit and gallantry, proving that the manufacturing system has not yet wholly destroyed the strength and energy of our population.

This account appeared in the *Mercury* on the streets of Leeds on Saturday 28 April. Immediately, a crowd gathered and a copy of the *Mercury* was tied to a pole with a piece of black crepe and born aloft as the crowd marched on the *Mercury* office where they burnt the offending paper to the accompaniment of hisses, booing and groans. That evening a far larger crowd assembled, bearing an effigy of Baines draped with banners proclaiming the stinging words which the radical, William Cobbett, had recently applied to the *Mercury* and its editor: 'The great Liar of the North'. Preceded by a brass band, the crowd marched past the *Mercury* office to the accompaniment of the 'Rogues March', then to the *Leeds Patriot* office where they gave three cheers, and then to the *Intelligencer* office where they gave three cheers and made the effigy bow down. They then marched to the homes of prominent supporters, including Sadler, where the band played 'God Save the King' and 'Rule Britannia' before returning to the *Mercury* office where they set fire to the effigy amid deafening shouts.[35] The *Intelligencer* reported these events in full, as well as devoting an editorial to refuting the *Mercury*'s derogatory report of the county meeting.[36] The *Mercury* reported the events with disdain as the work of ultra-Tories and ultra-Radicals, and warned,

---

35. This summary is taken from my account in *Revolutionary Britannia* (Manchester: Manchester University Press, 2000), p. 158, and is reproduced here by permission. The loyalist song *Rule Britannia* contains the appropriate line 'Britons never will be slaves'. The Rogues March was traditionally played when disgraced soldiers were literally drummed out of the army.
36. *LI*, 3 May 1832.

Talk of democracy! If the Tories are not with the proceedings on the Ten Hours Bill, and their other election manoeuvres getting up a democracy in Leeds and in Yorkshire that will one day overwhelm them, we are very much mistaken.[37]

The Factory Reform issue was soon overshadowed by political developments in Parliament. Two weeks after the *Mercury's* humiliation came further bad news for the parliamentary reformers: the *Mercury's* editorial heading told it all:

A GREAT CALAMITY HAS BEFALLEN ENGLAND
THE BOROUGHMONGERS HAVE TRIUMPHED!
THE REFORM BILL HAS BEEN STRANGLED!
THE KING HAS REFUSED TO MAKE PEERS! AND
THE GREY AND BROUGHAM ADMINISTRATION HAS RESIGNED!!![38]

Two weeks later, though, it was the turn of the *Intelligencer* to be disconsolate, as the King bowed to public pressure and agreed to create the necessary peers for Grey to carry the Reform Bill, which in turn led the Duke of Wellington to preserve the integrity of the House of Lords by allowing the Whig Bill to pass into law.[39] With the ensuing dissolution of Parliament, Sadler's Select Committee came to an end, its evidence for factory reform only half-collected.

In the first general election under the new franchise, the campaign was a bitter one: Marshall received 2,012 votes, Macaulay 1,964 but Sadler only 1,596. Thus Marshall and Macaulay were returned for Leeds and the *Intelligencer* had to console itself with the belief that Sadler had done well and that Macaulay was no more than a corrupt, career politician. There was no disguising, though, the triumph of the Bainesocracy and the *Mercury*.[40]

The passage of the Reform Act in 1832 brought to an end the first stage in Oastler's campaign. It is said that when news came of the

---

37. *LM*, 5 May 1832.
38. *LM*, 12 May 1832.
39. *LI*, 24 May 1832.
40. *LM*, 15 December 1832; *LI*, 20 December 1832.

5:6 Map of the
Parliamentary
Borough of
Huddersfield, 1832
(Huddersfield Local
Studies Library).

passage of the Act, it was greeted with cheers in the anti-slavery camp.
With the abolition of many rotten boroughs, the West Indies lobby of
MPs was severely weakened while a government committed to ending
slavery was greatly strengthened. But if the Reform Act also drove
Sadler out of the Commons and ended the work of his Select
Committee, his work and what he had stood for was not so easily
dismissed.[41] The evidence collected so far appeared damning and so

41. Sadler stood for the single seat at the Huddersfield by-election in 1833. The
    voting was Blackburne (Whig) 234; Sadler (Tory) 147; Wood (Radical) 108.

the new government did what governments often do when they wish to kick a difficult issue into the long grass: they set up a Royal Commission, suitably structured under the leadership of three Benthamite radicals: Edwin Chadwick, Thomas Southwood Smith and Thomas Tooke. Their task was to produce a politically more acceptable view than Sadler's Select Committee had been forming. The outcome was strangely mixed. In a way, the recommendations and subsequent Act, passed in 1833, were more radical than that for which Oastler and Sadler had been pressing. The Royal Commission recommended ending the employment in large textile factories of children under nine and limiting the hours of those between nine and thirteen to eight per day. The logic of this recommendation was accepted by Macaulay as being compatible with *laissez-faire* economics when he agreed that children were analogous to slaves because they were in the power of another, an argument that did not apply to adults.[42] Thus the reformers had won part of their case when the parallel with slavery was accepted by one of their most determined opponents, but the factory reformers had wanted more – a ten-hour limit because, since adult labour depended on child assistants, this would have meant Ten Hours for all. The factory masters were not prepared for such interference in their rights as employers and the apparent concession of a further two hours' reduction for children left open the possibility of working them in relays with a sixteen-hour day for adults, the majority of whom were women. A late amendment in the House of Commons weakened this prospect by cutting the hours of young people between thirteen and eighteen to twelve a day, so establishing in practice a twelve-hour day for adults. More importantly, the Benthamite principle of inspection was established with the creation of the factory inspectorate. The 1833 Act was in many respects a reasonable compromise, but one which left the factory reformers still dissatisfied and fighting for the ten-hour day as proposed by Wood to Oastler in 1830.[43]

---

42. Kydd, I, pp. 148–50.
43. Henriques, *Before the Welfare State*, pp. 83–9.

Oastler's leadership and the campaign he waged through the Leeds press between 1830 and 1832 had played a significant part in these events, but it was to have wider consequences in the wake of this partial defeat. The Radicals, and those who had organised the pilgrimage to York and taken part in the demonstration against Baines in 1832, continued their struggle for reform. The Bainesocracy had failed to win their support, even in the matter of parliamentary reform, but the Tories had not won them over either. Radicals and Tories could come together only on particular issues such as factory reform and the poor laws; they remained apart on the question of political reform, and so Tory-Radicalism could never be more than an uneasy alliance, dependent largely on certain issues and Oastler's personal popularity.[44]

The democrats' paper, the *Leeds Patriot*, closed in February 1833, after an acrimonious dispute with Oastler, but was replaced in June by a little penny unstamped paper edited by Joshua Hobson, one of those Huddersfield men who had gone to Fixby Hall in June 1831 to seek Oastler's support in the factory movement. Titled *The Voice of the West Riding*, it spoke the aspirations and anger of working people in the factory districts.[45] Then, in November 1837, Hobson published the first number of the *Northern Star and Leeds General Advertiser*, a newspaper to rival the middle-class press and which continued to give voice through the Chartist movement to working-class anger and aspirations. It took up both the Ten Hours question and the introduction of union workhouses and attack on welfare payments to people in their own homes imposed by the Poor Law Amendment Act of 1834.[46] The latter, like the exploitation of children in the factories, was an affront to Oastler's sense of the moral economy and Christian

---

44. Tory Radicalism and Christian Radicalism are discussed in Eileen Groth Lyon, *Politicians in the Pulpit. Christian Radicalism in Britain from the Fall of the Bastille to the Disintegration of Chartism* (Aldershot: Ashgate, 1999), pp. 143–50. See also Driver, pp. 507–13. The fragility of the alliance is illustrated by the failure of Sadler at Huddersfield in 1833.

45. See Chapter 4; and Stanley Chadwick, *'A Bold and Faithful Journalist'. Joshua Hobson, 1810–1876* (Huddersfield: Kirklees Metropolitan Council, 1976), pp. 12–14. The Short Time Committees and the Fixby House Compact are discussed in Driver, pp. 81–89. The *Voice* was published weekly from 1 June 1833 to 7 June 1834.

46. Hobson also edited the *Northern Star* between August 1843 and October 1845.

duty. He was never a Chartist but his leadership had inspired the movement that became Chartism.

The struggle for the Ten Hours Act was to continue for another decade and more, with further Acts in 1844, 1847, 1850 that went part of the way, extending protection while leaving loopholes which employers could exploit to prolong the hours that children and young persons were kept on factory premises. The 1853 Factory Act finally established an effective ten-and-a-half hours' day, which was the closest the ten-hour movement came to success in Oastler's life time. Though he and his followers remained dissatisfied with this less-than perfect outcome, it was nevertheless a great achievement.[47]

'The factory operatives of Huddersfield never cease to remember you, their friend', wrote John Leech of the Huddersfield Short Time Committee to Oastler in 1856.[48] As memories of the campaign between 1830 and 1832 sank deep into the consciousness of men and women from the industrial districts, Oastler continued to make a lasting impact on working people in the West Riding, particularly in the vicinity of Huddersfield where he had been so active among, and loved by, the people. This loyalty endured beyond the grave, as Honley postmistress, Mary Jagger, confirmed many years later. She had been born during Oastler's lifetime and was in her eighties in the 1930s when she recalled hearing in her childhood

> much about Richard Oastler, who so fervidly advocated the cause of factory-workers, especially the children. Oral accounts were always forthcoming of the great pilgrimage to York, when thousands from this neighbourhood walked to and from that city on foot and in pouring rain.[49]

---

47. Henriques, *Before the Welfare State*, pp. 99–113.
48. Kydd, II, p. 299.
49. Mary A. Jagger, *The Early Reminiscences of Mrs Jagger* (Honley: Dightam, 1934), (reprinted from articles in the *Huddersfield Weekly Examiner*, January and February 1931), p. 12.¹ Michael Craton, 'Slave Culture, Resistance and the Achievement of Emancipation in the British West Indies, 1783–1838' in *Slavery and British Society, 1776–1846*, ed. by James Walvin (London: Macmillan, 1982), pp. 100–22.

CRUELTIES OF THE FACTORY SYSTEM.

We copy the following case of cruelty and hardship from the *Standard*; and we can bear testimony that such are of almost daily occurrence in the manufacturing districts; indeed many cases not a whit less atrocious have come to our knowledge.

Joseph Habergam is a poor lad belonging to the parish of Huddersfield; he was sent to work in a factory at a very early age; he underwent the usual process of overwork, insufficient wages, and merciless beating; and, in his case, to such an extent did his master find it his interest to pursue the process, that at length his constitution sank under it; and, at seventeen years old, with the bones of his back and legs miserably and hopelessly distorted, his feeble and emaciated frame was spurned from the factory because no extremity of torture could any longer extract profitable labour from it, and he was thrown upon his parish. He was also, under surgical treatment, both at the Huddersfield and Leeds Infirmaries; he was, however, but very little benefitted, and, on his discharge from the latter institution, a week or two since, the medical man who had attended him, Mr. Hey, certified in writing that his complaint was such as to disable him from any longer pursuing his occupation in the factories. It was, therefore, thought best that his very laudable desire of acquiring knowledge, for "he is in sooth no vulgar boy," should be gratified; a small subscription was set on foot for that purpose, and confident hopes were entertained that, with a trifling assistance from the parish, a sufficient sum would have been raised to provide for his subsistence, while he gained knowledge enough to enable him to gain his livelihood as a teacher. But I am sorry to say that his application was rudely repulsed by the overseer, who not only threw his medical certificate in his face, and ordered him out, but absolutely took off the small pittance which had been before allowed him, and which I can assure you did not exceed, by a single stiver, the strictest limits of Malthusian parsimony. This extraordinary harshness is, in some degree, accounted for by the circumstance that the poor fellow had just been guilty of the deadly sin against the factory system, with which this high official personage is understood to be profitably concerned; he had absolutely dared to relate some few particulars of his tale of woe to the select committee of the House of Commons, in compliance with the chairman's summons!

This is a very frequent case with the witnesses who have given evidence in favour of the proposed regulation, and who are employed in factories. They are dismissed from their situations, either immediately on their return from London, or as soon afterwards as a plausible pretext can be devised against them; and then their applications for parish relief, which they have been repeatedly compelled to make, are treated in the same manner as Habergham's.

About £20 is wanted to rescue this unfortunate youth from the miserable death, to which his return to the factory will infallibly subject him; and it is confidently hoped that to his generous and benevolent fellow countrymen this appeal will not be made in vain; but that they will cheerfully contribute so small a sum to save him from being again tied to the wheel, and panting forth the last gasp of his existence beneath the thong of the factory tyrant.   X.

5:7 Article headed 'Cruelties of the Factory System' published in the *Poor Man's Guardian*, 28 July 1832.

So contemporary recollections were passed on to future generations in the twentieth century and beyond, shortening the years between the time when Yorkshire people fought against child slavery in their local mills and the present day with its own experiences of child exploitation on a global scale and the continued subjection of the weak to the power of the strong.

'Oastler is welcome': Richard Oastler's triumphant return to Huddersfield, 1844

JANETTE MARTIN

ON SHROVE TUESDAY 20 February 1844 Richard Oastler, the tireless champion of the factory slave and friend of the poor, returned to his adoptive town of Huddersfield after serving three and a half years in prison.[1] Oastler's return was deliberately timed to coincide with Shrove Tuesday, a half-day holiday when the operatives would be released from the mills at noon.[2]

6:1 View of Huddersfield from Longley Hall by William Cowen, 1850 (Kirklees Museums and Galleries).

1. Oastler's sentence was initially served at the Fleet Prison until November 1842 when it closed and he was transferred to the Queen's Prison, Cecil Driver, *Tory Radical: The Life of Richard Oastler*, (New York: Octagon Books, 1970), p. 422.
2. Mandatory holidays were laid down by factory legislation, a fact that would not have been wasted on the cheering factory hands, Driver, *Tory Radical*, p. 446.

6:2 The tracks and platforms of Brighouse Station, drawn and lithographed by Arthur Fitzwilliam Tait (1819–1905), on the Manchester and Leeds Railway, printed by Day and Haghe, lithographers to the Queen, 1845 (C.D. Helme Collection).

Despite fears of inclement weather, Tuesday dawned crisp and bright, adding to the air of festivity. It had been arranged that Oastler would travel by train to Brighouse on the 19 February 1844 (Huddersfield did not, at this time, have its own station) and from there continue to Huddersfield by carriage.

Throughout the morning supporters and well-wishers, drawn primarily from the labouring classes and from across the textile region, gathered to greet him at the Railway Hotel. As successive groups arrived they competed with one another in their enthusiastic welcomes. Some contingents brought their own musicians and a reporter counted at least seven rustic bands who entertained the crowds with their lively airs.[3] At one o'clock the mass of operatives, women and children were marshalled into some kind of order and a procession formed. At the head was an open carriage seating the 'Factory King' followed by several carriages conveying ladies and the better off, a contingent of horse riders and lastly a mass of pedestrians, cheering, singing and carrying flags and banners. As the procession marched towards Huddersfield, a distance of some four miles, it swelled in size as more and more people joined the marchers. By the time the parade reached Huddersfield the crowd was estimated to have numbered between

---

3. *Northern Star,* 24 February 1844, p. 8; Driver, *Tory Radical,* p. 447.

12,000 to 15,000 people, all of whom fell into a reverential silence as Oastler addressed them at length from a temporary hustings outside the Druid's Hotel, Halifax Road.[4]

OASTLER'S RE-ENTRANCE TO PUBLIC LIFE.

SIR,

I beg most respectfully to invite your attendance on Tuesday Morning next, at Ten o'Clock, at the Weekly Meeting of the Central Committee, at the Railway Hotel, Brighouse, when it is intended to present a congratulatory Address to Mr. Oastler on his re-entrance to Public Life. On that day Mr. Oastler will make his public entry into Huddersfield, and the Procession will leave Brighouse for that Town at One o'Clock, p.m., *to a minute.*

I remain, Sir,

Your's respectfully,

L. PITKEITHLEY, Secretary.

Feb. 15, 1844.

6:3 A printed letter from Lawrence Pitkethly dated 15 February 1844 inviting members of the Central Committee to present Richard Oastler with a congratulatory address on his return to Brighouse at the Railway Hotel on Tuesday 20 February 1844 (West Yorkshire Archive Service, Bradford DB27 C131).

4. Alfred* [Samuel Kydd], *The History of the Factory Movement,* (London: 1857), Vol. II, pp. 204–6. The scene of Oastler speaking to the crowds was captured by the artist J. O'Rourke whose pen and ink drawing is held in the Mary Evans Picture Library.

Richard Oastler was a renowned orator. During the 1830s his fiery and charismatic speeches denouncing factory exploitation and inhumane treatment of the poor had attracted large crowds of working people and inspired fierce devotion. This chapter will examine Oastler's return to Yorkshire and the significance of his first post-prison speech. Besides examining the spectacle of the procession, with its bands and banners, it will also examine the rhetorical qualities of Oastler's speech and how the event was reported and disseminated beyond Huddersfield. Oastler was adept at using oratory in the battle for public opinion, understanding that a public speech functioned at both the initial delivery and in its subsequent afterlife as reported speech in newspaper columns or in the shape of printed tracts. Oastler prepared rigorously for his public entry into Huddersfield in the expectation that his speech would be widely reported and that it would give him a unique opportunity to set out clearly his principles and explain his solutions for solving the problems of industrial Britain. Oastler's homecoming was a visual and aural demonstration of support. The large crowds vindicated Oastler's public career as an outspoken critic of factory exploitation and the new poor law and showed the affection in which he was held by the people of Yorkshire.

Richard Oastler had been imprisoned for debt under a politically motivated action brought by his former employer, Thomas Thornhill. Oastler's strong, impassioned language on the horrors of 'Yorkshire slavery' and the 'starvation laws' led to mounting tensions between himself and his employer, the absentee landlord of the large Thornhill estate.

6:4 View of Huddersfield from the Thornhill Estate at Cowcliffe by G. D. Tomlinson (Huddersfield Local Studies Library).

6:5 Extract from a letter of 2 January 1832 on estate business from Oastler to Thomas Thornhill, in which he describes his campaign for factory reform (Thornhill Papers RO 064-069).

in opening the Eyes of all parties & I can assure you the Factory
Bill has in a great measure taken the attention of the People, in this
Place of the Reform Bill — It is astonishing that a System
so destructive to the property & comfort of the Country sh^d
have been allowed to proceed so far, without being ex
mined into — I have now done my duty & have completely
succeeded, against the most powerful opposition —

      the Battle must next be fought in

      Parliament — & every Member of both

      houses who has any interest in supporting

      the Landed Interest & the Working Classes

for their interests are one & the Same, should Support
Sadlers Factory Bill against the empty headed Philosophy
of the day. —

    The other day the part of "Woodhouse" occupied by Bently
Morton next Geo Denhams — Fell in — They occupy
2. 21. 2. 20. You know the place, it cannot be repaired
If you rebuild I would do it more conveniently in one of the
fields — But I am sure you cannot get a rent equal
to the outlay — Two Houses would cost at least £450.
The families are without dwellings — but I do not see
that you can be expected to build them houses, when it

6:6 Cartoon of
Thomas Thornhill,
addressed to Mr R.
Oastler and signed
'your sincere friend
T. W. Thornhill'
(Kirklees Image
Archive k024393).

By May 1838 relations between Thornhill and Oastler had so
deteriorated that Oastler was dismissed from his post as Fixby Hall
steward and legal proceedings were initiated for recovery of debts owed.
Oastler, unable to repay his debts, was eventually committed to the
Fleet Prison until his friends could raise the considerable sum required
to liberate him. Not until the end of 1843, when another leading
advocate of factory reform, John Fielden MP, secured the outstanding
balance, was Oastler's release in sight.[5]

---

5. Stewart A. Weaver, 'Oastler, Richard (1789–1861)', *Oxford Dictionary of
    National Biography*, (Oxford: Oxford University Press, 2004).

During his long imprisonment Oastler was vilified in some quarters
and attempts were made to derail the efforts of the Oastler Liberation
Committees which had been formed in various localities.[6] Oastler's
reputation may have been unjustly damaged by the 'needle or the law'
controversy when, during a speech to the Blackburn Short Time
Committee in September 1836, Oastler had appeared to advocate
industrial sabotage in mill towns where employers and magistrates
wilfully ignored the provisions of the Factory Act.[7] Oastler, along with
the Revd J. R. Stephens, had made similarly incendiary statements

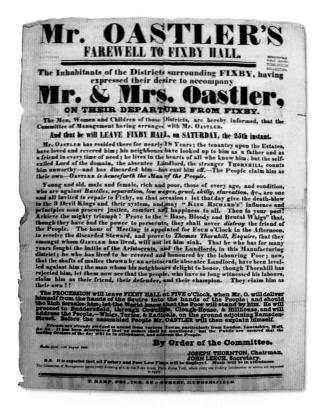

6:7 Poster advertising
events marking 'Mr
Oastler's Farewell to
Fixby Hall' after his
dismissal from
Thornhill's
employment (West
Yorkshire Archive
Service, Kirklees
KC174 Box 5 112).

6. See for example correspondence published in the *Preston Chronicle*, 23
    December, 1843, p. 3.
7. Oastler broadly hinted that factory children should protect themselves by using
    knitting needles to stop the machinery, Richard Oastler, *The Factory Question,
    the law or the needle* (London: 1836); G. D. H. Cole *Chartist Portraits*, (London:
    1941), pp. 99–100.

from the anti-Poor Law platform before thousands of working men. Such inflammatory rhetoric played into the hands of those who sought to marginalise Oastler as a dangerous demagogue.[8]

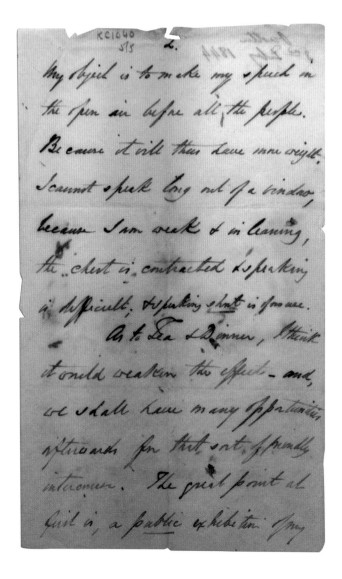

6:8 Letter of 3 February 1844 from Richard Oastler in the Queen's Prison to Lawrence Pitkethly outlining his wishes for his first speech on his return to Huddersfield (West Yorkshire Archive Service, Kirklees Pitkethly papers 1040/5/5).

8.   For example Oastler, at a mass meeting to protest against the new poor laws in Rochdale in 1838, allegedly said: 'before I would submit to such an Act, I would set the whole kingdom in a blaze' Jephson, *The Platform its Rise and Progress*, vol. 2, p. 219 (London: 1892).

As Oastler's release grew imminent, the Central Liberation Committee turned their attention from fund raising to managing Oastler's return to public life. Oastler was actively involved in co-ordinating these arrangements. He wrote several letters to the Committee's secretary, Lawrence Pitkethly, deliberating on the best way of managing his first public appearance. These letters reveal how Oastler and the Committee considered at length how Oastler should arrive in Huddersfield, where he should make his first address and before whom.[9] Oastler not only sought to restore his reputation but also to 'candidly and calmly' state his 'views [on] the causes and cures of England's disorder'.[10] Despite suffering weak health in consequence of his long confinement Oastler was adamant that he wished to make his first speech in Huddersfield at a mass meeting 'before all classes and all parties' not at a private tea party for his London supporters.[11] He envisaged that his words should be delivered verbally and later published:

> My object is to make my speech in the open air before all the people. Because it will have more weight – As to Tea and Dinner, I think that will weaken the effect – The great point at first is, a public exhibition of my principles to be published, not as delivered in a room, to scores or hundreds – but, in the open air to thousands. That speech could then be put into the hands of any who ask – what are Oastler's principles? [12]

His staged return to Huddersfield was a golden opportunity to answer his critics and set out his philosophy in the full glare of the early Victorian media. Yet as his opponents anticipated, the enforced reflection of a prison cell had tempered Oastler's appetite for confrontation. As we shall see this time he was determined to speak in more measured tones. Oastler's letters to Pitkethly also reveal that he was keen to avoid any action which might antagonise his old foe, Thomas Thornhill. Thus rather than passing through the heart of

---

9. WYAS: Kirklees, Lawrence Pitkethly papers, KC 1040/5/3-7.
10. Letter from Oastler to Pitkethly, 4 February 1844, KC 1040/5/6.
11. 'I cannot speak out of a window because I am weak and in leaving the chest is contracted and speaking difficult.' Letter from Oastler to Pitkethly 3 February 1844, KC 1040/5/5.
12. Letter from Oastler to Pitkethly 3 February 1844, KC 1040/5/5.

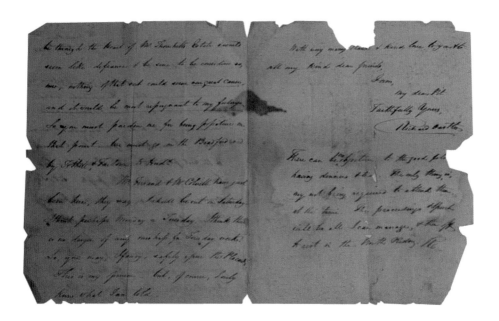

Thornhill's land which would 'seem like defiance and be sure to be considered so,' Oastler requested that the welcome procession be routed via Fartown rather than passing over Fixby Ridge.[13]

Oastler's public entry into Huddersfield was part of a long radical tradition of political martyrs being greeted by processions and mass celebrations. When Henry Hunt, the hero of Peterloo, made his triumphal entry into London after his incarceration at Ilchester prison on the 11 November 1822 he was greeted by large crowds.[14] His release was also marked elsewhere in the country (including Huddersfield) with bonfires, dinners and processions.[15] Some twenty years later Chartist prisoners were also paraded and publicly celebrated after their release from prison. Feargus O'Connor's release from York Castle in

6:9 Letter of 8 February 1844 from Richard Oastler to Lawrence Pitkethly outlining his wish to avoid the Thornhill Estate as to go 'through the Heart of Mr Thornhill's Estate would seem like defiance & be sure to be considered so now, nothing of that sort could secure our great cause, and it would be most repugnant to my feelings' (West Yorkshire Archive Service, Kirklees KC1040/5/7).

---

13. Letter from Oastler to Pitkethly, 8 February 1844, KC 1040/5/7.
14. The Peterloo Massacre took place on 16 August 1819, when the yeomanry charged into a crowd of 60,000–80,000 gathered at a meeting in St Peter's Fields, Manchester to demand the reform of parliament and extension of the franchise.
15. John Belchem, *'Orator' Hunt: Henry Hunt and English working-class radicalism*, (Oxford: Oxford University Press, 1985), pp. 163–4.

August 1841, for example, was marked by carefully orchestrated public celebration.[16] Oastler's Liberation Committee included Radicals such as Lawrence Pitkethly who, as Chartists, would have appreciated the propaganda value of such ceremonial displays. In addition to generating column after column of newspaper reports such public demonstrations of support reaffirmed the radical beliefs of those attending and strengthened the demand for social and political reform in the localities.

Oastler's warm welcome into Huddersfield needs to set against the broader political context. During Oastler's imprisonment the anti-Poor Law movement had been largely absorbed into Chartism and new leaders, such as Feargus O'Connor, had risen to prominence. Yet despite the initial promise of Chartism, by the time of Oastler's release, the Chartist movement was in the doldrums. Chartism had been weakened by the rejection of the 1842 mass petition, the strike wave of that year, and damaging internal splits among the leadership over the so-called 'New Move' and collaboration with middle-class suffragists.[17] The Chartist Land Plan had yet to fill the vacuum. The Owenite socialist movement, which was very prominent in Huddersfield, was also in decline because of difficulties concerning its Harmony Hall community (which failed the following year).[18] At a national level the benefits of Robert Peel's fiscal reforms, following his victory at the 1841 General Election, had not yet worked their way down to the working people of Huddersfield. Peel's other reforms, such as repeal of the Corn Laws (1846) and, later Morpeth's Health Act (1848), were still in the future. All of which made Richard Oastler's return particularly attractive. Oastler was untainted by the controversies that had dogged Chartism

---

16. Paul A. Pickering, 'Class without words: Symbolic Communication in the Chartist Movement,' *Past and Present*, No. 112. (Aug., 1986) pp. 157–8. Malcolm Chase, *Chartism: A New History*, (Manchester: M.U.P., 2007) p. 183.

17. Chase, *Chartism*, chapter 8; John A. Hargreaves, '"A Metropolis of Discontent": Popular Protest in Huddersfield c. 1780–c.1850 in *Huddersfield A Most Handsome Town*, ed. by E.A.H. Haigh (Huddersfield: Kirklees Cultural Services, 1992), pp. 215–17.

18. John F. C. Harrison, *Quest for the New Moral World: Robert Owen and the Owenites in Britain and America*, (London, 1969), pp. 172–3; Edward Royle, *Victorian Infidels: the origins of the British secularist movement, 1791–1866.* (Manchester, 1974), pp. 51–2.

6:10 Oastler's
triumphant
procession along
Cross Church Street,
Huddersfield,
attended by Lindley
Band (Huddersfield
Local Studies
Library).

since 1840. Moreover his popular appeal had been strengthened by his
enforced absence from public life.

Processions, rallies and mass outdoor meetings were popular in this
period as they united large numbers of working people in shared
grievances, creating a sense of purpose and solidarity. The entertainment
factor requires emphasis too. Part of the allure was the drama and
excitement of being part of a crowd, of participating in history. For
working people with little leisure time a grand procession, accompanied
by bands and banners and concluding in a rousing speech was a
welcome diversion. While Oastler's welcome home was heartfelt it
chimed with the people's desire for music and festivities. The
procession itself was a spectacle and, as Cecil Driver noted, 'all along
the route ballads and souvenirs were being sold by street hawkers
among the throngs of sightseers.'[19] The working people of textile
districts, freed for the afternoon from the factories, were making the
most of the day. After Oastler's speech ended the crowds dispersed but
later that evening 'the operatives held a high tea and a dance of their
own to complete the celebration'.[20]

Music was a key component of political mobilisation in the early
nineteenth century. Oastler's campaigns against Yorkshire slavery and

19. Driver, *Tory Radical,* p. 447.
20. Driver, *Tory Radical,* p. 448.

the new poor law were enlivened by the support of musicians.[21] The noise and spectacle of a parading band captured attention, drawing

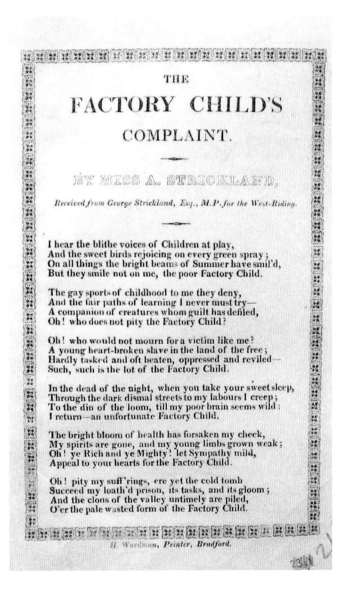

6:11 Poem: 'The Factory Child's Complaint' by Miss A Strickland (West Yorkshire Archive Service, Bradford, DB27/C1/21/1).

---

21. The role of bands in political protest is beginning to attract the attention of historians. Paul A. Pickering and Kate Bowan, 'Songs for the Millions: Chartist Music and Popular Aural Tradition,' in *Labour History Review* Vol. 74. No. 1, April 2009.

people into forming an audience or joining the campaign. The Lindley Band, which continues to this day, had a long connection with Richard Oastler. It accompanied those who walked to York in 1832 in a mass show of support for the ten-hour movement.[22] Twelve years later, the Lindley band was one of seven which marched in the procession from Brighouse to Huddersfield that Shrove Tuesday. Singing was also important. At least two ballads were specially written and sold by hawkers to mark Richard Oastler's release from prison and return to Yorkshire. The music and song and shouts of welcome which accompanied the marchers were mentioned in most newspaper reports. Another notable feature of the procession was the large numbers of children, many of whom carried small white flags inscribed with the slogans such as 'Welcome Good Old King' or 'Our King is Free'[23] The Short Time Committees had in the past utilised the propaganda value of small children. In May 1833, for example, during the Factory Commissioners' visit to Huddersfield, a mass of ragged factory children gathered outside the George Hotel where the Commissioners were housed – after presenting a written 'protest' the assembled children began singing the *Song of the Factory Children*.[24]

During Oastler's welcome the noise created by the musicians plus the regular cheers, shouts and singing of the crowd made the procession both a visual and an audible show of support. The *Northern Star's* reporter captured the atmosphere:

> As the solid, living mass of human beings moved down the hill – the floating white banners – the pealing cheers of the multitude – the infantile shout of 'welcome' – the sweet strains of the music, now swelling in full chords, and then dying away in distant melody – all these, combined with the absorbing thought that Richard Oastler was that day making his triumphant entry into his own loved Huddersfield, made up a scene at once affecting and spirit-stirring.[25]

22. Driver, *Tory Radical,* especially Chapter xiv 'The Pilgrimage to York'; W. R. Croft, *History of the Factory Reform Movement* (Huddersfield, 1888) pp. 59–62.
23. The slogan 'Our King is restored, the captive is free, Long may he live, and blest may he be,' was inscribed on the small white flags carried by children, *Northern Star,* 24 February 1844, p. 8.
24. Croft, *History of the Factory Movement,* pp. 85–86. According to Cecil Driver, the words of the *Song of the Factory Children* had been put to a popular tune of the day, Driver, *Tory Radical,* p. 230.
25. *Northern Star,* 24 February 1844, p. 8.

6:12 Huddersfield
Collegiate School,
St John's Road
Huddersfield
(Kirklees Image
Archive k011216).

Nor was the Chartist *Northern Star* the only paper waxing lyrical. *The Times* was also captivated by the enthusiasm of Oastler's welcome and the beauty of the day. Its reporter gave a romantic description of the hills and scenery and the awe inspiring spectacle as the parade climbed the long hill from Brighouse:

> For two miles the road lay over a rather steep ascent, which gave good effect to the moving mass as seen from afar, wending their way thought scenery so truly picturesque – while the acclamations of the thousands who lined the route, or stood on the adjacent rising grounds, mingling with the sounds of music, awoke the echoes of the surrounding hills.[26]

As the procession entered the principal streets of Huddersfield the school boys at the Collegiate School gave a hearty cheer. At the National Infant and Sunday School, flags were hoisted up, while the windows of the George Inn were crowded with the gentry of the neighbourhood. Three cheers were given and the procession temporarily halted at the spot where Oastler took leave of his friends in 1838. It was not till after three o'clock, more than two hours after

---

26. *Times*, 22 February 1844, p. 5.

6:13 Spring Street,
Huddersfield, the site
of the National
Infant and Sunday
School (Huddersfield
Local Studies
Library).

its departure, that the procession finally reached the hustings platform
next to the Druid's Hotel, at the bottom of Halifax Road.[27]

The crowds of working people who formed the welcome procession
that Shrove Tuesday thought nothing of the four mile walk to Huddersfield

6:14 George Inn and
Market Place,
Huddersfield
(Kirklees Image
Archive k015539).

27. *Northern Star*, 24 February 1844, p. 8.

6:15 Oastler in the
Fleet Prison. Oastler's
sentence was initially
served at the Fleet
Prison until
November 1842
when it closed and
he was transferred to
the Queen's Prison
(Mary Evans Picture
Library).

(indeed many had already travelled from places like Bradford, and Halifax and further afield on foot). The willingness of men, women and children to walk considerable distances to hear and see their heroes needs to be set into the context of the time. Working people in this period had little choice but to make the bulk of their journeys on foot. By today's standard their capacity for walking long distances was remarkable. So too was their devotion to Richard Oastler. The recollections of the former Chartist John Bates, for example, described how in 1838, in order to attend a meeting protesting Richard Oastler's dismissal from Fixby Hall, he and others 'walked from Queensbury to Rastrick, from Rastrick to Huddersfield, and then back to Queensbury after standing between three and four hours,' a walk of nearly twenty-two miles.[28] Yet even this journey pales into insignificance against the events of 1832 when Oastler led several thousand working men from Huddersfield and the surrounding areas on the Great Factory Reform 'pilgrimage' to York Castle.[29] On this occasion Oastler and his followers walked a return distance of over ninety miles. It was a key event in Oastler's public life. His determination to complete the journey on foot, alongside 'his men', proved his integrity and sealed his saintly reputation.[30]

Oastler is best remembered as an orator and while the *Fleet Papers* (edited from his prison cell) and Oastler's printed tracts were bought by his admirers it was on the platform that he had greatest impact.[31] Oastler cut an impressive figure: he was a powerfully built man, over six feet in height with a commanding presence. A contemporary described his voice as 'stentorian in its power and yet flexible, with a

28. Bradford Central Library: Local Studies Library, B920 BAT Misc articles on John Bates of Queensbury. See also *John Bates of Queensbury, the veteran reformer: a sketch of his life,* (Queensbury: 1895).

29. The 'pilgrimage' was made to draw attention to the factory campaign and to attend a vast outdoor county meeting, see Driver, *Tory Radical,* especially chapter xiv 'The Pilgrimage to York'. W. R. Croft, *History of the Factory Reform Movement,* (Huddersfield: 1888) pp. 59–62.

30. When Oastler arrived back at Fixby Hall 'the skin of his feet peeled off with his stockings', Driver, *Tory Radical,* p. 161.

31. G. D. H. Cole noted that Oastler was 'a speaker and organiser of immense energy, and not by instinct a writer,' G. D. H. Cole *Chartist Portraits,* (London: Cassell, 1989) p. 102.

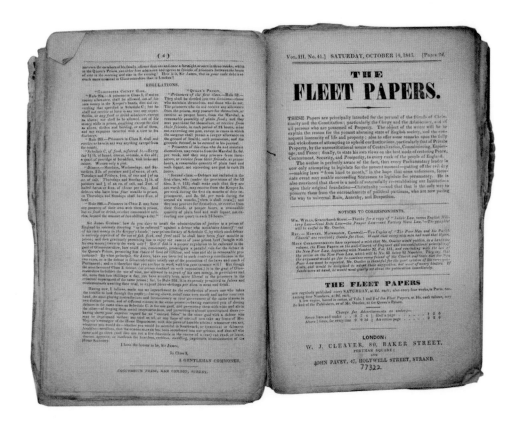

6:16 Fleet Papers
14 October 1843,
published in the
Queen's Prison
(University of
Huddersfield).

flow of language rapid and abundant'.[32] In the 1830s and 1840s oral
communication had many advantages over print. In the days before
mass literacy, radical political culture was shaped by visual and aural
displays such as processions, banners, marching bands, and the use of
effigies, emblems and symbols.[33] While literacy rates were rising by no
means all working men were competent readers, moreover tracts and
newspapers were often beyond the means of the factory operative. The
inanimate page was no match for the drama and excitement of the
charismatic orator and the experience of being part of a large event.
Oastler did not disappoint his hearers that Shrove Tuesday. He spoke

32. Thomas Adolphus Trollope, *What I Remember*, (1st edition, 1887, version
    edited by H. Van Thal, London: 1973) p. 132.

33. James Epstein, *Radical Expression: Political language, Ritual, and Symbol in
    England, 1790–1850*, (Oxford: 1994). Pickering, 'Class without words'.

at length and, according to *The Times,* the stillness that prevailed was 'the most remarkable' its reporters had ever seen at an outdoor meeting. That is not to say that the audience was silent and passive. The audience responded to Oastler's sentiments with cheers and applause, yet these heart-felt interjections were quickly suppressed 'lest one word he uttered should be lost'.[34]

Oastler, from the moment he appeared publicly at Brighouse railway station, played the part of an ageing and wronged king who had returned one last time to impart his reflective wisdom to his loyal subjects. The tone of his address was deeply religious, claiming that his liberation was God's will and concluding his speech by stating that God had allowed him to address them once more and that God would prevent him from leading them into error. His words were affectionate both in their references to shared memories and in the repeated use of words such as 'my own people,' 'friends' and 'neighbours'. Oastler humbly thanked the crowds for their support in securing his release, telling them that 'you are my benefactor and I am your purchased advocate', a phrase which reflected his ideas on duty and reciprocity.[35] His speech also displayed an emotive sense of place with endless references to his beloved Yorkshire. *The Times,* for example, recorded him as saying 'I thank you with a true Yorkshire heart for this right Yorkshire welcome'. For Oastler neighbourliness and duty were essential to society and the fear that these traits were being eroded lay at the heart of his objections to the new poor laws, which he felt encouraged the wealthy to shirk their moral responsibilities. As a Tory Radical, Oastler's politics centred on the constitution, crown and altar, sentiments which were very much in evidence during his post-prison speech.[36]

The impact of the prison cell was evident both in Oastler's frail physical appearance and in his attitude. The old Oastler, who dealt in firebrand rhetoric was no more. Incendiary words delivered in the heat of the moment were replaced by a carefully measured speech in which God, modesty and humility played a large part. Gone too were

---

34. *Times,* 22 February 1844, p. 5. The *Northern Star* also emphasised the decorum of the procession, *Northern Star,* 24 February 1844, p. 8.
35. Ibid.
36. Weaver, 'Oastler' *ODNB.*

personal attacks on his political enemies. After his inflammatory language for over a decade, his battle cry was now God and forgiveness.[37] He claimed not to even resent those who had insinuated

Upon arriving at a road-side inn, called the New inn, the procession was joined by one which had come thus far on the road to Huddersfield. From this point, and from Netheroyd Hill, the immense procession was seen to the best advantage. As the solid, living mass of human beings moved down the hill—the floating white banners—the pealing cheers of the multitude—the infantile shout of "welcome"—the sweet strains of the music, now swelling in full chords, and then dying away in distant melody—all these, combined with the absorbing thought that Richard Oastler was that day making his triumphant entry into his own loved Huddersfield, made up a scene at once affecting and spirit-stirring. The sight of Woodhouse Church produced an evident effect upon one who in years gone by was wont to worship within its sacred walls.

The procession entered Huddersfield in the order in which it had been previously arranged.

On passing the Collegiate School, the boys, who were drawn up in front, gave a hearty cheer as the procession passed by. Near the National Infant and Sunday School a blue flag was hoisted, evidently the work of juvenile hands, and inscribed "Home Trade." The procession was seen to the best advantage as it moved along New-street; it halted for a few moments opposite the George Inn, the windows of which were crowded with the gentry of the neighbourhood.

The procession entered the town by way of Northgate, and passed along Cross Church-street, Queen-street, (where it halted for the purpose of giving three cheers, this being the spot where Oastler took leave of his friends in 1838,) Ramsden-street, New-street, Market Place, Westgate, and Temple-street.

The place selected for the delivery of the speech by Mr. Oastler, was the spacious area in front of the Druid's Hotel, on the Halifax road. The procession did not arrive upon the ground until after three o'clock, and as it advanced up the street it presented a most imposing appearance. We have pleasure in adding, that throughout the entire route, and during the whole of the meeting, there was not the slightest attempt at disorder or interruption.

6:17 The account of Oastler's return published in the *Northern Star*, 24 February 1844 (British Library).

---

37. Ibid.

against him while in prison. Oastler, as his secretary Samuel Kydd noted, was a 'changed man; the energy of former years had been mellowed by experience and reflection, and chastened by experience'.[38] A change acknowledged by Oastler himself during his speech.

> It is my duty, my friends, to inform you that whilst I have been in prison I have lost all that feeling of animosity which was wont to occupy a portion of my mind ... I am bound hereafter to avoid every expression which is calculated to give personal offence to any ... I hope hereafter that passion will be supplanted by reason.[39]

Thus while he mentions factory children the highly emotive phrase Yorkshire slavery is notably absent. Rather than inciting factory children to arm themselves with their grandmothers' knitting needles to enforce their rights he presents a calm and rational explanation of the ills of an industrial society and how they might be mitigated. For the most part he succeeds, although when talking about the Poor Law we catch sight of the old Oastler. His description of the death of a London pauper lapses into the emotionally charged rhetoric which had earned him so much censure in the past:

> Dying of want on the streets of London ... hurried with such haste to the grave, that before death had made them his own, whilst the limbs are still quivering and the lungs are moving, and the heart is beating its last throe, they are dragged from the iron bedstead of your London workhouses, laid upon the undertakers board, and covered with a winding-sheet, whilst the muscles of the expiring man are quivering in the hands and moving the limbs (shame). There lies your New Poor-Law-created independent labourer!![40]

Such melodramatic oratory reflected the emotionalism of the day and was one of the tools used by skilled orators to elicit sentiment. In this example the sensational horror of Oastler's words led to cries of 'shame' from the audience. It is notable how easily nineteenth century

---

38. Kydd, *History of the Factory Movement*, p. 205.
39. *Northern Star,* 24 February 1844, p. 8.
40. Ibid.

MR. RICHARD OASTLER AT HUDDERSFIELD.

On Tuesday last, Mr. Oastler,—after an absence of upwards of three years, during which period he has been incarcerated in the Queen's prison, and from which he has just been rescued by the voluntary contributions of his friends,—made a public entry into the town of Huddersfield, with which he was formerly for a series of years intimately connected, as steward of the Thornhill estate, at Fixby. The day chosen for the occasion was one of the most auspicious, in regard to the state of the weather, that we have had for some weeks past, and possessed the additional advantage of being a public holiday.

In accordance with previous arrangement, Mr. Oastler was to have been met at the railway station, at Brighouse, by the central committee of the Liberation Fund, at ten o'clock on Tuesday morning; but this arrangement was rendered ineffectual by Mr. Oastler, who, it appeared, had made an earlier and unexpected entry to Brighouse, having left Leeds on Monday evening, and arrived at the Railway Hotel at that place by a late train. At this hotel he remained during the night, and in one of its spacious rooms, at about half-past eleven o'clock on Tuesday morning, he was presented with an address of welcome and congratulation, which emanated from the Central Committee, and which was received and responded to by Mr. Oastler under feelings of evident emotion. At this time two bands of music had arrived from places in the neighbourhood; and at one o'clock a public procession was formed, embracing the bands alluded to, about half a dozen vehicles (in the first of which sat Mr. Oastler and a few friends), several horsemen, and several hundred persons who had assembled opposite the hotel. In the procession were a few banners, chiefly white, and diminutive in size, most of them having the motto—

"Our King is restored ; the Captive is free ;
Long may he live, and blest may he be."

Displayed amongst the banners were also two Union Jacks; but, at the outset from Brighouse there was little in the aspect of the procession that was grand or imposing. The number of pedestrians, though at first somewhat meagre, received accessions (chiefly of the working classes, at every village en route; and on arriving at Huddersfield they might amount to five thousand, the procession then being several hundred yards in length; but no increase took place in the number of horsemen or vehicles. The procession passed through several of the principal streets of the town, and Mr. Oastler was repeatedly cheered, but the enthusiasm altogether came far short of that with which the people of Huddersfield have greeted him on many former occasions. Mr. Oastler appeared much thinner than we have seen him, and his pale countenance seemed to indicate a state of health much less vigorous than that possessed by him prior to his long imprisonment.

At the close of the procession the people congregated in a large open space of ground, at the foot of the new North-road, where a temporary platform had been erected, and from which it was expected Mr. Oastler would speak.

As soon as Mr. Oastler ascended the platform, Mr. SCHOLEFIELD, of Rastrick, presented to him a long address, welcoming him to his native county, and strongly eulogizing him on his past public efforts, in seeking the protection of infant labour and British industry in general.

The Rev. Mr. HOWARTH, Incumbent of Pudsey, having read aloud the address, which purported to emanate from the inhabitants of Huddersfield, and the various towns in the West Riding.

Mr. OASTLER then came forward and said, turning toward the gentleman who presented the address,—I receive this address from the Huddersfield committee with the most heartfelt gratitude, and it shall have my answer, as they have kindly postponed the time, when I shall be more at ease in my body, and more calm in my mind. Mr. Oastler, turning to the meeting, then said—Men of Huddersfield, it is once more my high privilege to address you as more than friends; you are now my benefactors, and I am your purchased advocate. Think for a moment, if you can, of the feelings under which I now stand in this town, the scene of so many of our labours, and at a time when you have not only emancipated me by opening the prison doors, but when the mind of England itself is emancipating, and those rights for which we have, under so much obloquy, so long pleaded, are now being adopted by almost every civilized country on the face of the earth ; and our own government are not only proceeding to adopt those schemes which we have propounded for the protection of factory labourers, but they are also, thanks be to God, receding in that grasp with which they have seized the poor of England, and are moving backwards from the Poor Law Bill. Allow me, my friends, before I proceed to explain myself, and to explain ourselves, for I know that England is listening to what shall proceed from these

6:18 The account of Oastler's return published in the *Leeds Mercury*, 24 February 1844 (British Library).

audiences could be moved to tears by a pathetic anecdote or heart-wrenching story. Audiences openly wept in theatres, they sobbed too while listening to pathetic instalments of Charles Dickens' latest

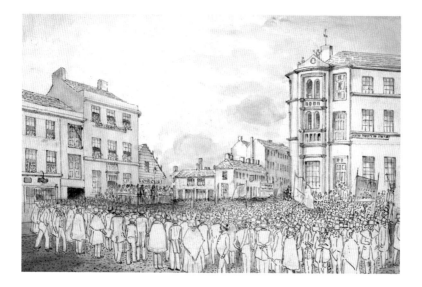

6:19 Oastler addressing the crowd of up to 15,000 people outside the Druid's Hotel, Westgate, Huddersfield on Shrove Tuesday, 1844, pen and ink drawing by J. O'Rourke (Mary Evans Picture Library).

novel.[41] A poignant public occasion might also elicit great emotion. Indeed when Oastler first appeared before the assembled crowds that day newspaper reports described how both old and young strove to restrain their feelings, until at last after battling with their emotions they were 'fairly overcome [and] burst into tears'. Oastler too was described as suffering from a surfeit of emotion, he sank back into his chair and was advised not to attempt speaking until later that day.[42]

Public speaking in this period was very much a two way process in which the audience helped shape and direct oratory by intervention in the shape of heckles, cheers and applause. A good orator was like a conductor, able to work the emotions of the crowd. The best speeches reflected back the audience's own perceptions, articulating and clarifying hazy grievances and offering a solution – a fact acknowledged by Oastler who, when briefly thanking his supporters prior to the procession's departure, promised the crowds that he would endeavour to 'mix the thoughts of my heart with the thoughts of yours', when he spoke at length later that day.[43]

---

41. Sally Ledger '"Don't be so melodramatic!" Dickens and the affective mode,' in *Interdisciplinary Studies in the Long Nineteenth Century*, issue 4, April 2007; Rohan McWilliam, 'Melodrama and the historians,' *Radical History Review*, 78, 2000.

42. *Northern Star*, 24 February 1844, p. 8.

43. Ibid.

At large outdoor rallies, without the benefits of modern sound amplification, it has been estimated that only ten per cent of the audience were actually in earshot of a speaker.[44] While the prevailing silence and Oastler's power as an orator assisted audibility it is unlikely that those at the back caught every word that fell from his lips. For those unable to hear the verbatim reports printed in newspapers were particularly valuable. In this period newspapers were still taxed and to counter the high cost and varying levels of literacy working people often bought newspapers communally to be read out loud before gathered friends, family and work colleagues. Indeed research into the Chartist newspaper the *Northern Star,* which enjoyed great popularity in the West Riding, suggests that its official circulation figures require substantial upward revision. It has been calculated that each copy on average reached at least twenty people (whether read silently or aloud).[45] The *Northern Star* devoted almost an entire page to Oastler's return and it seems plausible that many Radicals present that Shrove Tuesday relived the experience via printed reports the following Saturday.[46]

As Oastler hoped his address was also reported extensively in the local and national press. *The Times* printed a verbatim account of Oastler's speech and aided his political rehabilitation by a sympathetic editorial which excused his bankruptcy by pointing out that many other noble men had neglected 'their private affairs in the zealous prosecution of a public cause'.[47]

Even the *Leeds Mercury,* a paper owned by Oastler's political enemy Edward Baines, published a near verbatim report of his address. Indeed, as Driver noted in his biography of Richard Oastler, it was the first time in well over a decade that the *Leeds Mercury* had reported Oastler fairly.[48] Key political speeches operated both during the drama and emotion of the initial delivery and subsequently via the printed page.

---

44. Pickering, 'Class without words,' p. 153.
45. James Epstein, 'Feargus O'Connor and the Northern Star,' *International Review of Social History*, vol. XX1 (1976) pp. 51–97, p. 70.
46. *Northern Star*, 24 February 1844, p. 8.
47. *Times*, 13 February 1844, p. 6; 22 February 1844, p. 5.
48. For the first time the *Leeds Mercury* also referred to Oastler as a gentleman throughout the article, Driver, *Tory Radical*, p. 449.

Thus while Oastler's immediate audience comprised thousands of working people in Huddersfield his words were also consumed in print by wealthy Londoners via the pages of *The Times,* and by readers of newspapers as varied as the *Aberdeen Journal, Birmingham Advertiser* and *Lloyds Weekly.*[49] The poignant return of Richard Oastler was recorded in several histories of the period, including W. R. Croft's *History of the Factory Movement* which described it as a 'red-letter-day in the annals of Huddersfield'.[50] As time passed Oastler's return lived on in folk memory as those present recounted their experience to their children and later grandchildren.[51] This process of commemoration was assisted by the ballads that were sung by the crowds and sold by hawkers as souvenirs. Such songs played on the historical significance of Oastler's return. The ballad *Oastler is Welcome,* for example, made specific reference to the event's place in Yorkshire's history:

> The twentieth day of February,
> Eighteen Hundred and Forty-four,
> Will be a story o' Yorkshire's glory,
> When Poor Law Bastilles are no more! [52]

If the ballad's jubilant conclusion fell wide of the mark, Oastler's stage-managed return and carefully considered speech ensured that the memory of the 'Factory King's' homecoming endured.

6:20 Ballad 'Oastler is Free!' (*The Making of the Modern World.* Gale 2009. Gale, Cengage Learning. University of Leeds. 24 July 2009<http://galenet.galegroup.com).

6:21 Ballad 'Oastler is Welcome' (*The Making of the Modern World.* Gale 2009. Gale, Cengage Learning. University of Leeds. 24 July 2009<http://galenet.galegroup.com).

49. For verbatim reports see *Times,* 22 February 1844, p. 5; *Northern Star,* 24 February 1844, p. 8; *Leeds Mercury* 24 February 1844, p. 6. Summaries were also reported in the *Lloyds Weekly Newspaper,* 25 February 1844, p. 9; the *Aberdeen Journal,* 28 February 1844 p. 2; *Age and Argus,* 24 February 1844, p. 8. Driver, *Tory Radical,* pp. 447–8 refers to reports in the *Birmingham Advertiser* and *Wakefield Journal.*
50. Croft, *History of the Factory Movement,* p. 129.
51. A reporter for the *Birmingham Advertiser* described the event as one which 'it is certain, will be named to generations yet to come and by fathers to their children'. Cited in Driver, *Tory Radical,* p. 448. The *Leeds Intelligencer* too commented on the historical significance of the day, *Leeds Intelligencer,* 24 February 1844, p. 6.
52. *Oastler is free!: Oastler is welcome!.* [s.l.], [1844?]. *The Making of the Modern World.* Gale 2009. Gale, Cengage Learning. University of Leeds. 24 July 2009<http://galenet.galegroup.com/servlet/MOME?af=RN&ae=U360642468 3&srchtp.=a&ste=14>.

OASTLER IS FREE!

EXALT your voices high,
Behold your friend draws nigh
 Your tribute bring,
Unto the Patriot, who
Suffer'd so much for you,
Show your allegionce to
 The factory child's king.

Welcome the captive home
From a dark dungeon's gloom
 No more bewail,
Tho' long he's captive lain,
Broke is the tyrant's chain,
Richard's himself again;
 Hail, Oastler, hail.

This day the factory slave
Will a great triumph have
 Oastler is free,
Lift up your voice and sing,
Until the welkin ring.
Welcome our good old "king"
 To liberty,

Come ye who are oppress'd
From North South East & West,
 Come, children. come,
Let every heart elate,
Great labour's advocate
And from the prison gate
 Welcome him home

Exalt your voices high
The "king" of the poor draws
 Welcome is he, (nigh,
Thousands to greet him stay
While the glad music play,
 'Tis labour's holiday.
  Oastler is Free.

OASTLER IS WELCOME

YOU sons of labour pay attention,
 Join in chorus while we sing,
In honour of our friend and champion
Richard Oastler, the poor man's "king",
  CHORUS.
Welcome Richard Oastler, welcome
Sons of labour swell his train,
Cheer him, cheer him with songs of wel-
Unto Yorkshire back again. (come,

The Lords of the bastile he offended,
Tha factoty hypocrite and knave
When against them he defended,
The helpless poor and factory slave

His words of truth the tyrants galled,
So they plotted his downfall,
The mean-soul,d 'squire when they called
Drove our "king" from Fixby Hall;

By trickery the knaves succeeded,
And labour's friend in prison laid,
But soon their deeds shall be rewarded
Now Oastler's free and his ransom's paid.

Four long years' incarceration,
Cou'd not break our champion's mind,
With labour's sons in tribula,ion,
His heart it was more closely joined.

They come, they come from every mountain
Hill and valley, moor and plain,
In numbers far beyond the counting
To welcome Oastler back again.

The factory children raise their voices,
While banners wave and music play,
The toil-worn strve for once rejoices
And gives dull care an holiday.

The twentieth day of Febru ary,
Eighteen Hundred and Forty-four,
will be a story of Yorkshire's glory,
When Poor Law Bastiles are no more!

'Treading on the edge of revolution?' Richard Oastler (1789–1861) a reassessment

JOHN A. HARGREAVES

RICHARD OASTLER'S TWENTY-FIRST century biographer Stewart Angas Weaver, concluded in 2004 that Richard Oastler 'for ten turbulent years trod the edges of revolution' paradoxically enough, in the name of 'homestead and hall, church and cottage, craftsmanship and harmony of function'.[1] He observed that Oastler is remembered 'not as a thinker, nor as a writer', but, as his first modern biographer, Cecil H. Driver, suggested in 1946, as the embodiment of a Tory Radical 'folk-dream which had an especial cogency in the days of transition to an industrial economy'.[2] Reviewing this paradoxical characterisation of Oastler as a Tory Radical in 1991, Felix Driver remarked that 'the theme of Tory Radicalism has been used to represent that peculiar combination of revolutionary spirit and reactionary hope which inspired popular protest before Chartism'.[3] This chapter offers a re-evaluation of Weaver's assessment of Oastler as a quasi-

---

1. S.A. Weaver, 'Richard Oastler', *Oxford Dictionary of National Biography*, (Oxford: Oxford University Press 2004). I am grateful to Professor Edward Royle of the University of York and Professor Keith Laybourn of the University of Huddersfield for their comments on an earlier version of this chapter.
2. C.H. Driver, *Tory Radical: the life of Richard Oastler*, (New York: Oxford University Press, 1946), pp. 128–29.
3. F. Driver, 'Tory Radicalism? Ideology, strategy and locality in popular politics during the eighteen-thirties', *Northern History*, XXVII, 1991, 120–38. Felix Driver was careful to point out that he was not related to Cecil H. Driver.

EVENINGS AT HOME
TEN HOURS BILL
1ST MAY 1848

7:1 Medal commemorating the passing of the Ten Hours Bill. The obverse depicts Queen Victoria with the legend 'GOD SAVE THE QUEEN ROYAL ASSENT 8th JUNE 1847' (West Yorkshire Archive Service, Calderdale FLD/991).

revolutionary figure within a broader historiographical context which has consistently emphasized the paradoxical attributes and conduct of this extraordinarily influential figure in the campaign against child labour in the second quarter of the nineteenth century.

It will re-assess Richard Oastler's contemporary impact and historical significance as an anti-slavery campaigner and factory reformer, focusing particularly upon his astute application of the analogy of working conditions for children on transatlantic slave plantations to those of children in the Yorkshire worsted industry, and also on his extension of the metaphor to his subsequent campaign to denounce the liberal utilitarian proposals for the reform of the system of poor relief. It will argue that to characterise Richard Oastler as a quasi-insurrectionary figure in the context of his campaign to improve factory working conditions for children fails to distinguish between the inflammatory rhetoric which he occasionally undoubtedly employed in the heady atmosphere of the arena of contemporary popular protest and its actual expression through the campaigning strategy underpinning the re-invigorated factory movement which his rhetoric inspired and his indefatigable campaigning orchestrated. When the rhetoric, which fell considerably short of the sustained advocacy of revolutionary action, translated into the reality of campaigning tactics, it scarcely amounted to a demonstration of revolutionary intent. Rather, it exemplified a generally more restrained exercise of extra-parliamentary pressure in the dogged pursuit of a single-issue, political objective, challenging powerfully entrenched vested interests, which, it must be added, proved no less susceptible than Richard Oastler to occasionally utilising alarmist rhetoric in defence of their case.

The most unequivocal sense in which Richard Oastler may be represented as 'treading on the edge of revolution' is perhaps the first tentative steps he took in infancy following his birth in Leeds in the year of the outbreak of the French Revolution in 1789, some six months after the fall of the Bastille. Indeed, the despised name of the Parisian fortress and prison would be employed frequently in Oastler's vocabulary nearly half a century later to denounce the new union workhouses after the Poor Law Commissioners moved north in 1837 to implement the provisions of the Poor Law Amendment Act (1834). But as Asa Briggs reminded readers of the *Yorkshire Post* in 1961 in an article commemorating the centenary of Richard Oastler's death in 1861, Oastler also 'lived to see an industrial revolution in the West Riding' and 'it was this revolution which created the problems which he found so disturbing both to his mind and his conscience. By 1830 when Richard Oastler wrote his celebrated letter to the *Leeds Mercury* condemning 'Slavery in Yorkshire', the textile industry of the West Riding was being transformed under the influence of steam power and the factory system, some three decades after the similar transformation of the cotton industry in Manchester and the North West. In other circumstances, Briggs remarked, Oastler might have lived quietly and unobtrusively, since he was conservative both by temperament and by conscious choice. Indeed, Briggs concluded, it was because other people were revolutionaries that he chose to become a Tory radical'.[4]

---

4.   Asa Briggs, 'Richard Oastler, King of the Factory Children' in *The Bed Post. A Miscellany of The Yorkshire Post*, ed. by K. Young, (London: Macdonald, 1962), pp. 24–27.

Briggs argued that 'Tory Radical' was an appropriate descriptive label 'since Oastler had no sympathy with the political radicalism of Tom Paine or of most of the West Riding Nonconformist mill-owners whom he bitterly disliked'.[5] Other historians have also emphasized the conservative instincts that underpinned his political attitudes. Twenty years earlier, G.D.H. Cole had described Oastler as 'a Church and State Tory', whose motto was 'The Altar, the Throne and the Cottage'.

Thirty years later, Felix Driver defined Oastler's political sympathies as those of a Tory traditionalist who professed himself to be 'the champion of factory children and the poor, rather than as the representative of any party'.[6] Indeed his enduring support for the Corn Laws introduced by Lord Liverpool's government in 1815 and his persistent opposition to Roman Catholic Emancipation would seem to deny him even the designation of 'Liberal Tory' in the period before 1830.[7] Moreover, his own definition of conservatism in a conversation

7:2 Oastler's seal, depicting his motto of 'the Altar, the Throne and the Cottage' and the principles of Charity, Mercy and Justice which motivated his campaign against child labour (Tolson Memorial Museum, Huddersfield).

5. Ibid.
6. G.D.H. Cole, *Chartist Portraits*, (London: Macmillan, 1941), p. 81; Driver, *Northern History*, 1991, p. 121.
7. Driver, *Northern History*, p. 121; *Richard Oastler: King of Factory Children; Six Pamphlets, 1835–61*, ed. by K.E. Carpenter, (New York: Arno Press Reprints, 1972), p. 16; 'Richard Oastler', *Concise Dictionary of National Biography*, (Oxford: 1992), p. 2214.

which he had with the Duke of Wellington in June 1832 revealed a highly paternalistic view of society with everything in its proper place:

> The King, happy serene, and venerated in his palace, – the nobles, happy secure, and honoured in their castles, – the bankers, merchants and manufacturers, happy, secure, and beloved in their mansions, – the small tradesmen and shopkeepers happy, secure, and respected in their houses; and the labourers happy, secure, and as much respected as the best of them in their cottages.[8]

Descended from yeomen farmers at Kirby Wiske, a small, remote Swaledale village in the North Riding of Yorkshire, his father, an early convert to Wesleyanism, later became a linen merchant in Thirsk before moving to Leeds, where his friend John Wesley famously blessed the infant Richard Oastler in 1790 on his last visit to Yorkshire. Consequently, Richard Oastler's formative early childhood years were spent in a 'thoroughly Tory atmosphere' before his father's secession to the Methodist New Connexion in 1797 introduced a decidedly more radical complexion to the family's Nonconformity. This might explain why Richard Oastler later expressed sympathy for King George IV's estranged wife, Queen Caroline in 1820 and why he cut his political teeth organising his employer's tenants to refuse to pay their tithes to the new Vicar of Halifax in 1827 and condemned the sentences of transportation imposed on the Tolpuddle Martys in 1834.[9] However, this does not appear to have deterred Oastler from assuming the role of surrogate Squire of Fixby Hall, cultivating relationships with the local gentry and Anglican clergy, living in style in the elegant Arcadian mansion conveniently vacated by the absentee Thornhill family and managing a thousand-strong tenantry and a rent roll of nearly £20,000, after succeeding his father on his death in 1820 as steward of the Norfolk family's Yorkshire estates.[10] Moreover,

---

8. Cole, *Chartist Portraits*, p. 103; Driver, *Tory Radical*, pp. 187–89.
9. Driver, *Tory Radical*, pp. 4–5; Cole, *Chartist Portraits*, p. 82; T. Koditschek, *Class Formation and Urban Industrial Society*, (Cambridge: Cambridge University Press, 1990), p. 415; J.A. Hargreaves, 'Religion and Society in the Parish of Halifax c1740–1914', unpublished Ph.D. thesis, Huddersfield Polytechnic, 1991, pp. 227–28.
10. Driver, *Tory Radical*, p. 24.

G.D.H. Cole, observed that with another prominent Tory Radical, Michael Thomas Sadler, Oastler's closest colleague in the earlier phases of the struggle for factory reform, Oastler opposed the Great Reform Act of 1832 and, unlike his friend the Revd J.R. Stephens (1805-1879), who has perhaps rather more aptly attracted the soubriquet of 'Revolutionary Tory', never joined 'in any phase of the Chartist agitation as such'. Indeed, Cole quoted an article written by Oastler in Henry Hetherington's *Twopenny Dispatch* in 1835, when he proclaimed candidly that:

> My opinion on Universal Suffrage is, that, if it were the law of the land next week, it would in a very short time produce 'universal confusion' and would inevitably lead to 'despotism'.[11]

By contrast, for his revolutionary rhetoric, which included the proclamation of himself as 'a revolutionist by fire, a revolutionist by blood, to the knife, to the death' in 1839, Joseph Rayner Stephens, the former Wesleyan minister, Lancashire factory reformer and anti-Poor Law agitator was sentenced to eighteen months imprisonment for his advocacy of the right and duty of resistance to bad laws rather than allow factory slavery to continue or the New Poor Law to be enforced.[12]

Some contemporaries, however, clearly viewed Richard Oastler's oratory in a similar vein. He was denounced on one occasion by no less a figure than the Lord Chancellor in a speech in the House of Lords as 'a criminal incendiary' and by political opponents echoing the charge in the 1837 Huddersfield election campaign as 'an incendiary, an assassin and a madman'.[13] Indeed a leader in the *Manchester Guardian*, which Oastler dismissed disdainfully as 'the Cotton Lords' Bible', alluded to the 'diseased' state of Oastler's mind, whilst the contemporary novelist and journalist Thomas Adolphus Trollope (1810–92), who

---

11. G.D.H. Cole, *Chartist Portraits*, 1941, p. 81; J.T. Ward, 'Revolutionary Tory: The life of Joseph Rayner Stephens of Ashton-under-Lyne (1805–1879)', *Transactions of the Lancashire and Cheshire Antiquarian Society*, LXVIII, 1958, pp. 93–116.
12. Cole, *Chartist Portraits*, pp. 63 and 79.
13. Driver, *Tory Radical*, pp. 4, 348.
14. D. Ayerst, *The Guardian Omnibus 1821–1971*, (London: Collins, 1973), pp. 68–69; Driver, *Tory Radical*, p. 404.

observed Oastler campaigning, dubbed Oastler 'the Danton of the Factory movement'.[14] However, dismissive repudiation of Oastler as insane or a revolutionary in the mould of Georges Jacques Danton (1759-94) fail to withstand close scrutiny. Another contemporary newspaper editorial in *The Times* commended Oastler as 'the providential organ of the oppressed and suffering poor' and although Danton, the intensely patriotic Jacobin mob orator of the French Revolution like Oastler championed the oppressed and faced accusations of financial indiscretion, he proved more personally ambitious, more pleasure-seeking and more politically unscrupulous than Oastler.[15] While Oastler's financial mismanagement certainly proved his Achilles' heel, for which he paid the heavy penalty of three years and two months imprisonment with all its Dickensian deprivations first at the Fleet and then at the Queen's Prison, Oastler's alleged revolutionary fervour remained confined within his own fertile imagination and his inflammatory rhetoric and it is misleading even to suggest that he trod on the edge of revolution throughout the decade in which he was most actively engaged in his campaigns for social justice.

This is not to deny, however, that his language was sometimes intemperate or even that he contemplated publicly employing industrial sabotage in 1836 to ensure that recent factory legislation enacted by Parliament in 1833 was properly enforced. Nor is it to deny that he threatened direct action in 1837 in his condemnation of the New Poor Law or that his passionate verbal criticisms of the Poor Law Amendment Act's unsuitability for the manufacturing districts of the West Riding contributed to the intensity of the violent resistance to the implementation of the new legislation. But in neither of these instances was revolutionary posturing the outcome of his protestations, and closer examination of both of these episodes underlines their expression of rhetorical threat rather than revolutionary intention. 'The Law or the Needle' controversy arose out of his concerns at Blackburn where magistrates had contemptuously dismissed complaints that the 1833 Factory Act, which banned the employment of children under nine from working in all textile factories and limited the hours of employment of other juvenile workers, was being infringed, referring to the Act disparagingly as 'Oastler's Law'. Recognising some of these

---

15. Driver, *Tory Radical*, p. 4.

magistrates in the audience at a public meeting he was addressing in
Blackburn, Oastler declared:

> If the law of the land, intended to protect the lives of the factory
> children, is to be disregarded, and there is to be no power to enforce
> it, it becomes my duty, as the guardian of the factory children, to
> enquire whether, in the eye of the law of England, their lives or your
> spindles are most entitled to the law's protection.

Turning to the general body of his audience, Oastler then remarked:

> If, after this, your magistrates should refuse to listen to your
> complaints under the Factory Act, and again refer you to me, bring
> with you your children, and tell them to ask their grandmothers for a
> few of their old knitting-needles, which I will instruct them how to
> apply to the spindles in a way which will teach these law-defying mill
> owner magistrates to have respect even to 'Oastler's law', as they have
> wrongly designated the factory law.[16]

When Oastler reiterated his advice in a pamphlet, *The Law or the
Needle*, his comments created a furore which led to protests from many
of the mill-owner supporters of factory reform and a public disavowal
of his remarks by some of his closest associates in the campaign for
factory reform, notably Parson Bull, John Wood and Lord Shaftesbury
and also his employer, Thomas Thornhill. His advice was undoubtedly
ill-considered and proved a temporary setback to his campaign, but if
this was inflammatory revolutionary incitement, then it is surely the
first occasion in which an alliance of grandmothers and children was
called upon to form a revolutionary vanguard by utilising domestic
utensils, notably discarded knitting needles, as their weaponry. Not
surprisingly, there is no evidence of his advice ever having been
implemented. Moreover his defence of his remarks in a letter to the
editor of the *Manchester Guardian*, emphasized that the real targets of
his opprobrium were the mill owners who chose not to respect the law
and the magistrates who declined to enforce it and not the government

---

16. Cole, *Chartist Portraits*, pp. 99–100.

whose 'great Whig leader, Lord Althorp' had introduced the ameliorative legislation and so the real question for Oastler was whether 'the law and the government and myself be overcome by the mill owners and the magistrates' or whether 'the latter yield to the former'.[17]

In relation to the second episode in which Oastler's rhetoric provided ammunition for his political opponents, in a heart-felt pamphlet published in 1837 in opposition to the New Poor Law, he declared unequivocally:

> I tell you deliberately, if I have the misfortune to be reduced to poverty, that that man who dares to tear from me the wife whom God has joined to me, shall, if I have it in my power, receive his death at my hands! If I am ever confined in one of those hellish Poor Law Bastilles, and my wife be torn from me, because I am poor, I will, if it be possible, burn the whole pile down to the ground. This will I do, if my case shall be thus tried, if I have the power; and every man who loves his wife, and who is unstained by crime, will, if he can, do the same.[18]

This enabled the liberal press at the May 1837 Huddersfield election to dub Oastler 'an incendiary, an assassin and a madman'. It also prompted them to remind voters of his calls for industrial sabotage in *The Law or the Needle*, provoking Oastler to denounce 'the bloody, base and brutal Whigs', who had transported the Dorchester labourers, frustrated further factory reform and introduced the iniquitous Poor Law Amendment Act.[19] However, this exchange of comments is entirely explicable in terms of the vituperative nature of this early post-Reform election campaign following Oastler's intrusive entry into a contest for a seat regarded as effectively a pocket borough of the dominant local Whig landowners, the Ramsdens.[20]

---

17. R. Oastler, letter to the editor of the *Manchester Guardian*, Fixby Hall, 26 September 1836, cited in Ayerst, *Guardian Omnibus*, pp. 66–68.

18. R. Oastler, 'Damnation! Eternal Damnation to the Fiend-begotten Coarser-Food New Poor Law' in G.D.H. Cole and A.W. Filson, *British Working Class Movements*, (London: Macmillan, 1965), pp. 334–35.

19. Driver, *Tory Radical*, p. 348.

20. A. Porritt, 'Richard Oastler', *T(ransactions) (of the) H(alifax) A(ntiquarian) S(ociety)*, 1965, p. 34.

If both episodes reveal the use of intemperate language and the counselling of illegal behaviour on Oastler's part, in neither of these instances was the rhetoric he utilised ever translated into reality. Felix Driver has cautioned that Oastler's role in the Huddersfield anti-Poor Law agitation should not be exaggerated and that repeatedly during 1837, despite his commanding leadership of the factory movement in Yorkshire, his ability to control the protesters 'was shown to be distinctly fragile'.[21] Moreover, in a speech in August 1838 the leader of the emergent Chartist movement, Feargus O'Connor, condemned 'the vile and false press of London' for stigmatising such men as Stephens and Oastler as 'agitators and madmen, men who sought to lead the country into ruin and bloodshed' and for branding them as 'incendiaries', maintaining that 'he had never heard them recommend the use of arms in the course of his life', while in 1848, an informed observer commented that 'in all his agitations and torchlight meetings, Oastler faithfully … kept his followers from outrage'.[22] Indeed, even in the heady atmosphere of 1842, a year of acute depression, widespread unemployment and wage reductions, Oastler cautioned his northern supporters not to be provoked into violence by the Anti-Corn Law League, warning 'if the Leaguers urge you to violence, leave that work to them!'[23] Furthermore, Oastler was later commended for his promotion of class conciliation rather than his class division by John Walter (1776–1847), chief proprietor and joint editor of *The Times*, albeit a leading opponent of the New Poor Law, who, addressing the citizens of Huddersfield in 1843 declared:

> Such a man as Oastler had the strongest claims upon every friend of humanity, – upon every parent, – and not only upon parents, but upon all classes of society.[24]

Oastler was also featured in the *Illustrated London News* gallery of national portraits in 1844 and was accorded not only an announcement

---

21. F. Driver, *Power and Pauperism. The workhouse system, 1834–1884*, (Cambridge: Cambridge University Press, 1993), pp. 125–26.
22. *Birmingham Journal*, 11 August 1838.
23. J.T. Ward, *Chartism*, (London: Batsford, 1973), p. 162.
24. Carpenter, ed., *Richard Oastler: King of Factory Children*, p. 4.

of his death but also a full obituary in the *Gentleman's Magazine* not to mention a public statue unveiled by an earl in the centre of Bradford, one of the fastest growing towns of northern England in the nineteenth century – all unlikely tributes to a quasi-revolutionary demagogue. He was also featured in an official publication commemorating the opening of the new Leeds infirmary in 1868, with the only extant photograph of him ever to have been published, as one of the sixteen 'eminent' figures in the history of his native Leeds. Moreover, over a century later, on 1 January 1972 the Richard Oastler School, was opened by the City of Leeds Education Committee in Leeds for children with special educational needs.[25]

How then do we assess the historical significance of Richard Oastler? Oastler's anti-slavery commitment dated back to his youth when he had engaged actively in the campaign against the transatlantic slave trade, writing his first letters to the press and making his earliest speeches on the issue, thereby gaining experience of a highly organised and remarkably successful campaign which succeeded in obtaining parliamentary legislation for the abolition of the slave trade in March 1807.[26] Cecil Driver has suggested that Oastler's abhorrence of slavery derived from his Methodist upbringing and his Moravian education at Fulneck from 1798–1806, which also produced another passionate opponent of slavery in the radical hymn-writer, James Montgomery (1771–1854).[27] During his abortive apprenticeship to an architect in Wakefield Richard Oastler witnessed at first hand the 1807 Yorkshire election, one of the most bitterly contested elections in the history of the West Riding, which provided him not only with 'a training in public affairs and the skills of the platform, but also with 'an apprenticeship in the art of agitation'.[28] He threw himself 'heart and soul' into William Wilberforce's campaign, working zealously on behalf of the great leader of the movement for the abolition of the slave trade,

---

25. *Gentleman's Magazine*, 1861, pp. 449, 689; *Illustrated London News*, 9 March, 1844; Anon, *Memoirs of Eminent Men of Leeds*, D. Green and Sons, Leeds, 1869, frontispiece and title page; *Richard Oastler School*, Leeds Education Department Festival of Education, 1987.
26. Porritt, *THAS*, 1965, p. 24.
27. Driver, *Tory Radical*, pp. 15–16. I am grateful to Ruth Strong for discussing with me Oastler's Fulneck connections.
28. Driver, *Tory Radical*, p. 20.

speaking at many meetings and on one memorable occasion even deflecting a brickbat intended for Wilberforce on the hustings, an incident which he often reminded his audiences of in the years ahead.[29] Later, in the 1820s, he joined the drive for slave emancipation in the West Indies, when Wilberforce resumed his campaign. Indeed, after he became involved in the campaign for the Ten Hours Bill, Oastler did not desert the West Indian slave and was outspoken in his condemnation of the Whig government's decision to grant twenty million pounds compensation to the former slave owners.[30] 'Willingly lend your assistance to emancipate black slaves' he constantly urged 'but imperatively require from those ... who solicit your aid in favour of the blacks, that they shall prove their sincerity, and that they really do hate slavery, by encouraging and signing petitions in favour of "ten hours a day" as the limit of your children's work'.[31] Oastler's passionate support for the campaign to end colonial slavery was a product of his Evangelicalism, his humanitarianism and his sense of social justice and these same impulses propelled him into the related campaign to end factory slavery in Yorkshire.

Richard Oastler, however, was neither the founder of the factory movement nor even the first to employ the slavery metaphor to the wage labourers of the industrial north. Lancashire manufacturers like the first Sir Robert Peel and operatives like John Doherty had been active since the turn of the century in campaigning for factory reform and as G.D.H. Cole observed in 1941 the slavery metaphor 'had, of course, occurred to many other people long before' and had been for many years, for example, one of William Cobbett's favourite themes'.[32] Indeed, William Cobbett wrote in his *Political Register* in November 1824:

> It is to be a despicable hypocrite to pretend to believe that the slaves in the West Indies are not better off than the slaves in these manufactories ... Some of these lords of the loom have in their employ

---

29. Driver, *Tory Radical*, p. 19.
30. Betty Fladeland, '"Our Cause being One and the Same" Abolitionists and Chartism' in J. Walvin, ed., *Slavery and British Society, 1776–1846*, 1982, p. 78.
31. Ibid., pp. 75–76.
32. J.T. Ward, 'The Factory Movement' in *Popular Movements c1830–1850*, ed. by J.T. Ward, (London: Macmillan, 1970), p. 65; Cole, *Chartist Portraits*, p. 84.

thousands of miserable creatures. In the cotton-spinning work, these creatures are kept, fourteen hours in each day, locked up, summer and winter, in a heat from eighty to eighty-four degrees. The rules, which they are subjected to, are such as no Negroes were ever subjected to.[33]

But Oastler was incontrovertibly the author of the phrase 'Yorkshire Slavery' which was to have such powerful resonance in the county of his birth in the 1830s, reinvigorating the campaign to regulate child labour, in his celebrated 1830 letter to the *Leeds Mercury*, which exposed the plight of thousands of children who worked a thirteen hour day 'in those magazines of infantile slavery – the worsted mills in the town and neighbourhood of Bradford'. His subsequent publications included a devastating tract entitled *Slavery in Yorkshire. Monstrous Barbarity !!!*, published in Bradford in 1835 with a bitter attack on the Leeds Liberal MP and editor, Edward Baines, who had published the original letter. Theodore Koditschek has argued that the reaction of liberal manufacturers and nonconformists to Oastler's letter reinforced his increasingly right-wing political stance.[34]

Oastler claimed to have had no inkling of the problems of child labour in local factories until his meeting in September 1830 with John Wood a successful worsted spinner and progressive manufacturer who lived at Horton Hall, near Bradford.[35] However, it is hard to imagine that the tragic fire early one February morning in 1818, which started on the ground floor of Thomas Atkinson's cotton mill at Colne Bridge not far from Fixby, managed to escape the attention of such a well-informed proponent of the factory regulation, since it had accelerated Sir Robert Peel the elder's introduction of a Factory Act in 1819 prohibiting the employment of children under nine in cotton factories. It claimed the lives of seventeen young girls, was widely reported and even discussed on the floor of the House of Commons and a monument

---

33. J.A. Hargreaves, *Factory Kings and Slaves: South Pennine Social Movements, 1780–1840*, (Hebden Bridge: Pennine Heritage, 1982), p. 2; see also J.A. Hargreaves, ' "A Metropolis of Discontent": Popular Protest in Huddersfield c. 1780–c.1850' in *Huddersfield. A most handsome town*, ed. by E. A. Hilary Haigh (Huddersfield: Kirklees Cultural Services, 1992), especially pp. 209–14.
34. Hargreaves, *Factory Kings*, p. 10; Koditschek, *Class Formation*, p. 416.
35. Porritt, *THAS*, 1965, p. 27.

to the fire was erected near the young girls' graves at Kirkheaton Parish Church around the time Oastler arrived at Fixby in 1821.[36] However, when John Wood, the Evangelical Bradford worsted manufacturer asked Oastler at the famous meeting in September 1830 if when he pleaded for the far off slave-trade it had never occurred to him that similar evils existed on his own doorstep, Oastler's awakening to the problem of child labour was likened to the dramatic conversion of Saul of Tarsus to Christianity on the road to Damascus.

Oastler's letter to the *Leeds Mercury* compared the condition of women and children in Bradford mills with that of slaves in the colonial plantations and described the system as 'horrid and abominable'. With a stroke of the pen he had raised the profile of the languishing factory movement in Yorkshire by linking it with the most enduring and successful extra-parliamentary protest movement in Yorkshire to date. He had succeeded in making Yorkshire factory conditions a central issue of debate in 1830 when other major issues were already dominating the political agenda, notably parliamentary reform and the campaign for the abolition of colonial slavery. Its impact was nothing less than sensational and proved the spur to an official enquiry and the legislative intervention of the Whig government. A public meeting of radicals in Huddersfield as early as 1830 adopted a resolution thanking Oastler for exposing the conduct 'of those pretended philanthropists and canting hypocrites who travel to the West Indies in search of slavery, forgetting that there is a more abominable and degrading system of slavery at home'.[37] In diverting attention exclusively from colonial slavery Oastler had challenged the dominance of Wilberforce and the influential Clapham Sect and scored an unprecedented publicity coup for the factory movement.

G.D.H. Cole's observation that 'the pen was not Oastler's natural weapon' and that he was more 'a speaker and organiser of immense energy, and not by instinct a writer' may have had some truth in relation to his later writing, notably his editing from prison of his weekly *Fleet Papers* in the early 1840s, and his magazine *The Home* in the 1850s, but it seriously underestimates the impact of his journalistic

---

36. Hargreaves, *Factory Kings*, p. 10.
37. G.B.A.M. Finlayson, *England in the 1830s*, (London: Arnold, 1969), p. 38.

and propagandist skills in the emergence of the factory movement in the 1830s, when Fixby Hall became the springboard and then the control centre of operations for conducting the campaign for factory regulation.[38] His celebrated letter on 'Slavery in Yorkshire', arguably the most influential letter ever written to a Yorkshire newspaper, was but the first of a plethora of letters, articles, broadsheets, pamphlets and tracts arguing the case for reform. Francis Place, a contemporary radical observer, pronounced Oastler 'a ready writer and fluent speaker of undoubted courage . . . writing and speaking incessantly, making an abundance of friends amongst the poor and a like abundance of enemies amongst those who employed them' and the historian Theodore Koditschek commended his considerable polemical talents in unmasking the 'canting oppressing capitalists' of Bradford 'who would not extend the freedom they demanded for the black West Indians to the English children who worked in their mills'.[39]

Indeed, Oastler's Sheridanesque polemical verbosity had a field day in his *A Letter to those Sleek, Pious, Holy, and Devout Dissenters Messrs. Get-all, Keep-all, Grasp-all, Scrape-all, Whip-all, Gull-all, Cheat-all, Cant-all, Work-all. Sneak-all, Lie-well, Swear-well, and Co., the Shareholders in the Bradford Observer, in Answer to their attack on Richard Oastler, in that Paper of July 17, 1834*, published in Bradford in 1834. In the same year, he offered in a more economically titled tract: *A Well Seasoned Christmas-Pie for 'The Great Liar of the North', Prepared, Cooked, Baked and Presented by Richard Oastler*. Later a memorable pamphlet denouncing the New Poor Law was entitled: *Damnation! Eternal Damnation to the Fiend-begotten, Coarser-food New Poor Law*, 1837, titles which have appeared over-lurid to some later readers but which resonated with the language of contemporary radical indignation and prophetic revivalism and connected effectively with Oastler's growing constituency of support.[40]

The historian D.G. Wright emphasized the considerable impact of his histrionic oratory as well as his journalistic skills and reports of some meetings recorded him bursting into tears as he described particularly horrific accidents in mills involving children.[41] Asa Briggs

---

38. Cole, *Chartist Portraits*, p. 102.
39. Driver, *Tory Radical*, p. 542; Koditschek, *Class Formation*, p. 416.
40. Driver, *Tory Radical*, pp. 564–65.
41. D.G. Wright, *Popular Radicalism*, (London: Macmillan, 1988), p. 102.

pronounced him a brilliant speaker, with his square jaw, set chin and 'scornful curl' of the lips as valuable assets as his rich voice, who knew his audience and could identify himself with it.[42] He was a powerfully built man over six feet in height with an impressive presence, which contemporaries readily recognised. T.A. Trollope and his mother Fanny, touring the north to research material for Fanny Trollope's industrial novel *Michael Armstrong* found Oastler 'the most remarkable individual with whom this journey brought us into contact'. They witnessed the dramatic power of his oratory in halls 'filled to suffocation, besieged by crowds around the door'. Thomas Trollope described Oastler's voice as 'stentorian in its power and yet flexible, with a flow of language rapid and abundant'.[43] The *Illustrated London News* commented on 'his vigorous oratory' and 'the extraordinary control which he exercises over the minds of great assemblages of working men, the secret of which', it maintained, was 'his long-tried honesty, and his disposition and ability to promote the real interests of the poor and the oppressed'.[44] Moreover, George Searle Phillips, Secretary of the Huddersfield Mechanics Institution, offering a critical appraisal of Oastler in 1848, felt bound to conclude that 'no one man ever had more power over a multitude' than Richard Oastler.[45]

His ability to control an angry crowd in this early phase of the factory movement is best illustrated by an incident during the great demonstration in support of factory reform held at York in April 1832, when working people from all parts of the West Riding clothing districts converged on the city. Oastler had organised the 'pilgrimage' and personally led a contingent from Brighouse and Rastrick, carrying the banner which now hangs in the Tolson Museum and acquiring sorely blistered feet on the long and arduous march. When angry resentment arose as the thousands of wet and hungry marchers reached the Knavesmire outside York to discover that the bread and cheese rations, which had been ordered for the crowd to consume with the ale had not arrived, creating a situation likely to result in rioting, Oastler, who had gone ahead into the city to meet with the organisers

---

42. Briggs in Young, *Bed Post*, pp. 26–27.
43. Porritt, *THAS, 1965*, pp. 31–32.
44. *Illustrated London News*, 9 March 1844.
45. G.S. Phillips, *Walks around Huddersfield*, (Huddersfield: Bond and Hardy, 1848), p. 8.

was informed of the problem. He at once mounted a horse and arrived at the Knavesmire where he found Lawrence Pitkethly, one of the Huddersfield operative leaders trying to appease the angry crowd. When Pitkethly saw Oastler he shouted: 'The King! The King!' and instantly the mood of the assembly calmed. The protesters cleared a passage for Oastler to the racecourse's grandstand and cheered him wildly as he humoured the huge gathering back into orderliness. An eye-witness commented: 'It was a critical moment. But for the good Providence and the magnanimity of "King Richard" there might have been havoc'.[46]

The soubriquet of 'Factory King' originally employed in derision by Oastler's opponents had been appropriated by Oastler and his supporters and became the name by which he is known to posterity. In his article marking the centenary of Oastler's death, Asa Briggs wrote: 'Not every commoner earns the title of king. Richard Oastler ... was the uncrowned king of the factory children of the West Riding'. His name became known and respected on both sides of the Pennines and articles appeared about him not only in London, but also across Europe.[47] By 1861, Oastler was even signing some of his correspondence 'Richard Rex'.[48] The relationship of mutual respect in which he was held by Pitkethly and the Huddersfield working men had developed after the famous Fixby Hall Compact, an alliance between Oastler and the leading members of the Huddersfield short-time committee, sealed June 1831, in the struggle for the regulation of factory labour. Felix Driver reviewing the concept of Tory radicalism in 1991 concluded that the co-operation of leading Huddersfield radicals such as Lawrence Pitkethly and William Stocks with Oastler was 'for the most part tactically rather than ideologically motivated', whilst Stewart A. Weaver has argued that the phenomenon was consequently illusory, concluding that 'as a determining popular influence Tory Radicalism scarcely

---

46. Porritt, *THAS*, 1965, pp. 30–31.
47. Briggs in Young, *Bed Post*, pp. 24–27.
48. Letter to Squire Auty 4 June 1861, quoted in 'Sketch of the Life of the late Richard Oastler with an account of his funeral obsequies', Bradford, 1861 in Carpenter, ed., *Oastler: King of Factory Children; Six Pamphlets, 1835–61*, (New York: 1972), p. 5.

existed'.[49] However, Theodore Koditschek has pronounced Oastler 'the most important of the new Tory Radicals' on account of his extraordinary success in organising perhaps the last major 'extra-parliamentary movement ... by conservative leaders along traditional lines' (until the pro-hunting demonstrations of the Blair decade), while other historians, notably Patrick Joyce, have detected an enduring legacy of Tory Radicalism in both industrial Yorkshire and Lancashire.[50]

Oastler viewed the campaign against the New Poor Law as an extension of the campaign against 'Yorkshire Slavery'. Some years later, justifying his stand, he argued that the two issues were 'inseparably connected' commenting that:

> The New Poor Law was intended to be used to perpetuate slavery in factories. The Ten Hours Bill was intended to destroy that slavery. It was in evidence that the New Poor Law was intended to decrease the wages of the factory operatives. The Ten Hours Bill was, as I always believed and maintained, calculated to increase those wages.[51]

Whereas, the factory movement aimed to eliminate the 'monstrous barbarity' of child labour, the resistance to the New Poor Law was designed to protect the elderly from the workhouse after a lifetime of toil. 'I will not submit to it' Richard Oastler bluntly declared, justifying his opposition as he had justified his opposition to child labour, with an appeal to conservative principles:

> It is an act of TREASON against the constitution, against Christianity, against the State, and against the King as well as the Poor.[52]

49. Felix Driver, 'Tory Radicalism? Ideology, strategy and locality in popular politics during the eighteen-thirties', *Northern History*, XXVII, 1991, pp. 120–138; A.S. Weaver, *John Fielden and the Politics of Popular Radicalism, 1832–1847*, (Oxford: Clarendon Press, 1987), p. 296.
50. T. Koditschek, *Class Formation*, pp. 415, 442; P. Joyce, Work, Society and Politics: the Culture of the Factory in Later Victorian England, (Brighton: Harvester, 1980), pp. 325–26.
51. Driver, *Tory Radical*, pp. 334–35.
52. Koditschek, *Class Formation*, p. 442.

John Knott, a historian of the anti-Poor Law Movement, has demonstrated how Huddersfield provided 'the model for resistance to the New Poor Law'.[53]

However, Oastler's involvement with radicals in open defiance of the law put him at odds with his employer Thomas Thornhill after the Fixby township refused to elect a Poor Law Guardian in 1837 and alienated him from his remaining supporters in the conservative camp, including Parson Bull, and as a result of his dismissal as Thornhill's steward and his subsequent imprisonment for debt he was effectively removed him from the Yorkshire resistance movement in 1838.[54]

In rousing the North in the cause of the factory movement and the anti-Poor Law Movement Richard Oastler paved the way for Feargus O'Connor's campaign for the People's Charter, although Oastler himself did not support universal suffrage and never officially joined the Chartists, he did not oppose industrialism itself as did O'Connor.[55] At least one later historian, W.H. Chaloner, approved of Oastler's controversial inclusion in G.D.H. Cole's *Chartist Portraits* since like John Fielden and Joseph Rayner Stephens whom Cole also included, all three radical leaders 'used Chartist platforms to further the causes in which they were primarily interested – factory reform and agitation against the New Poor Law'.[56] Moreover, the latest historian of Chartism, Malcolm Chase, has described Oastler as 'one of Chartism's inspirational figures' and commented particularly on Feargus O'Connor's affinity with him on the eve of the launch of the new movement, and noted that at least one infant in a Chartist household had her birth registered in 1842 under the name of Fanny Amelia Lucy Ann Rebecca Frost O'Connor McDouall Leach Holberry Duffy Oastler Hill Boden![57]

---

53. J. Knott, *Popular Opposition to the New Poor Law*, (London: Croom Helm, 1986), p. 183.

54. Ibid., p. 441; Driver, *Tory Radical*, pp. 342–43.

55. Cole, *Chartist Portraits*, pp. 10–11, 26, 80–105; Fladeland, in Walvin, ed., *Slavery and British Society*, p. 76.

56. W. H. Chaloner, introduction to Mark Hovell, *The Chartist Movement*, (Manchester: Manchester University Press, 1966) edition, pp. vi–vii.

57. M. Chase, *Chartism*, (Manchester: Manchester University Press, 2007), pp. 15–17, 50 and 267.

7:3 Portrait of Richard Oastler, frontispiece, *Sketch of the Life and Opinions of Richard Oastler* published by Joshua Hobson in 1838 (University of Huddersfield Special Collections).

Thousands of poor people attended Richard Oastler's funeral service conducted by his old friend Parson Bull at St Stephen's Church, Kirkstall, Leeds in 1861, including representatives of the factory movement's Short Time Committees from all over the north and some of the pall bearers had signed the Fixby Hall Compact three decades earlier.

Eight years later in 1869, when Lord Shaftesbury unveiled a bronze statue by J. Birnie Phillips of Oastler in Bradford, 100,000 people were said to have been present. 'Their enthusiasm', wrote Shaftesbury, 'knew no bounds' and medals were struck commemorating the event.[58]

---

58. Porritt, *THAS*, 1965, p. 42; E. Hodder, *The Life and Work of the Seventh Earl of Shaftesbury*, (Cassell, 1892), p. 636.

DEATH
OF
RICHARD OASTLER.

WITH unaffected sorrow—a sorrow in which thousands in this district will participate—we have to announce the demise of RICHARD OASTLER—a man who, in his day and generation, has "done the State some service;" one who was, in his public and private dealings, Generosity and Disinterestedness personified ; one who for a lengthened period dwelt in this locality, and was regarded with no common feelings of respect as a neighbour and a friend ; one who, now that his earthly race is run, goes down to the grave full of years and honour, deeply regretted by all who knew him personally—and their name was legion—carrying with him the sympathy and love of the entire community of Factory Workers for his heroic devotion to their cause, and for the material, social, and educational benefits which his herculean and disinterested labours contributed principally to secure for them and their posterity.

The mournful event we have to record occurred at High Harrogate on Thursday morning last. For now some time, Mr. OASTLER's home has been at Conway, in North Wales, where, blessed with the society and the devoted attention of his adopted daughter, Miss MARIA TATHAM, he enjoyed all the happiness which this life could give, and found that rest from labour—mental and physical—which was necessary to a frame shattered and almost worn out by previous over-exertion. About Christmas last, during the very severe cold of that season, he became subject to a painful illness—obstruction to the action of the bowels—of a most dangerous nature. Under the assiduous attention and medical aid of his brother-in-law, Mr. THOS. ROBT. TATHAM, surgeon of this town, and the careful nursing of his household, the extreme danger that then threatened was happily averted for the time, and the patient partially recovered. But never since that period has he passed a month without a return of the attack, more or less severe, until at last nature has sunk beneath them.

It was Mr. OASTLER's wont, when well enough to travel, to pay a visit annually to his Yorkshire friends. At the time he was seized with his last illness he was in the act of performing this, to him, pleasurable duty. He had been to Neesham Abbey, near Darlington, on a visit to a nephew and neice, and was on his way from that place to Bowling Hall, the seat of his firm

he was the indomitable leader and the faithful guide, that were ever inscribed on the Statute-book of any nation. His work and fame are thus a portion of the History of the country. A good part of that work was performed amongst us—*here*, in Huddersfield. He then lived in our neighbourhood, mixed in Huddersfield society, took part in our affairs, used our press, and adorned our platform. It was *here* that many of his soul-stirring addresses—oratorical efforts that roused the nation almost to madness—were delivered. It was *here*, too, that twice within four months, he was a candidate for a seat in Parliament, with the enthusiastic approval and support of the great bulk of the labouring community, and with the votes of nearly one-half of the constituency recorded in his favour. Huddersfield was, therefore, the arena in which most of the gigantic labours of Mr. OASTLER were performed. Nearly a quarter of a century, however, has now passed since he was resident amongst us. In that period a new generation has sprung up, which knows little of the terrible struggle which had to be undertaken, and the almost superhuman efforts that had to be made, ere the measures of which *they* are enjoying the blessing could be secured. That *they* may know something of the man who disinterestedly and heroically fought for them, and conquered for them ; and that others who took part in the agitations with which Mr. OASTLER was connected may recall to mind some slight reminiscences of the stirring times they passed through, we present the following, abridged from a publication of our own many, many years ago. It is from the pen of one who well knew the facts he recorded—one who also took a foremost part in the struggles he notices : —

MEMOIR
OF THE
"FACTORY KING."

"Son of light
In a dark age, against example, good,
Against allurement, custom and a world
Offended : fearless of reproach and scorn,
Or violence, he of their wicked ways
Shall them admonish ; and before them set
The paths of righteousness, how much more safe
And full of peace."

RICHARD OASTLER was born in St. Peter's-square, Leeds, on the 20th of December, 1789. He was the son—the youngest of eight children—of ROBERT OASTLER, whose father lived on the paternal estate at Moorhouse, Kirkby Wiske, in the North Riding of Yorkshire. His forefathers and the forefathers of the present Earl of HAREWOOD were substantial yeomen, occupying neighbouring farms, following the same pursuits, and connected together by business and friendship for many generations.

7:4 Oastler's obituary in the *Huddersfield Chronicle*, 21 August 1861 (Huddersfield Local Studies Library).

Subscriptions from a public appeal across the textile districts of
Yorkshire and Lancashire had realised the considerable sum of £1,000
and voting by the subscribers for the location of the monument is
revealing. A mere five votes were cast for Halifax, in whose parish
Oastler had resided as steward of Fixby Hall and where he had cut his
political teeth in the anti-tithe protest of 1827; eighty-eight votes were

7:5 Statue of Richard
Oastler in Northgate,
Bradford (University
of Huddersfield).

cast for Huddersfield, where he had forged his extraordinary alliance with the Short Time Committee, campaigned against the union workhouse, contested two elections and received a Mandela-like reception on his release from prison in 1844; 119 votes were cast for Leeds, where he had been born in 1789 and buried in 1861 and a massive 1,472 votes for Bradford where he had experienced the Damascene conversion which launched his campaign against 'Yorkshire Slavery' in 1830 and Bradford Corporation offered a site for the statue opposite the Midland hotel in Forster Square. Huddersfield workpeople, however, provided their own monument to 'The Factory King' at Christ Church, Woodhouse, Huddersfield, where he had worshipped when residing at Fixby Hall from 1820–1838.

Memorials to Oastler were also unveiled at St Stephen's, Kirkstall in 1864, at St Mark the Evangelist's Church, Longwood and in Leeds Parish Church in 1925.[59] Most recently, in the ancient parish of Halifax a public house in a former Wesleyan chapel was named in his honour.

All three major agitations in which Richard Oastler engaged brought significant results during his own lifetime: the slave trade was abolished in 1807; slaves in the British Empire were emancipated in 1833 after serving a seven-year apprenticeship; factory regulation and machinery for its enforcement were introduced into all textile industries between 1833 and 1853 and the operation of the New Poor Law was modified in the north of England through the continuation of outdoor relief after 1837.[60] This was a remarkable achievement for extra-parliamentary protest in an age when the beneficiaries of these ameliorative policies remained largely un-enfranchised in an era which saw the rejection of three well-supported Chartist petitions.

Writing in the year of the centenary of Richard Oastler's death in 1961, Asa Briggs observed that 'Oastler is a largely forgotten figure today … He is forgotten not only because the details of his life are unfamiliar but because the extraordinary circumstances which drew him into prominence seem complex and remote'. This observation would have been equally true in the year of the bi-centenary of the

---

59. Porritt, *THAS*, 1965, pp. 42–44.
60. P. Horn, *Children's Work and Welfare, 1780–1880s*, Economic History Society, (Basingstoke: Macmillan, 1994), pp. 55, 59–62.

7:6 Memorial to Richard Oastler, outside the entrance of Christ Church, Woodhouse, the church attended by the Oastler family during their period of residence at nearby Fixby Hall (Kirklees Image Archive k025058).

abolition of the slave trade in 2007, notwithstanding a total of nearly 20,000 Oastler-related websites by that year. He deserves to be even better known. Theodore Koditschek has argued that while Oastler may have failed to inaugurate a new urban industrial paternalist age in the early nineteenth century, he nevertheless 'laid some of the foundations of the future welfare state'.[61] Oastler has also been claimed as an influential figure in the evolution of one-nation Conservatism and his concept of the social state finds resonances in Tory social philosophy from Benjamin Disrael's 'Two Nations' of the mid-nineteenth century

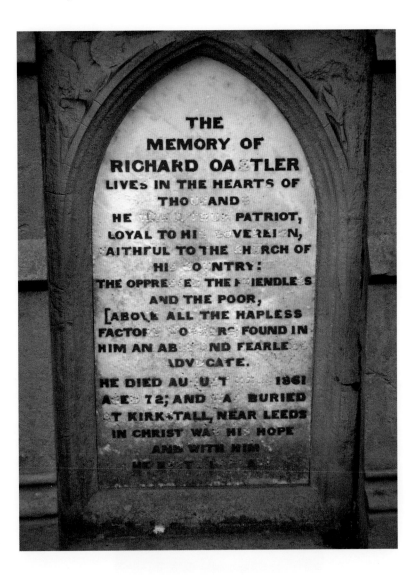

7:7 Close up of the inscription on the Oastler Memorial at Christ Church Woodhouse (Photograph: E.A.H.Haigh).

THE
MEMORY OF
RICHARD OASTLER
LIVES IN THE HEARTS OF
THOUSANDS
HE ... PATRIOT,
LOYAL TO HIS SOVEREIGN,
FAITHFUL TO THE CHURCH OF
HIS COUNTRY:
THE OPPRESSED THE FRIENDLESS
AND THE POOR,
[ABOVE ALL THE HAPLESS
FACTORY ... R FOUND IN
HIM AN AB ... ND FEARLESS
ADVOCATE.
HE DIED AUGUST ... 1861
AGE 72; AND A BURIED
AT KIRKSTALL, NEAR LEEDS
IN CHRIST WAS HIS HOPE
AND WITH HIM
...

61. Koditschek, *Class Formation*, p. 435.

to David Cameron's 'Broken Society' of the early twenty-first century. Some of the issues Oastler raised, health and safety at work, fair trade, the work-life balance, the employment of children as child soldiers, child prostitutes and in sweat shops in various parts of the world have a continuing relevance today. Campaigners estimate, for example, that some 700 people close to where Oastler operated his campaign against Yorkshire Slavery have died of asbestos-related diseases linked to Acre Mill, Hebden Bridge since 1939, making it not only Britain's worst industrial disaster with victims surpassing the grim total of 439 miners

7:8 Stained glass window depicting Richard Oastler with two factory children, in in the Church of St Mark the Evangelist, Longwood, Huddersfield (Photograph: Peter Pearson).

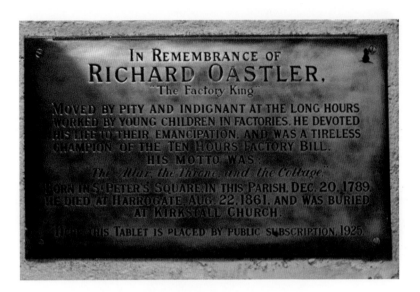

In Remembrance of
RICHARD OASTLER,
"The Factory King"

MOVED BY PITY AND INDIGNANT AT THE LONG HOURS
WORKED BY YOUNG CHILDREN IN FACTORIES. HE DEVOTED
HIS LIFE TO THEIR EMANCIPATION. AND WAS A TIRELESS
CHAMPION OF THE TEN HOURS FACTORY BILL.
HIS MOTTO WAS
"The Altar, the Throne and the Cottage."
BORN IN S! PETER'S SQUARE IN THIS PARISH. DEC. 20, 1789,
HE DIED AT HARROGATE AUG. 22, 1861, AND WAS BURIED
AT KIRKSTALL CHURCH.

THIS TABLET IS PLACED BY PUBLIC SUBSCRIPTION. 1925.

7:9 Memorial plaque in Leeds Parish Church (Photograph: Jonathan Emery).

killed in the Senghenydd mining disaster in Wales in 1913, but an ongoing tragedy.[62]

Instinctively conservative, Oastler was consumed with a humanitarian passion for social and economic change, which was rooted, like that of William Wilberforce, in his Evangelicalism. In identifying slavery with the factories of the county of his birth he was identifying it also with the county which had spearheaded the campaign to abolish slavery under the leadership of Wilberforce and he succeeded in raising the profile of the factory movement in the way that his fellow Yorkshireman, Wilberforce, raised the profile of anti-slavery movement. Both recognised the value of propaganda: printed broadsheets, sermons, tracts, posters and letters to the press. Oastler was arguably more in tune with the hopes and aspirations of working men than Wilberforce. Occasionally Richard Oastler's language was intemperate in marked contrast to that employed by Wilberforce. It was a product of the passion he felt for the causes he endorsed: the injustice of colonial slavery, the extortionate exaction of tithes, the oppression of child labour in factories and the bureaucratic and inhumanitarian operation of the New Poor Law. Occasionally Oastler appeared to advocate criminality and violence. However Weaver's

---

62. *Telegraph Magazine*, 6 October 2007.

7:10 A rare photograph of Richard Oastler in his later years which appeared in C.S. Spence's *Memoirs of Eminent Men of Leeds*, which was published to mark the opening of the new infirmary in Leeds on 19 May 1868 by H.R.H. Edward Prince of Wales (British Library).

suggestion that in the 1830s Oastler was 'treading on the edge of revolution' ultimately conveys a misleading impression. Oastler was no more a Danton-clone than was Feargus O'Connor, 'the lion of freedom' whose rhetorical bark proved louder than his revolutionary bite.

7:11 Signature of Richard Oastler from a letter written during his period as Steward to the Thornhill Estate (Thornhill Estate Archive).

Notes on contributors

JOHN A. HARGREAVES was born and educated in Burnley and later at the University of Southampton, where he obtained a BA honours degree in history and a post-graduate certificate in education. He has taught history on both sides of the Pennines, including twenty years at King James's School Almondbury and retired as Head of Humanities at Batley Girls' High School in 2006. He obtained his MA with distinction and his PhD following part-time study at the University of Huddersfield, where he is currently Visiting Research Fellow in History. He is also an Associate of the Leeds Centre for Victorian Studies and has taught in both higher and adult education throughout West Yorkshire. He is author of a history of Halifax (1999; second edition 2003) and is currently writing a history of Huddersfield. He has contributed numerous articles to the *Oxford Dictionary of National Biography* and is a Fellow of the Royal Historical Society, a Fellow of the Historical Association and a Fellow of the Society of Antiquaries. He is General Secretary of the Wesley Historical Society and Vice-President of the World Methodist Historical Society and has received three Yorkshire History Prize Awards and a Personal Achievement Award from the British Association of Local History in 2009.

E.A. HILARY HAIGH was born in Honley and educated at Holme Valley Grammar School and the University of Leeds before training as a librarian in Aberystwyth and an archivist at the University of Liverpool. She served as Huddersfield CB Local History Librarian and Archivist from 1964 to 1974; as Kirklees Metropolitan District Archivist and Local Studies Officer from 1974 to 1982 and as the Polytechnic and later University of Huddersfield Archivist from 1991 to 2010. She is Visiting Research Fellow at the University of Huddersfield.

She obtained a Master of Philosophy in History at the University of Leeds in 1988 for *An Edition of Documents relating to the Township of Thornhill in the West Riding of Yorkshire, c.1684 to c.1789* and is joint founder and the first Honorary Secretary of the Huddersfield Local History Society from 1978 to 1998. She has compiled and edited several publications relating to Huddersfield, including *Huddersfield Maps from 1634* (1971), *Huddersfield's Canal Age* (1974) and *Kirklees Camera 1: Local Transport 1870–1940* (1978); *Honley Parish: A History of the Church of St. Mary the Virgin* (1986); *Huddersfield: Snapshots in Time* (1990) and the prize-winning *Huddersfield. A Most Handsome Town: Aspects of the History and Culture of a West Yorkshire Town* (1992).

JAMES WALVIN WAS born in Manchester and after graduating in History and Politics from Keele University, he obtained his M.A. in History at McMaster and his D.Phil. at the University of York where he taught from 1966 until his retirement as Professor of History. He has written numerous books and articles on modern British social history and is a leading authority on the history of slavery. His numerous publications have included *Black and White. The Negro and English Society 1555–1945* (1973), which won the Martin Luther King Memorial Prize, and a collection of edited essays, *Slavery and British Society 1776–1846* (1982) examining the impact of New World slavery on British society in the late eighteenth and early nineteenth centuries; *Black Ivory: A History of Black Slavery* (1992); *An African's Life. The Life and Times of Olaudah Equiano* (1998); *Making the Black Atlantic* (2000); *Britain's Slave Empire* (2000) and *The Trader, The Owner, The Slave. Parallel Lives in the Age of Slavery* (2007), published to mark the bicentenary of the abolition of the slave trade.

D. COLIN DEWS worked for five years as a clerk with the Yorkshire Electricity Board, before training as a secondary school teacher at the Methodist Southlands College, Wimbledon, Parkside. He then spent the next thirty-five years until retirement, at Park Lane College of Further Education, Leeds, first as a lecturer and subsequently as the Health and Safety Officer. A fifth generation Methodist, he is a local preacher and Leeds Methodist District Archivist. He has served as Secretary of the Wesley Historical Society (Yorkshire) since 1975, collecting and indexing items for the Society's library now deposited with the University of Huddersfield Archives and Special Collections. He has a specialist interest in Primitive Methodism and Nonconformist architecture and is a member of the Ancient Monuments Society, the Chapels Society, the Victorian Society and the Wesley Historical Society.

EDWARD ROYLE was born in Huddersfield and educated at King James's School in Almondbury, and Cambridge University. He returned to Yorkshire in 1972 to teach at the University of York where he is now Emeritus Professor of History, specialising in modern British social history. He is also a Fellow of the Royal Historical Society, President of the Wesley Historical Society and Chairman of the Wesley Historical Society, Yorkshire. He has written extensively on Chartism, Owenism , Secularism and aspects of Victorian religion. His most recent publications include an edition of *Bishop Bickersteth's Visitation Returns for the Archdeaconry of Craven* (2009) which examines the condition of the Church in 1858 in what is now West Yorkshire; *A Church Scandal in Victorian Pickering*, Borthwick Paper 117 (2010) and 'From Philistines to Goths: Nonconformist chapel styles in Victorian England' in *New directions in local history since Hoskins*, ed. C. Dyer and A. Hopper (2011). A third edition of his study, *Modern Britain, a social history, 1750–2011*, has been published by Bloomsbury in 2012.

JOHN HALSTEAD studied at Highburton Church of England elementary school, Penistone Grammar and the London School of Economics. He was a civil servant for ten years, leaving the administrative class at the Home Office in 1965 for a career teaching coal miners, steel workers and other industrial workers at the University of Sheffield. He is former Chair and currently Vice-President of the Society for the Study of Labour History. His recent publications include essays on 'labour history', in *The Oxford Companion to Family and Local History* (2008 edition), and on the history of 'adult education in South Yorkshire', for a volume celebrating the twenty-fifth anniversary of the *Northern College* (2004). John's forbears were fancy weavers during the early years of the nineteenth century and since his retirement he has remained active in social enterprise, co-operative and labour politics and tutors a School of Democratic Socialism.

JANETTE MARTIN was born in Dewsbury and spent much of her childhood in Brighouse where she attended Brighouse Girls' Grammar School before studying history at Lancaster University. Her interest in nineteenth century radical history began while working as an archivist at the Labour History Archive and Study Centre at the People's History Museum in Manchester. Janette completed a Ph.D at the University of York in 2010 on the relationship between public speaking and political mobilisation in northern England during the Chartist years. During her doctoral research she studied Richard Oastler's powerful oratory in defence of the factory children and his speeches denouncing the new poor law. She is now a lecturer at the University of Huddersfield and is currently working on a book on nineteenth-century political oratory.

Index